MW01103634

Policy and Research in Education

"In institutional and academic circles, the notion of educational leadership stands out as the most traditional. As Curry Stephenson Malott points out in clear revolutionary code, leadership in education is laced with undiluted power and a forthright intention to control the societal and cognitive rhythms of the academy by way of its white supremacist, hegemonic ideology tolerant of nothing less than the standardized knowledge industry emanating from the values of Anglo-centric capitalism. In this exciting book, Malott offers optional world views of educational leadership as a struggle for including actionist research qualitatively driven with critical theory and pedagogy coupled with an indigenous analysis of being in the world with little or no resemblance to the educational leadership as invented by white, European or North American civilization. The colonial models of educational leadership need not be any longer; and the reliance on the racialized socio-historical project of educational leadership can become truly transformative and begin to work in the interest of communities as they really are rather than on notions about who they should be. A must-read for all educational leaders."

Hermán S. García, Regents Professor, New Mexico State University

"This book is a long-overdue challenge to the very foundations of leadership ideology in Western nations. Curry Stephenson Malott boldly takes on the founding fathers of leadership, organization, systems, and behaviorist theories, and clears a new path for thinking about leadership in a democracy. By reuniting Western educational leadership with its historical roots in capitalism and colonialism, dissecting it via Marxist analysis, and contrasting it with often-untold histories of African and indigenous histories, he reveals Western leadership's intrinsically anti-democratic and oppressive nature. The text goes beyond critique as Malott provides historical and contemporary alternatives to hegemonic leadership models, as well as critical pedagogical frameworks for knowledge workers to rethink the face of leadership so that it may foster rather than quell democracy. As a true alternative to the hierarchical leadership models that have dominated Western education for centuries, this is a must-read for not just leaders or leaders-in-training but for all educators who envision education as the foundation for liberation and democracy."

Tricia Kress, UMASS Boston

"Curry Stephenson Malott's command of a personal, protagonist[ic,] and critical analysis of educational leadership is a timely and necessary contribution for creating transformative educational spaces. This collection inspires and challenges educators to think beyond the way things have been done, to how they could be when we direct our praxis to socially just alternatives."

Nathalia E. Jaramillo, Purdue University

"For those of us who, like John Dewey, believe that a fundamental purpose of education is to deconstruct rather than reinforce the social injustices of a hegemonic society, Curry Stephenson Malott's groundbreaking work provides us with a new way to understand and achieve a practice of criticality around educational leadership—a framework that is greatly needed within today's educational landscape."

Kecia Hayes, Assistant Professor, Montclair State University

"Curry Stephenson Malott, one of the most important voices in critical pedagogy over the last five years, has done it again! In *Policy and Research in Education* he applies his not inconsiderable critical analytical talent to the world of academic administration; as a 'junior administrator' myself in higher education, one who is driven by notions of socialist libertarianism, I found Malott's latest volume inspirational and reinvigorating. This is a must-read for all students of education, social work, public policy, and critical theory!"

Marc Pruyn, New Mexico State University

"The critical perspective necessarily comes from those being led, those historically marginalized by leaders. In the tradition of Howard Zinn's history from the people's perspective, Curry Stephenson Malott offers a critical look at leadership, applying Freire's call for a move from authoritarian to authoritative and therefore the empowerment of all. Malott challenges the norms that reduce leadership to hierarchies and recognizes the historical/political/social dynamic that is often traditionally masked by mechanistic claims of objectivity. This is a discussion fully human and made so by honoring the humanity of all involved in the pursuit of empowerment and democracy through education."

Paul Thomas, Associate Professor, Furman University

"In *Policy and Research in Education*, Curry Stephenson Malott turns educational leadership on its head. This book is not only intended for a typical leadership audience, which . . . enhances its value and impact. Malott dissects what leadership involves without the pretense of suggesting that pre-fabricated programs, standards, rubrics, and tools may be the remedy for the problem that is ailing our society. There are no easy answers, and employing a vigorous critical pedagogical framework allows Malott to explore how power is infused into the educational project . . . *Policy and Research in Education* willingly engages the reader in a range of discourses that highlight how leadership in education can become a more instructive, beneficial, and meaningful form of engagement. This is an important book, one that could be used inside and outside of the educational leadership realm."

Paul R. Carr, Youngstown State University

Policy and Research
in Education

M. Christopher Brown II

GENERAL EDITOR

Vol. 4

PETER LANG
New York • Washington, D.C./Baltimore • Bern
Frankfurt • Berlin • Brussels • Vienna • Oxford

Curry Stephenson Malott

Policy and Research in Education

A Critical Pedagogy for Educational Leadership

PETER LANG
New York • Washington, D.C./Baltimore • Bern
Frankfurt • Berlin • Brussels • Vienna • Oxford

Library of Congress Cataloging-in-Publication Data

Malott, Curry.
Policy and research in education: a critical pedagogy
for educational leadership / Curry Stephenson Malott.
p. cm. — (Education management: contexts, constituents,
and communities; vol. 4)
Includes bibliographical references and index.
1. Educational leadership. 2. Education and state.
3. Critical pedagogy. I. Title.
LB2806.M2236   371.2—dc22   2010012819
ISBN 978-1-4331-0830-3 (hardcover)
ISBN 978-1-4331-0829-7 (paperback)
ISSN 1947-6256

Bibliographic information published by **Die Deutsche Nationalbibliothek**.
Die Deutsche Nationalbibliothek lists this publication in the "Deutsche
Nationalbibliografie"; detailed bibliographic data is available
on the Internet at http://dnb.d-nb.de/.

The paper in this book meets the guidelines for permanence and durability
of the Committee on Production Guidelines for Book Longevity
of the Council of Library Resources.

© 2010 Peter Lang Publishing, Inc., New York
29 Broadway, 18th floor, New York, NY 10006
www.peterlang.com

Printed in the United States of America

TABLE OF CONTENTS

In Their Words: Educational Leadership in K-12

In Their Words: Educational Leadership in Higher Education

Conclusion

INTRODUCTION

A CALL TO ACTION FOR EDUCATIONAL LEADERSHIP

Policy and Research in Education: A Critical Pedagogy for Educational Leadership was conceptualized not from the perspective of a principal, a superintendent, a department chair, or a dean, and not from the assumed *neutral* and *objective* position of the *unbiased* Western scientist/researcher, but from the experiences of being a worker and therefore subject to the leadership practices of the dominant, white supremacist, patriarchal, capitalist society. It is therefore *a view*—a largely Western counter-hegemonic view—from below. That is, it represents one of many subjugated knowledges of the working class, the poor, the colonized, the enslaved, and the generally devalued and disrespected multitude. It is therefore, in many ways, an address to the leaders by one of the masses they are charged with leading.

More importantly, however, the intended audience of *Policy and Research in Education* is the *led*, the worker (i.e., the teacher, the professor, the adjunct, the Ph.D. student, and the teacher education student), interested in better understanding the larger historical/political context in which their labor power is externally commanded or directed—in both hegemonic *and* counter-hegemonic ways—through policy and educational leadership. The goals of achieving such critical class-consciousness includes intervention in not only the democratization of leadership *style*, but also in the *purpose* of leadership and education in general. That is, in our non-negotiable support for humanity and the Earth *to be* and *become* free from oppression and external coercion, we endorse an educational movement dedicated to the mobilization of an empowered population endowed with the critical thinking skills conducive to reading both the word and the world for paradigmatic transformation—that is, for life *after* capitalism. Ultimately, *Policy and Research in Education* is an invitation to *all* stakeholders in education (teachers, administrators, students, parents, grandparents, sisters, uncles, religious leaders, organizers, activists, revolutionaries, and other community members) to transform the nature and purpose of education in general and educational leadership in particular from the ground up through a movement of raising critical consciousness and engaging in direct-democratic action.

However, the notion of a *purely* counter-hegemonic position within the present hegemony is a romantic and dangerously simplistic vision. That is, while *Policy and Research in Education* was written from the perspective of a critically self-conscious worker, it was conceptualized by a *white* worker, and therefore from the position of an often invisible white privilege (especially to whites) due to the simple fact that the author was *raised white in America*, despite his rejection of the historical project of *whiteness*. Important here is the rejection of whiteness, which is part of a larger rejection of the compulsory form of social organization based on hierarchy and exploitation, in a word, capitalism. Because critical pedagogy, with early roots in Latin America, is fundamentally anti-colonial, and because whiteness is part of the ideological perpetuation of the colonial project, our critical approach to educational leadership must therefore be informed by this rejection of whiteness/hierarchy. Peter McLaren and Ramin Farahmandpur (2005) place whiteness within this larger political-economic, historical context, noting that it was "introduced by the seventeenth-century Anglo-American and U.S. ruling class" and is therefore "fundamentally linked to the practice of Anglo-European and U.S. colonialism" (McLaren and Farahmandpur, 2005, p. 106).

That is, whiteness was deployed in America to divide the Africans, Europeans, Native Americans, and others who were forming coalitions and alternative societies in their resistance against the highly exploitative *plantocracy* that began soon after the first shipment of indentured laborers were brought to North America by British investors in the sixteenth century. It was within the wake of devastation left by the violent process of primitive accumulation that "some Europeans brought to American shores, against their investors' will, saw a more promising future within Native societies as did many Africans brought as chattel slavery" (Malott, 2008, p. 104). In practice, whiteness was intended to provide the bosses with a larger base of support by convincing poor Europeans that their true comrades were their European over-lords because of their shared Euro-ancestry. Whiteness, in short, was employed to maintain the basic structures of colonial, and later, capitalistic, power. Resistance against colonialism and capitalism, for many Marxist critical pedagogues, therefore includes the rejection of whiteness and its core, implicit hierarchies. Our critical pedagogical approach to educational leadership, as argued above, has a lot to learn from these historical insights.

Situated within this white supremacist context of the dominant society (i.e., an institutionalized racial hierarchy) that assumes Western civilization (i.e., neoliberal capitalism) represents the most advanced stage of human cul-tural development, whites in America, regardless of their political orientations, are automatically located *above* those who do not fit within current conceptualizations of whiteness or do not possess white cultural, economic, and political capital. Consequently, this hegemonic reality that takes the content of whiteness, such as Euro-centrism and the capitalist relations of production, as a non-perspective or objective reality, makes it difficult for white radicals to understand how whiteness is central to the colonialist project, thereby limiting their counter-hegemonic potential. This awareness is especially important for those charged with leading and influencing and constructing policy.

This *qualification*, if you will, is not intended to *disempower* the white critical pedagogue, but rather, is a challenge to ensure we are as critically effective and enlightened as possible. That is, in our work as critical educators and educational leaders we do not want to unknowingly and naively reproduce Euro-centric views of the world, and therefore, Euro-centric policies and practices (i.e., pro-capitalist). This is the danger of whiteness and the power of hegemony—it gets reproduced unconsciously. If our worker rebellion and attempts to offer an effective critical pedagogy for educational leadership are successful, then we must confront the ways we unconsciously internalize and reproduce white supremacy and capitalism as a result of being raised in a white supremacist, capitalist society—this applies to whites and people of color alike.

If this complexity were not enough, *Policy and Research in Education* also takes inspiration and guidance from its author's experiences as an organic, non-institutionalized leader of students and workers. This point of view—the point of view of a small-scale, radical-democratic movement leader—made the manifestation of this project a possibility. The story of this experience begins in Las Cruces, New Mexico, which is worth pausing for a moment to briefly reflect upon.

Democratic, Ground-Up Leadership: The Justice Stand

In 1998 as a graduate student and part-time, weekend college, sociology faculty member at New Mexico State University in Las Cruces, New Mexico I helped to establish *The Justice Stand* with a few fellow graduate students. The Justice Stand was inspired by the post-Black Panther Party for Self-Defense street organizing culture in Oakland California—a tradition that is dedicated to raising critical awareness and organizing actions and campaigns against police brutality and other abuses of power. The Justice Stand was constructed around this model of physically being on the streets every day talking with people and offering analyses and connections between larger structures of power, current events, and local policies and injustices. The Justice Stand started as a simple card table placed in front of the student union Monday through Friday. The table was stocked with fliers and a few signs and staffed by about five graduate and undergraduate students dedicated to dialogue and the democratic values that fundamentally oppose the hierarchical, anti-democratic nature of colonialism's current form—neoliberal, global capitalism.

One of the primary local *issues* addressed by The Justice Stand was the practice of canalizing cows within the University's College of Agricultural, Consumer, and Environmental Sciences. The practice includes surgically creating a large hole in the side of a cow and inserting a door with a spring mechanism resembling a push bin garbage can with a lid that seals tightly. The cattle are then sent out into the greatly degraded desert for grazing. Because the desert lands of the South Western regions of the United States are highly exploited, they do not provide cattle with sufficient nutrients for maximum weight gain and value production. The canalized cows, after grazing for a few days, are then brought back to the laboratory where scientists are able to empty the contents of their stomachs to be analyzed for nutritional value. Based on the results of this ongoing study, scientists are able to supplement the cow's diet with minimal waste and therefore maximum efficiency and profitability. These emaciated, sickly looking canalized cows are kept in outdoor pens right on campus. We therefore took pictures of them, and made posters and literature for The Justice Stand. Our position was that this practice was a grossly unjust and unethical use of science. Canalization represents the *purpose* of education and how science is used within the colonialist project, which is the subjugation of the Indigenous communities and imported labor, an on-going process needed to extract the maximum amount of value out of the land, animals, and human labor power. The Justice Stand therefore struck a nerve with the University's administration because we were challenging the financial heart of the institution and the underlying value system of the larger colonial-ist/capitalist dominant settler-state/society.

From a student perspective, on the other hand, The Justice Stand was an instant success. It generated widespread participation and discussion. An overt culture of transformative resistance was quickly flowering on campus. It is therefore not surprising that the University's administration—its educational leaders—withdrew its support only a few weeks after it began and declared it no longer allowable or legal. As the University had a *Free Speech policy*, our Justice Stand had to first be approved, rendering the exercise of organized speech on campus not really *free* or without unusual limitations. This action, that is, *shutting us down*, as it were, transformed the Justice Stand into a free speech campaign. We prophetically called our campaign *Speech is Coming* because NMSU's restrictions on speech were eventually lifted as a result of our initiative.

The Justice Stand, and quickly thereafter, *Speech is Coming*, was always informed by a deep commitment to democratic leadership, and consequently, about having fun and raising awareness about issues that affect our lives and communities. We were inspired by what the social movement literature termed *new social movements* because of their non-hierarchical, rotating leadership structure making the identification of a single leader a challenge for those dominant forces working to disrupt and neutralize movement and revolutionary agency. Operating *in* Southern New Mexico and operated *by* a few conscious Chicanos we naturally looked to Mexico's Indigenous Revolution led by the Zapatistas as the quintessential example of the new social movement, which was, in fact, an ancient model indigenous to Native America.

We consciously attributed our democratic, non-hierarchical structure to our popular success because, by not intending to direct and control people as movement leaders, but rather, committed to opening up democratic spaces for dialogue and creating non-hierarchical challenges to dominant forms of power, many people felt that the Justice Stand's *Speech is Coming* campaign offered an opportunity where they could have a direct impact, and not get lost in the nameless masses of a large movement. We were advised by veteran organizers in Oakland, California to maintain an independent existence, resisting attempts to turn our movement into a student organization. Following what we understood to be the democratic will of the movement, however, we eventually created a student organization, and our sometimes-daily meetings went from spontaneous street gatherings to scheduled events in designated conference rooms.

Shortly thereafter the spirit of the Justice Stand dissolved itself, reemerging in other forms. For example, after the Justice Stand days a few of its core members became heavily involved with developing off-campus, non-university affiliated *Cop Watch* and *Migra Watch* street-actions/education, calling the group, *Anonýmo*. Justice Stand and Anonýmo activists also started a few social justice-oriented Latino-punk rock fusion bands playing a significant role in Las Cruces' underground music scene. One of these groups, Ajogún, continues to maintain a web page (see www.myspace.com/ajogun), write and record new music, and has plans for future performances. As the years march on we continue to find increasingly radical and creative ways to take *a Stand for Justice*, careful not to forsake our critical pedagogical approach to leadership. What follows is therefore a brief introduction to a critical examination of educational leadership informed by the democratically radical spirit of *The Justice Stand* and the *Zapatistas*.

Educational Leadership in a Larger Context

Within the educational leadership literature there exists a lively debate around the pedagogy of leaders that constructs the world of leadership on a continuum where one end represents the extreme authoritarian leader who views *his* workers (i.e., teachers) as having absolutely no decision making skills and in need of external control. On the other end of this continuum exists the democratic leader who draws on the strengths, interests, and abilities of *colleagues* to perform the tasks the system demands. Many scholars advocate for a position that falls somewhere in the middle (see chapter four). While these debates are an indispensable component of a critical pedagogical approach to educational leadership, they tend to leave the internal curriculum or *purpose* of leadership largely unexamined. Because of the underlying significance of critiquing educational leadership from this perspective, let us restate it in a slightly different light before we continue.

We might therefore note that there tends to be an emphasis in the discipline on *styles* and *practices* at the expense of *context* and *purpose*. Again, in the literature there is a move away from traditional conceptions of *the* leader as the *rugged individual who single-handedly directs his institution or program to success with the aggressive discipline of a military commander*, coupled with a simultaneous shift toward the *compassionate leader* who works with *her* or his colleagues to develop goals and strategies in a less hierarchical context. While this shift is significant and a representation of real progress, it does not disrupt the underlying *purpose* of education—that is, the perpetuation of the capitalist social and economic system and its Euro-centric hegemonies.

As you read the following chapters of *Policy and Research in Education*, you will notice that in making my case for a critical pedagogy for educational leadership I spend a considerable amount of time examining the many complex and contradictory ways that education supports capitalism and the basic structures of power. For example, in settler states, such as Canada and the United States, education has supported elite interests through its ability to assimilate both voluntary and forced immigrants and Indigenous peoples, with the help of Christian missionaries (although there are also many examples of Christian missionaries acting counter-hegemonically), and an active militia, into consenting wageworkers. What has become clear through the process of engaging this study is that when one finds oppression, one finds an equally intense spirit of agency, and in North America (and throughout the world) it has a long history that has developed into a thoroughly entrenched *culture of resistance* permeating entire populations. It is this culture of resistance where an organic, democratic, and critical approach to leadership can be found and encouraged by cultural workers and critical pedagogues.

However, the purpose (supporting the basic structures of power) of traditional models of educational leadership, and the system of education more generally, is not overt. Rather than being portrayed as an instrument of social control, education has been paternalistically held up by progressives and conservatives alike, as *the great equalizer* or democratizer—defined here as a system that allows all citizens an equal chance to compete with each other on the market for the best wage and social position or rank. Consequently, capitalism and colonial occupation have been normalized and naturalized to such an extent that their practices are not *named* but are presumed to represent the natural, objective outcome of human progress linearly marching forward toward a one-world empire of Euro-centric domination.

Again, what tends to be absent in educational leadership are discussions regarding the *purpose* of schooling as a form of social reproduction within the larger context of capitalism and the colonialist project initiated by Columbus in 1492. That is, the Columbian presence and legacy in the Americas, and around the globe, have been marked by a vicious form of leadership that reduces people, ecosystems, biodiversity, sources of fresh water, etc., to their wealth generating potential. In this paradigm leadership serves the function of

managing the accumulation of wealth by any means necessary, including genocide and an assault on the viability of life itself on planet Earth. Challenging
this destructive process—a process that does not spare even its most loyal followers, white people—is the task of critical pedagogy in the twenty-first century.

Informed by this spirit of radical resistance in *A Call to Action: An
Introduction to Education, Philosophy, and Native North America* (2008) I challenge teacher education students to consider how their roles as future teachers are institutionally designed to socialize the next generation of the settler
state to perpetuate the process of colonialist plunder as consenting wage earners. Towards these ends students are invited to consider the significance of the
land on which the United States and Canada, for example, are situated on, in
their preparation as future teachers. Consider:

> Because colleges of education in the United States and Canada, at their core, are
> informed by Western philosophical traditions, yet are situated on land whose people
> have their own unique process of knowledge creation and wisdom, which tend not to
> be institutionally represented, except within the schools controlled by those Indigenous
> to North American, we must ask: "Why?" In the process of answering this question we
> will inevitably uncover the on-going war waged by the occupiers against Native peo-
> ples and their cultures and philosophies motivated by an effort to extract the maximum
> amount of wealth and use value…from the people and their land, even if it means
> destroying everything that is (including themselves). (Malott, 2008, p. 4)

In *Teaching Native America Across the Curriculum* we draw on this contextualization in our proposal for universal curricular reform. Highlighting this
approach in the context of the social studies we explain:

> The social studies, irrespective of form, unifying and democratic *or* reductive and
> hierarchical, was constructed to be part of the process of Western colonization, that
> is, native national *dis*placement, foreign invading *re*placement, and hegemonic con-
> tinuation. Underscoring where power lies and how it operates can lead to a social stud-
> ies that is counter-hegemonic. For example, from the perspective outlined in *A Call
> to Action* (Malott, 2008), *no responsible party* would question teaching the history of the
> Americas from a Native American perspective, thereby challenging the hegemony of
> the settler state. An Indigenous social studies would situate the United States in the
> context of Indigenous democracy, the colonization of the Americas, and the genocide
> of America's First Nations. From this perspective settler-state social studies curriculum
> and instruction is understood as embodying the tension between the settler-
> community's ruling class and the settler community's working class marginalizing
> Indigeneity and the enslavement and genocide of millions of Africans in the process.
> The tension we refer to is the product of these two antagonistically related settler class-
> es' historic struggle over the distribution of wealth extracted from lands violently

denationalized from Indigenous Nations. (Malott, Waukau, Waukau-Villagomez, 2009, p. 95)

In other words, teachers are challenged to reflect on how common schooling was, and continues to be, an important mechanism for manufacturing the consent needed to perpetuate the colonialist project of land occupation and wealth extraction. Teachers in training are therefore engaged in the process of constructing their own philosophies of education with the opportunity to imagine what their future practices might look like if they were constructed *against* global capitalism, the most recent manifestation of colonization, rather than *for it*. Similarly, this introduction to *Policy and Research in Education* is designed to engage educational leaders and other education workers in considering what an anti-colonialist/capitalist model of educational leadership might look like in practice. Towards these ends, we must first outline the traditional model of educational leadership and what it tends to look like in schools and universities.

In understanding Western colonialist-oriented leadership, it is useful to consider what Noam Chomsky (2007) considers to be the two axioms of state policy. First, invoking the memory of Thucydides and the ancient world of Greece, Chomsky (2007) notes that, "large nations do what they wish, while small nations accept what they must" (p. 41). The second axiom that, according to Chomsky (2007), guides the policies and leadership practices of Western nations (and beyond) is derived from the insights of Adam Smith regarding the context of eighteenth century England. Summarizing this second axiom Chomsky (2007) paraphrases Adam Smith: "the 'principal architects' of state policy, the 'merchants and manufacturers,' make sure that their own interests are 'most particularly attended to,' however 'grievous' the consequences for others" (pp. 41–42) including domestic populations.

This image of the self-serving leader, or the leader as *lion for capital*, continues to serve as the dominant archetype in the contexts of not only foreign policy and corporations, but in education. It is therefore not surprising that a great deal of the literature in educational leadership (see *The Jossey-Bass Reader on Educational Leadership*, 2007) draws significantly from the work in corporate leadership/management, such as the work of Jim Collins (2007), which seeks to identify characteristics that contribute to enduring and profitable companies, such as *strong* leaders. Outlining the characteristics of this lionized leader Jerome Murphy (2007), in his critique of what he argues are the unrealistic expectations of education leaders, summarizes:

> Leadership is back in fashion in education, and the conventional wisdom suggests a heroic boss who meets at least six expectations. First and most insistently, leaders are supposed to possess a clear personal vision. A sense of purpose is central to success, and center-stage leaders define it for their organizations. Second, leaders are extremely knowledgeable; they have the right answers to the most pressing problems. Third, leaders are expected to be strong: to display initiative, courage, and tenacity. Fourth, leaders communicate forcefully, using their knowledge to convey their vision aggressively and persuasively. Fifth, leaders amass power and use it for organizational improvement. Finally, leaders are take-charge individuals who solve knotty problems along the way as they move toward achieving their personal visions. (p. 52)

Murphy (2007) argues that this mythic figure is unrealistic and therefore sets leaders up for failure. Other critics point to the thoroughly patriarchal nature of this model of leadership that has historically excluded women and people of color based on sexist and racist stereotypes. For example, Cherry Banks (2007) notes that "in the early 1900s, and then again in the 1960s and 1970s" a "trait theory" approach to leadership assumed that leaders were characterized by particular traits "such as intelligence, self confidence, high energy, and persuasive skills" (p. 302), which were traits often implicitly attributed to white males, thereby excluding women and people of color from leadership positions. It has been argued that women in general are too emotional, irrational, weak, and subjective, and thus, unfit to lead.

While these foci of critique are helpful for beginning to understand how the dominant culture and institutions discriminate, they fall short by assuming that the basic structures of institutional and social power that the leader serves are fundamentally correct or so thoroughly hegemonized, that is, normalized and naturalized, that they are viewed as a non-perspective and, as mentioned above, *just how it is*. In other words, we are not only interested in questioning and democratizing how the leaders or managers of the empire govern and are selected, but we are equally interested in challenging the very legitimacy of the colonialist project itself. This requires a paradigm shift, that is, a change of values, and the transformation of how one perceives the world and the relationships between entities within it. Rather than viewing the world as *potential wealth* and the leader as *grand enforcer*, a critical pedagogy for educational leadership views the world as a vast and complex living entity where the leader's responsibility is to ensure policy that does not betray the spirit of democracy and the right of all life to live without oppression and subjugation. A fundamental component of this critical pedagogical approach is self-rule or communities selecting their own leaders and form of social organization.

Approaching educational leadership from this *critical pedagogical* perspective we can begin by asking a series of questions:

~ What is the *purpose* of education and educational leadership?
~ How, and by whom, has education been historically constructed?
~ What kind of relationships, citizens, and society are educational institutions designed to foster?
~ What are the paradoxes or contradictions of education as it is current-
ly designed in Western societies such as the United States and Canada?
~ How does education differ for different people, especially across racial
and class lines?
~ Why is there an ever-growing number of educational researchers and
practitioners arguing that educational leadership tends to support capitalism, and the larger colonialist project, beginning with Columbus,
it represents?
~ What is the evidence for and against this position or conclusion?
~ How can educational leaders work counter-hegemonically within the
atmosphere of No Child Left Behind (NCLB) that has transferred a
great deal of the institutional power of principals and superintendents
to the federal government?
~ What kinds of knowledge, characteristics, and dispositions might critical pedagogical educational leaders operating in today's increasingly
restrictive pro-capital environment need to be successful and survive?

Considering the implications of these questions we might conclude that it is
wise to be weary of efforts to reform the hierarchical, top-down approaches to
educational leadership that do not question the underlying purpose of education. For example, we might be cautious when we hear our educational leaders call for *shared governance* and *common purpose* because we know that such
calls can too easily become *behaviorist* strategies designed to manipulate workers (in this case teachers and professors) to be more productive for *the bosses*
without addressing the underlying relationships and *purpose* of education. For
a truly democratic approach to educational leadership we argue that a critical
perspective is indispensable. We are interested in forms of educational leadership that can successfully guide education so it becomes part of the global movement against oppression, exploitation, and human suffering. A critical pedagogy
for educational leadership refuses to accommodate the view that education is
a technical or mechanical act decontextualized from the political economy it
serves. These kinds of *critical pedagogies for educational leadership* are what this

book is intended to make a contribution to. However, before we transition into Chapter One, we first provide a brief summary of the sections and chapters of this book.

The Contents Herein: A Summative Introduction

The first two sections in this volume, "The Foundations of Educational Leadership: Toward a Critical Pedagogy" (Chapters One and Two) and "Educational Leadership Critically Examined: Two Historical Examples" (Chapters Three and Four) are designed to provide the reader with a multitude of critical theoretical lenses to view the policies and practices of educational leadership. Chapter One situates educational leadership in a broad historical framework highlighting the three major trends in the discipline, from the social efficiency model of Frederick Taylor, to the behaviorism of Skinner, and, more recently, the systems theory approach. Chapter Two introduces the ways in which policy and research *are* and *might be* connected to the theory and practice of educational leadership. Chapter Three explores the tendencies of educational leadership within the African American context, which began after the Civil War. Within this chapter we explore the critical agency and organic leadership structures of the enslaved and devalued African community in America that explain why they have been able to survive in this white supremacist, exploitative context. We take a non-romanticized approach here (and in the book more generally) and explore the challenges and setbacks, as well as the achievements and successes, of African American leadership. Chapter Four examines the system of education for Native Americans developed by Captain Richard Pratt during the late 1800s around the last of the United States' *Indian Wars*. This *education*, as we see, was designed to kill the Indian and save the man within. This chapter pays special attention to the Native American-led education initiatives designed to restore Native languages (i.e., culture).

The next two sections, "In Their Words: Educational Leadership in K-12" and "In Their Words: Educational Leadership in Higher Education," contain four chapters, each one representing the perspectives and experiences of an educational leader. These chapters provide invaluable insights for current and future educational leaders interested in democratizing their practice. They also provide invaluable insights for educational workers (i.e., teachers and professors) who are interested in better understanding how their bosses think as a way of adding depth and perspective to their agency and class-consciousness. The chapters in these two sections came to be as a result of the interviewees agreeing to answer my questions. They can only be held accountable for the content in *their* individual chapters. The remainder of the book is my responsibility alone. That is, it is *not* safe to assume that the contributors necessarily agree with and endorse the analyses and conclusions that I have come to in the rest of the book.

The final section and chapter in this volume concludes the project by attempting to bring it all together through the lens of research. I argue that the critical pedagogical approach to educational leadership advocated for throughout the book, while political in nature like all education, irrespective of perspective, is supported by cutting edge research in teaching and learning. The message I want to portray is that this is the power of critical pedagogy. That is, critical pedagogy is not only informed by the democratic values of social justice and cooperation, but it is supported by science and what we know about the essence of the human mind. In other words, I argue that a critical pedagogy for educational leadership is inclusive of a postmodern politics of difference as well as a Western scientific approach to objectivity. While modern and postmodern theories tend to be situated as antagonistically related to one another, in this volume we treat them as mutually useful and beneficial. What we do *not* support, however, are policies and practices that coddle the aggressor and perpetuate abuse and indoctrination, which can employ either modernism *or* post modernism as a vehicle for transmission.

THE FOUNDATIONS OF EDUCATIONAL LEADERSHIP

Toward a Critical Pedagogy

· 1 ·

LEADERSHIP, THE WORLD, AND KNOWING

Organization theory or the theory of administration and management, since the beginning of the twentieth century and the rise of large scale industrialization in the Western world, is typically divided into three major eras: scientific management, behaviorism, and systems theory. Analyzing these models from a philosophical perspective reveals various assumptions about the world and knowing embedded within them. What follows is a relatively linear analysis of these three periods, which serves as part of the contextualized, critically complex, theoretical foundation of later chapters. However, before we begin our review of the educational leadership literature, we briefly explore the roots of hierarchy in Western civilization because it is within this tradition that contemporary management practices are firmly grounded.

The Roots of Hierarchy in Western Civilization

Institutionalized forms of mass education in the Western world, almost without exception, are structured hierarchically. That is, one of the primary philosophical building blocks of Western institutions of education is an *ontology of hierarchy*. The core of this reasoning can be traced back to ancient Greece to Plato's ideas of intelligence as naturally unevenly distributed where the small minority (the "gold metal" people) were endowed with a special gift for ideas, reasoning and therefore leading and managing the affairs of commerce, the gods, and governance. The silver metal people, although not as advanced as the gold metal people, were still honorable and able to demonstrate a respectable level of intellectual capacity. The "bronze metal" people of ancient Greece, the brutes and slaves (labor), on the other hand, were considered to be exclusively of the body or the flesh, and therefore had no capacity for intelligence, humility, and self-control, and could thus not be trusted to participate in the democratic process, relying on people of higher quality and moral fiber to make decisions for them.

Constructing a system of education based on the assumption that there naturally exists an unequal distribution of intelligence, with high cognitive function being a rare occurrence, has rendered the notion of leadership a paternalistic occupation with policy taking the form of a top-down system of *orders* or *dictations* intended to control the labor power of teachers, assumed to be *incompetent technicians*, who are expected to similarly control *their* students. The *elite few natural leaders* paradigm of education is so entrenched that it is rarely challenged.

Rather than arguing for the sharing of power this research outlines the ways that leaders can lead democratically within the hierarchy by tackling such issues as institutional tracking policies. While this literature is relevant and important for working within the system that currently exists, it is missing the long-term vision aimed at challenging basic structures of power and decision-making. As a result, much of the research that examines educational leadership does not question the punitive authority administrators have over teachers and students. In other words, knowledge is produced that constructs an image of the world as naturally unequal, leaving the only fluctuating variable being the leadership choices of the naturally superior.

That is, do leaders *take care of* and *love their* student/teacher children, or do they punish them for their infuriating deficiencies and inadequacies? By framing research around issues of *what* leaders do with their political power some of the more interesting and relevant questions go unasked, such as, *is the hyper concentration of administrative power over curriculum and pedagogy socially just?* And *are teachers, who tend to have vivid knowledge of how students learn and what their lives are like, better suited to develop effective pedagogies and curricula than federal administrators with no teaching experience?* Unless we ask these and other questions we leave unexamined the dichotomy between powerless practitioners and all powerful policy makers and administrators.

I am therefore arguing for the proliferation of knowledge about teaching and learning, and therefore *leading*, which affirms and contributes to the healthy development of boys and girls. To support this agenda in the long term a model of leadership would have to be implemented that is similarly informed by what we know about human nature, the mind, and what it requires. We might find, for example, that a leadership style that best fits human need looks more like a horizontal line of small rotating circles representing the sharing of power, than a pyramid with a small minority with all the power and the vast majority with very little. Before we further explore these critical pedagogical approaches to educational leadership, we will review the history of what we might call *the boss's approach to managing human labor power*.

Efficiency and the Scientific Management of Labor

It has been argued that the publication of Frederick Taylor's *The Principles of Scientific Management* (1911) transformed the relationship between the managerial or *specialized* class and the working class in fundamental ways. In essence, the argument goes, Taylor intensified capital's ability to control the labor power of the working class by reducing production into multiple simple procedures, each step precisely measured, clocked, and standardized to ensure every second of a workers' *paid* time was most efficiently generating value, therefore contributing to the *bottom line*. With the amount of labor hour units needed to perform a particular task significantly reduced by eliminating, for example, unnecessary procedures or steps, the capitalists' profit would therefore increase resulting in their ability to pay higher wages, reasoned Taylor. Based on what we know about the *laws* of capital and the structure of the corporation where CEOs are legally charged to *always* act in the interests of the share holders even if it means sacrificing the labor force, that is, the public, Taylor's (1911) approach was not only mechanical in nature, as we will see below, but it was ideological as well, designed to "train" workers to believe that *scientific management* would result in a fair and unbiased society and industry because *science* is neutral.

Taylor's ideas, as outlined below, continue to influence the standardization movement in education, informing every aspect from curriculum development to "selecting educational materials, in developing structural systems, and in other aspects of educational administration" (Sergiovanni, 1979, p. 14). While this statement was made thirty years ago, we can look to the more contempo-rary No Child Left Behind Act (NCLB) as representative of a hyper-inflated standardization policy that, for the first time, dictates learning outcomes and objectives at a federal level. Consequently, Sergiovanni's (1979) observation remains true thirty years later. Sergiovanni (1979) observes that while the lan-guage changes, the practice of scientific management remains the same. For example, the discourse of "behavioral objectives, state and national assess-ment, [and] cost benefit analysis" (Sergiovanni, 1979, p. 14) is language that refers to Taylor-like practices that were not only common in the 1970s, but con-tinue to be heard, echoed by current policy makers such as Arne Duncan and his support of NCLB's emphasis on accountability, efficiency, and control.

Underlying this system of control is the belief that human behavior can eas-ily be manipulated by economic rewards and punishments alluding to an envi-ronmental theory of intelligence. Ignored is the human need for creativity and autonomy that have been linked to psychological health and thus intimately linked to the notion of human nature or essence. Summarizing these assump-tions Sergiovanni (1979) notes that "since persons are primarily motivated by economic and other extrinsic incentives, they will do that which brings them the greatest extrinsic gain" (p. 14). Classrooms are clearly managed according to these cognitive assumptions with grades and future employability as the pri-mary incentive to consent to the hierarchical structure with teachers as the uni-lateral disciplinarians and teachers being scientifically managed in a similar way with curriculum and outcome objectives handed down unilaterally from state and federal policy makers.

**

Born in 1856 in Philadelphia Taylor developed his approach to human man-agement during a time in history when the United States of America was beginning to emerge as a soon-to-be super power. Consequently, the nascent settler-state was also suffering from the social ills of large-scale industrial pro-duction such as rampant poverty, hunger, alienation, pollution and environ-mental degradation, leading to an increasingly radicalized and violent working class. America's manufacturing and banking classes were not only becoming wealthy, they were becoming scared and nervous that the bewildered herd would trample them under.

Frederick Taylor offered a solution to the angry throng's growing militancy—scientific management where the workers are trained and educat-ed not to think, that specialized occupation was reserved for the responsible men who understand that power and privilege need to be respected. In other words, leaders and managers organize the highly complex productive apparatus, and workers follow orders carrying out their tiny repetitive part of the larger system too big for their tiny brains to comprehend. In short, Taylor's method reduced humans to interchangeable parts of a vast industrial machine incorporating all aspects of society including education. Taylor's work can therefore be understood as part of the imperial process marked by colonial expansionism.

The Principles of Scientific Management provided a blueprint for leadership/management that we can call *modern industrial efficiency*, which, in many ways, has become so hegemonized, that is, normalized and naturalized, that it is almost invisible in contemporary times. In other words, our schools and training facilities tend to ignore the philosophy behind accepted leadership practices, which incorrectly send the message that they are neutral or science-based. It is only when we challenge those practices that it becomes apparent that scientific management is not just *the natural order of things*. The power structure, or ruling elite, when Taylor developed his so-called *science*, was marked by:

~ The end of the last major *Indian Wars* and the domination of the physical space that is now the United States

~ The determination to re-write history from a Euro-centric perspective, ignoring the multiple ways the non-European world generously assisted Europe out of the Dark Ages and into Enlightenment

~ The desire to manage and lead the planet, that is, to rule and dominate it, with an iron fist

~ The invention of *intelligence testing* that claimed to be able to quantify and measure innate, predetermined cognitive ability offering managers and leaders an *unbiased* method of sorting and ranking the population

~ Hereditability of particular characteristics, such as intelligence, refers to the percentage of variation within "populations" being due to genetic factors, which assumes intelligence and populations are well-defined properties

~ The other half of the theory looks at "the percentage of variation in the characteristic due to all other factors." Considering intelligence, researchers examine "prenatal and perinatal biological factors, environmental factors of a biological nature such as nutrition, and social factors such as education and experience" (Nisbett, 2009, p. 22), as contributing to variability among particular populations. Again, intelligence and population characteristics such as race are assumed to be well-defined and thus measurable.

~   The debate among behaviorists is therefore over what percent of intellectual variability is due to genetic factors and what percent is due to other factors. Neither *side*, if you will, questions intelligence as a knowable entity. They both assume it is well defined and measurable. For environmentalists like Nisbett (see below), the new culture racists or deficit theorists, intelligence testing only measures twenty to forty percent of actual genetically-determined cognitive ability. Nisbett concedes that what IQ testing is actually measuring is culture. However, for Nisbett (2009) this just reaffirms the Euro-centric notion that white culture produces more intelligent people, even after admitting that IQ testing is more of a measure of how white a person is than how smart or intelligent they are.

Taylor's work, situated within this context, can be understood to be informed by the same ontological and epistemological hierarchy as the larger colonial or *postcolonial* U.S. society. It is within this larger context of domination and colonization that Taylor's work can be best understood. For example, it is evident that the social engineering and scientific management of Taylorism, designed to discipline and control the body, is part and parcel of the imperial call of *manifest destiny* to *tame the Wild West* and expand the empire westward. In his first paragraph of *The Principles of Scientific Management* Taylor (1911) situates his work within the framework of then President Roosevelt's charge that conserving the Nation's natural resources is part of the process of developing *national efficiency*. While it is obvious to most citizens when *our* forests disappear and *we* squander *our* other natural resources, reasons Taylor (1911), *our* biggest waste, that of "human effort" (p. 5), tends to be less apparent to most people. Summarizing this point Taylor (1911) notes:

> Awkward, inefficient, or ill-directed movements of men leave nothing visible or tangible behind them. Their appreciation calls for an act of memory, an effort of the imagination. And for this reason, even though our daily loss from this source is greater than from our waste of material things, the one has stirred us deeply, while the other has moved us but little. (pp. 5–6)

Taylor, of course, is writing from the perspective of the ruling class for it is businessmen and investors who lose profit when the labor power they hire for a wage far less than the value it produces is not producing as much value as it could given different management practices. In other words, when Taylor mentions "our interests" he means the interests of the bankers, investors, and industrialists who gamble with the Stock Exchange, winning and losing the wealth generated by the working class. The interests of those who rely on a wage to survive are not mentioned here. As we will see below, Taylor's intention is to indoctrinate or train workers to believe that capitalism can be fair and organized in a way where the interests of capital and labor are not antagonistic but one and the same.

The ontological perspective informing Taylor's work clearly views the world as naturally structured hierarchically where the labor power of those assumed to be *common people* is a natural resource the intellectually superior leaders of industry are just as entitled to exploit as rivers, forests, mountains and oceans. Because his approach is hierarchical, it is paternalistic. That is, Taylor's thesis is based on the false assumption that advanced intelligence is exceptionally rare, rendering those uniquely endowed with this special gift the natural leaders—the bosses—which renders them morally obligated to civilize the savage, of whatever cultural, ethnic or regional background—*the* white man's burden. Put yet another way, Taylor's model is based on the belief that only the few, elite, responsible men know what is best for the vast, ignorant majority. Consequently, Taylor (1911) argues that his approach provides a solution to the antagonistic relationship between labor and management. Consider:

> …A large part of the organization of employers, as well as employees…do not believe that it is possible to arrange their mutual relations that their interests become identical. The majority of these men believe that the fundamental interests of employees and employers are necessarily antagonistic. Scientific management, on the contrary, has for its very foundation the firm conviction that the true interests of the two are one in the same; that prosperity for the employer cannot exist through a long term of years unless it is accompanied by prosperity for the employee, and vice versa. (p. 10)

Painted here is an ontology that conceives the world to be naturally divided into leaders and workers, brains and bodies, that, rather than at odds with one another, are dependent on one another. This is the *we're all one big happy family* discourse that was constructed to demonize and disrupt the labor movement during the period around the Great Depression of 1929. The argument was that unionization is the result of *outside agitators who want to disrupt the harmony because of their evil dispositions*. Marxist scholars point to this as an example of social reproduction or hegemonic indoctrination because workers do not need bosses; the bosses are an impediment to their humanization and ultimate liberation as a creative species whose nature it is to be free from external coercion.

Taylor goes on presenting this analysis as a compromise where bosses take a more "liberal policy" and pay slightly higher wages, and, in return, workers who "begrudge" capitalists for accumulating vast fortunes off the unpaid labor hours of men and women are similarly "led" to "modify" their views. Again, it should be noted that this *we're all one big happy, harmonious, family* discourse is a clever tactic on the part of Taylor because it takes attention away from the legal structure of the corporation that renders the notion of harmony within this system deceitful or perhaps just naïve. It seems as though Taylor's true purpose here is to teach leaders and managers how to ideologically train their workers to buy into the system. Supporting this speculative analysis Taylor (1911) makes the case that a smart steward of the vast majority, what we might paternalistically call *the mediocre masses*, does not merely search for the most competent or best trained bodies to do the work required, but rather, *he* takes it upon *himself* to "systematically" "train" and "make" a "competent" (p. 6) work force. Only then, Taylor (1911) boasts, "shall we be on the road to national efficiency" (p. 6).

Summarizing his new vision, Taylor (1991) charges that "in the past the man has been first; in the future the system must be first" (p. 7). Cautious *not* to imply that the natural hierarchy of intelligence or competence can somehow be eliminated or dismantled through the leveling effect of equal systematic training rendering the need for leaders or managers redundant, Taylor firmly states:

> This in no sense, however, implies that great men are not needed. On the contrary, the first object of any good system must be that of developing first-class men; and under systematic management the best man rises to the top more certainly and more rapidly than ever before. (p. 7)

The educational supporters of big business and the ruling elite, who advocated for a model of social education that was based on the assumption that the curriculum should be constructed to fit the indoctrinating needs of business and nationalism following the strict disciplinary reductionism of subject matter, found a useful tool in Taylor's patriarchal ideas. This traditional model of education is based on the idea that educational resources should be tightly controlled to ensure the regimentation of knowledge production and the development of habits and dispositions conducive to the needs of business. This model of education assumes:

~ There is knowledge of an objective reality, the assumed content of *pure science*, that exists outside and independent of the mind and politics.

~ If knowledge exists outside the realm of human intervention, then *truth* can be absolutely known and externally imposed mechanically irrespective of the learners' and educators' culture, context, and relationship to dominant forms of power.

~ The problem with schools is that students are not committing enough objective, predetermined *facts* to memory.

~ The pedagogy of teachers is inefficient therefore failing to deposit as much knowledge within students as is possible.

Again, Taylor's approach promised managers and leaders a *scientific* solution to all forms of social organization concerning current and potential oppressed and agitated populations because it is grounded in the assumptions of mechanical philosophy that views humans as fully-programmable machines, despite the fact that Newton had debunked the approach through his discovery of *action at a distance* or free will/consciousness, which Galileo and others praised as the species' most *noble gift*. However, Newton had no scientific explanation for *free will*, that is, the *absurd* notion of being animated by an independent (not divine), non-material, perhaps spiritual, entity. Three hundred years later science still cannot explain free will or the phenomenon of consciousness. Traditional psychology, through behaviorism, has attempted to solve the problem by denying the problem, arguing that *free will is an illusion because humans are designed like machines that only respond according to external conditioning*. That is, humans, according to the behaviorists, are not *designed* to be *free*.

However, this explanation is inadequate at best, and dangerous at worst, because we know that humans suffer when our creative capacities are externally controlled as wageworkers, for example, rendering the concept of extreme importance for educational leaders. Many critics have therefore concluded that the notion of *scientific management* and behaviorism are pseudo-sciences because they appear to be more concerned with fulfilling social and ideological needs of power and privilege than a rigorous engagement with accepted values and ideas of the scientific community (Chomsky, 1987). Consequently, behaviorism can be understood as an extension of Taylor's ideas. That is, behaviorism appears to be an effort to transform a crude method and theory of social control into a respected academic discipline and legitimate *science*. It is therefore not surprising that many contemporary behaviorists consider themselves to be scientists.

Behaviorism

Challenging the claim that behaviorism is founded upon scientific principles and is therefore a legitimate science, internationally renowned professor emeritus of linguistics at the Massachusetts Institute of Technology (MIT), Noam Chomsky (1987), argues that the notion of human malleability, which, again, assumes that free will is an illusion, is an outdated, pseudo-scientific generalization of the nineteenth century. It is a *generalization* because it *is* true that people can be manipulated and trained to be obedient workers acting against their own class and human interests, but there are limits to human malleability not recognized within behaviorism. Founding figure of critical pedagogy, the late Brazilian Paulo Freire, developed an approach to teaching and learning that continues to disrupt the central underlying assumption behind behaviorism, that is, that we are only, and can only ever be, the product of our external conditioning.

Rather, Freire (2005), drawing on the work of Vygotsky, observed that we are in fact the product of what we inherit *and* what we acquire. What he was alluding to was that while people can be conditioned or indoctrinated through behaviorist pedagogy, we are not machines or computers, and therefore have the ability to become aware of our socially-constructed schemas and alter them through *purposeful action* utilizing the intellectual gifts we are endowed with as a species. Again, assuming that humanity is *wholly malleable* therefore fails to acknowledge the omnipresence of our biological endowments and, consequently, the existence of agency and resistance to oppression among even the most indoctrinated, uneducated (according to Euro-centric Western standards), and isolated communities.

This is an epistemological and ontological leap behaviorism is not willing to make because, as a discipline, it is based on the assumption that there is no internal reality hidden from science as Newton and others have suggested. For behaviorists, everything that is real is external, factual, observable, and fully knowable. The behavior patterns and decision making of humans, from this perspective, have nothing to do with a non-material, intelligent consciousness, but are the result of environmental conditioning. From a leadership perspective, the goal of behaviorist research is therefore to understand teacher and student behavior patterns and how they are caused by environmental conditions thereby more efficiently designing leadership strategies to obtain the desired behavior or outcome. It is the managerial act of manipulation that is touted as a science. As a result, behaviorists claim to be uncovering the laws of behavior, and, as a result, believe they are able to devise universal strategies to universally control them.

As we will see in the pages that follow this conclusion is not the result of objective science, but is the West's arrogant attempt to control nature and harness its value-generating potential. Indigeneity has a lot to offer here. When people attempt to transform the balance inherent within natural ecosystems by clear-cutting forests, damming rivers, and polluting the world's bodies of water, for example, we do not make life better as we believe we are. What we do, on the other hand, is suffocate life, and because all life is connected, all life, including human life, suffers. While it is true that ecosystems are not static entities, and are therefore always in some stage of evolutionary development, the source of nature's progress is not external, but rather internal. Because of human intelligence and our unique ability to transform the world like no other species, we also have a unique responsibility not to abuse our intellectual powers or gifts. The current gross imbalances among people and between people and the rest of the world are the product of a mechanical philosophy that is informed by a reductionism that separates values, politics, and culture from science and industrial society.

Edward Thorndike

Edward Thorndike is considered to be the scholar and researcher most responsible for the ascendancy of experimental psychology (Pinar, Reynolds, Slattery and Taubman, 2000) that presupposes the mind and consciousness are knowable and measurable properties as a challenge to the views informed by Newton and other Western scientists who maintain that the force or cause of our movement is a largely unknowable and mysterious entity. Paradoxically, Thorndike disregards the established knowledge of the scientific community by referring to its content as *philosophical*, and thus not as *objectively true* as the *facts* generated through his more *scientific* methodology. It is therefore not surprising that the field of education, which continues to be informed by a neomechanical paradigm, tends not to be taken seriously by the scientific community and institutions of higher education (outside of colleges and departments of education) more generally. A transformative educational leader, in this context, demands that pedagogy and curriculum be informed by what the scientific community agrees are the most up-to-date ideas and knowledge regarding the cognitive nature of humanness. Towards these ends, we will briefly explore the assumptions embedded within Thorndike's approach to teaching and learning, which, I argue, are essentially philosophical.

Thorndike's paradigm, represented most fully in *Educational Psychology* (1910), stands in stark contrast to where scientific knowledge *was* and *is* in regards to human nature and the mind. For example, in *Educational Psychology* (1910) Thorndike's pedagogical place of departure is the presupposition that the primary responsibility of the educator is to control student behavior, which is falsely assumed is possible due to the machine-like quality of the mind. Education, from this perspective, is a mechanical act interested in discovering the most efficient methods of achieving the predetermined outcomes of behavior modification. While Thorndike does acknowledge that there are some qualities and cognitive endowments that are innate or inherited, he places special significance on those that are variable due to environmental factors, such as formal education.

While the scientific community tends to be wary regarding the measurability of little known properties such as intelligence, Thorndike assumes it is well defined and therefore absolutely knowable, measurable, and subject to external manipulation. Beginning his study with this presupposition Thorndike (1910) notes that, "exact knowledge of the nature and amount of individual differences in intellect, character, and behavior is valuable to educational theory and practice..." (p. 3). The educational significance here, for Thorndike (1910), is that it leads to "knowledge of what human beings are," enabling educational leaders and educators to "choose the best means for changing them for the better" (p. 3). The underlying assumption is therefore an ontological hierarchy where the vast majority are viewed as deficient and therefore in need of *being* educated. The legitimacy of the educational leader as manager and, at times, although increasingly less frequently, policy maker, in this context, comes from their superior knowledge or intellect.

Consequently, Thorndike (1910) believed that some differences between individuals, such as mental ability or cognition, were due to what he called *remote ancestry*. By this he meant that the more a group has remained isolated and can therefore trace its lineage back within that same group, the more a distinct race they will be. The more distinct, the more unique physical and mental qualities they will possess. Summarizing this point Thorndike (1910) reasons, "an individual may thus, by original nature, possess certain racial mental tendencies. His position on the scale for any mental trait may be due in part to his membership in a certain race" (p. 51). However, Thorndike (1910) offers a modest qualification, noting that because of the high degree of integration between all of the peoples of the world in the modern era, "the influence of remote ancestry...cannot be isolated for measurement...perfectly" (p. 51).

Despite the difficulty in untangling what is the result of biological endowment and what is the result of social experience and intervention, Thorndike (1910) concludes that, "the most noticeable fact about the races of men seems to be their great mental variety" (p. 64).

Thorndike's conclusions here, while they supported the white supremacist dominant socio-political-economic order of his own time, were not grounded in valid scientific methodology and rigor. Descartes' (1637/1994) observation that "good sense is, of all things among men, the most equally distributed" (p. 3), had not been refuted by science although the eugenicists certainly tried. Even Darwin acknowledged that the notion of race is a social construct.

For example, during the mid-1800s when Darwin was engaged in his studies it was commonly argued that "races were so distant from one another that interbreeding was impossible" (Zimmer, 2007, p. 226). Darwin, on the other hand, who, at his best, was truly a man of science, "considered many of the differences between peoples to be minor," so minor in fact that he did not "think natural selection had shaped them" and that our species is "variable" like "dogs or pigeons" (Zimmer, 2007, p. 227). Summarizing these conclusions he reached after years of rigorous academic, field-based, study Darwin comments,

> The great variability of all external differences between the races of man…indicates that they cannot be of much importance; for if important, they would long ago have been either fixed and preserved, or eliminated. In this respect man resembles those forms, called by naturalists protean or polymorphic, which have remained extremely variable, owing, as it seems, to such variations being of an indifferent nature, and to their having thus escaped the action of natural selection. (p. 274)

Darwin's scientific habits of mind, at their best, clearly led him away from the false hierarchy of white supremacy and about as far from the so-called *social Darwinism* that attempts to inscribe the racial biases of conquest and capital on his work through the imposition of natural selection, which, to reiterate, was never considered a factor in determining human variability or race. In other words, while Darwin concluded that natural selection must be responsible for human intelligence, it is not related in any way to the socially constructed concept of race, rendering intellectual variability among the species completely random, as suggested by Descartes and others.

Thorndike's mechanical racialized approach that assumes human behavior is as predictable and malleable as a machine, which relies on a static, reducible, unchanging conception of the world, can therefore be understood as not based on science but on the political motivation of the accumulation of wealth through the exploitation of human labor power, which requires a certain amount of control over the human mind. Behaviorism therefore claims to be based on science and therefore non-political, but is informed by biased and ulterior motives. Behaviorist psychology therefore does not foster an education that is based on intellectual growth and human advancement according to the Enlightenment values of social justice, democracy and equality, in which science is supposed to be grounded.

B.F. Skinner

One of the most well-known founders of behaviorism, Burrhus Frederic Skinner, born in Pennsylvania in 1904, like Taylor and Thorndike before him, advanced the mechanical approach to human nature that is inherently hierarchical and conducive to indoctrinating practices. Regarded as one of the most important psychologists of the twentieth century, Skinner spent the later part of his career as a professor at Harvard. By his many supporters Skinner is deemed a progressive utopian visionary while his critics interpret his work as an attack on the very core of the human essence—our independent creative nature referred to above as *free will*. What follows is a brief critique of Skinner's (1971/2002) *Beyond Freedom & Dignity*, where these ideas are most fully explored and elaborated on.

Skinner (1971/2002) begins his analysis making the case that science and technology are simultaneously both the cause *and* solution of the major social problems of his day such as homelessness and industrial abuses to the natural environment. Skinner recognizes that science, as a tool, is well equipped to fashion technologies that could lay the ground work for the development of a just and responsible society. Aware that science does not work without human agents Skinner (1971/2002) rightfully concludes that:

> The application of the physical and biological sciences alone will not solve our problems because the solutions lie in another field. Better contraceptives will control population only if people use them...and the environment will continue to deteriorate until polluting practices are abandoned. In short, we need to make vast changes in human behavior...(p. 4)

Among these problems Skinner (1971/2002) includes "the disaffection and revolt of the young" (p. 4). This statement suggests that his work supports the interests of the ruling elite who become nervous when working people organize and take political action in ways that can be perceived as being done on behalf of their own class interests. To avoid such problems Skinner (1971/2002) proposes the development of a "technology of behavior" (p. 5). Toward these ends, Skinner (1971/2002) clearly breaks from accepted truths within the scientific community, with origins in the work of Newton, Hume, Descartes, Priestley, Chomsky, and others, arguing that "it is easy to conclude that there must be something about human behavior which makes a scientific analysis, and hence an effective technology, impossible, but we have not by any means exhausted the possibilities" (p. 7). Skinner undoubtedly is referring here to that notion of *free will* or consciousness that has been credited as the *cause* of human behavior tending to be *inclined* to act in certain ways given specific environmental conditions, but not *compelled*, making absolute predictability utterly impossible. Skinner (1971/2002), however, argues that in contemporary times, "intelligent people" no longer attribute the causes of human behavior to "indwelling agents" (p. 9).

Reflecting on Skinner's (1971/2002) *Beyond Freedom & Dignity* Chomsky (1987) notes that, "his speculations are devoid of scientific content and do not even hint at general outlines of a possible science of human behavior" (p. 158). A leading scientist in his own right, Chomsky's (1987) objective here is to disassociate science from Skinners' work because:

> He appears to be attacking fundamental human values, demanding control in place of the defense of freedom and dignity. There seems something scandalous in this, and since Skinner invokes the authority of science, some critics condemn science itself, or "the scientific view of man," for supporting such conclusions…(p. 158)

What has been particularly objectionable about Skinner's ideas is that they represent an industrialized, mechanical science that is devoid of soul and spirit, that is, freedom and dignity, because they are "merely the relics of outdated and mystical beliefs" (Chomsky, 1987, p. 159), suggesting that the objective of society's leaders and managers is not to promote independent thinking citizen participants, as our democracy promises, but rather, to institute effective social controls to ensure *the static, unchanging, survival of the culture.*

A. Maslow

Responding, in part, to the growing criticism against behaviorism, in 1968 Abraham Maslow offered an updated psychology that more centrally acknowledged the existence of an "inner nature" that is intrinsic, unchanging, and essentially "good" as it tends toward the well being of self-actualization. However, Maslow (1968) is clever, he contends that while our inner nature "rarely disappears in the normal person," it is, paradoxically, "weak" and therefore when people are exploited by the "slave owner" or the "dictator" (funny he does not mention the capitalist or colonizer), "most people do not protest …they take it" (p. 8). As a result, the oppressed tend to live unfulfilled, miserable lives.

The role of the psychologist or the educational leader is thus to "tell" the oppressed "how to be good, how to be happy, how to be fruitful, how to respect himself, how to love, how to fulfill his highest potentialities" (Maslow, 1968, p. 4). Maslow therefore arrives at the same place as Skinner, that is, because of the deficits of the general population, external conditioning is the moral responsibility of those more supremely endowed. Maslow's complete silence regarding the pathology of the oppressor serves only to leave intact the hierarchy of class society.

Again, Maslow advances an ontology of hierarchy where the exceptional few, who are able to retain their internal structure under the stress of external forces, possess a moral responsibility to paternalistically empower and train the structurally unsound masses. Within the imagined universe of this hierarchy it is only the strong who possess the fortitude to grasp and hold on to the truth. Leadership, from this perspective, is equally concerned with controlling information and depositing predetermined factoids and knowledge about the world and how to be better than his predecessors and contemporaries. The act of discovery and learning, rather than attributed to anything internal within the learner, is attributed to the proper administration of efficient and productive behavioral modification technologies.

While the work of Maslow and Skinner, by some standards, might seem outdated and old, their ideas continue to hold sway in the public domain and in public schools and their training programs in particular, and therefore continue to stand as an impediment to democratic practice.

R. Nisbett

For example, contemporary figures such as James Flynn, Emeritus Professor of Political Studies at the University of Otago in Dunedin, New Zealand and author of the influential *What Is Intelligence?* (2007), and Richard Nisbett, leading scholar in cultural psychology and intelligence and Distinguished University Professor at the University of Michigan, Ann Arbor and author of *Intelligence and How to Get It* (2009), have, essentially, advanced an environmental-behaviorist approach to intelligence that suggests that Western culture produces smarter people, and schools should therefore, the reasoning proceeds, be reformed accordingly. Because Nisbett's (2009) work, unlike Flynn's, is situated specifically in the context of education, what follows is a brief analysis of *Intelligence and How to Get It*.

Like his predecessors, from Taylor to Maslow and Skinner, Nisbett (2009) begins by attempting to connect his work to legitimate science and the discourse of progressivism, arguing that, "results of recent research in psychology, genetics, and neuroscience, along with current studies on the effectiveness of educational interventions, have overturned the strong hereditarian position on intelligence" (pp. 1–2). Nisbett is clearly referring to the white promotion of the many discursive constructions that have assumed that people of color are genetically inferior. However, he does not mention the role these discourses served in justifying the enslavement and acts of genocide committed against Africans and Native Americans (Menchaca, 1997), for example. Taking what may appear to be a position for social justice, Nisbett (2009), rejecting genetic causes of intelligence, proclaims, "intelligence is highly modifiable by the environment" (p. 2). Careful not to lose his culturally conservative audience, in the very next line, Nisbett (2009) reassuringly notes that, "without formal education a person is not going to be very bright" (p. 2).

Consequently, Nisbett (2009) does not challenge the policy makers and educational leaders who control and monitor the validation process that deems some knowledge valid and other knowledge invalid or wrong. Knowledge produced from Marxist, Indigenous, postformal, and other non-dominant epistemologies, thus, tends not to be validated in formal institutions of education, especially in the K-12 context during the developmentally formative years. In other words, Nisbett and others are saying that there are millions of people around the world who are not "very bright" because they have not been properly *trained* how to think and how to *behave* through the *scientific management technologies* of Western schools and demonstrated appropriate levels of competence and internalization of accepted values and facts, which happen to be increasingly influenced by corporate interests and saturated with a deeply entrenched Euro-centric culture of deficit thinking.

Returning to the core data and philosophical assumptions of *Intelligence and How to Get It*, what becomes apparent is Nisbett's supposedly objective conclusions seem thoroughly entrenched in the same deficit thinking he has attempted to disassociate himself from. For example, after his initial discussions Nisbett (2009) exposes his behaviorist orientation commenting "the environment counts for a lot in determining IQ and could conceivably account for more if we could think of the right ways to change it" (p. 22). Intelligence, in this context, is something to be externally controlled and manipulated by those properly trained. Alluding to this cultural bias Nisbett acknowledges the high degree of cultural bias embedded within IQ tests but does not find it important enough to question the assumptions behind the belief that intelligence is knowable and measurable.

***

Behaviorism and its recent manifestations—manifestations that may not always self-identify as behaviorist, but are nevertheless informed by very similar constructs—therefore promote a mechanical, hierarchical ontology that conceives the world of humans as nothing more, or very little more, than the manifestation of efficient or inefficient, conscious or unconscious, social engineering— the notion of an internal, independent, *will*, *consciousness* or *spirit*, in the behaviorist paradigm, is assumed to be a primitive, mystical, unsophisticated superstition of the unenlightened, uneducated, ignorant masses.

The leadership goal here is therefore to develop human engineering tactics that most efficiently and mechanically deposit sanctioned truths and reinforce desired behaviors facilitating the development of student dispositions and skills most conducive to the needs of wealth and power, such as *being a team player* or *works well with others*, which translates into *does what they are told, follows directions, is obedient, does not talk to others when the teacher is talking* and so on. Coincidentally, these dispositions represent the needs of corporations with their hierarchical structures and concentrated wealth and decision-making. This system would be meaningless and ineffective if its traditional, hegemonic keepers of knowledge production and education did not assume that their approach was objectively superior, or representative of the one right answer to social organization. This one right answer approach or one correct way to understand and view the world has legitimated itself by claiming to be based on the neutral, objective facts of science, which exist outside the realm of politics and human error and bias.

Again, leadership, in this context, is not a shared activity between equal stakeholders, but a paternalistic act that is either *done to* or *on behalf of*. Managing teaching and learning is therefore always informed by the presupposition that intelligence is either naturally unequally distributed or it varies according to objectively inferior and superior cultures, and middle-class educational leaders, working in middle class and working class schools, are therefore assumed to be better equipped to make curricular and pedagogical decisions than those most directly affected, teachers and students.

However, despite behaviorism's failure to hold up to the rigorous scrutiny of the scientific community, it continues to inform the training and practice of educational leaders. It should therefore not be surprising that behaviorism, like Taylorism, continues to inform much of what goes on in schools from leadership/administration to classroom teaching.

Systems Theory

More recently, however, a new discourse has emerged, the language of systems theory, which equates social systems to biological systems rendering the former as objective and politically neutral as the latter. Proponents of this model argue that social systems, like biological systems, are comprised of four basic "components," "inputs," "processes," "output," and "feedback loops" (Chance, 2009, p. 41).

For example, in schools inputs include a wide range of *external sources* like laws and policy, such as the No Child Left Behind Act (NCLB), as well as human resources such as teachers and paraprofessionals. The processes in an educational system refer to the institutionally defined roles of each of the participants, or the division of labor. That is, it is the task of teachers to teach, of students to learn, and administrators to administer. The outputs then, are the results of the processes. These include exam scores, student dispositions, beliefs and values, and their overall performance. Feedback comes from those who identify their interests as being connected to these outcomes, such as students, parents, and business leaders (Chance, 2009).

This system, like other biological systems, so the argument goes, tends to function properly because it is *normative*. That is, schools, as systems, "have an established system of sanctions that can be brought to bear on those who do not behave in the manner which is expected of them" (Chance, 2009, p. 44). This internal feedback structure therefore functions to ensure stability and harmony. Leadership roles, from teachers to principals, therefore tend to be designed to enforce "ascribed roles in the social system to maintain equilibrium" (Chance, 2009, p. 45).

However, this is not a *natural* system, it is a political system constructed by the minds of men and women designed to present itself as normal and natural, and thus hegemonized or taken for granted as a non-perspective. Within this slightly adjusted mechanical approach to scientific management, the purpose of schooling is not questioned. What is questioned is the practice of management. In other words, curricular considerations are sacrificed for a decontextualized pedagogy of efficiency as the focus of inquiry. Educational leaders here are merely technicists charged with managing and carrying out the orders handed down from above in a standardized, one-size-fits-all format. Even adjusted versions of the *systems* approach that takes into consideration the uncertainty of the individual are ultimately designed not to transform the system but to perpetuate its existence through the establishment of harmony/equilibrium/social stability.

Consequences of Modern Day Mechanics in Education

Distributed Leadership

Current *innovation* in educational leadership tends to conform to the same view of the world established by social efficiency behaviorism. That is, social organizations exist as they do because they are functional. The purpose of leadership is therefore to ensure that the systems operate as they were intended, serving the interests built into their internal logic. *Distributed leadership*, for example, has been identified by leading scholars in the field, such as James Spillane (2003), as representing a "potentially fruitful direction for research on educational leadership" because it is "grounded in a concern with leadership for improving teaching and learning" (p. 344).

However, the notion of *improving* here does not imply challenging the view of what it means to learn, but rather, it implies more efficiently carrying out the agenda that was established by existing policy makers. In other words, it does not mean questioning the increasing role that high stakes standardized testing has played through NCLB in determining what students and what schools are effective. Success, according to mainstream leadership theory, is equated with the ability to most efficiently comply with the Adequate Yearly Progress goals set by NCLB guidelines.

The Euro-centrism and White Supremacy of Social Efficiency

The one-size-fits-all approach that has emerged from the hyper-reductionism of Cartesian philosophy and science that claims it is not only possible, but desirable, to disconnect facts and knowledge from politics and the larger context in which humans always construct knowledge, has clearly had the effect of ignoring the white-Euro perspective informing the Western science of capital. As a result of this privileging of whiteness (it is the white perspective that is present-ed as the non-perspective), those who do not construct knowledge from this perspective tend to not be recognized for their intellect and higher order think-ing skills. It is therefore not surprising that dropout rates, especially among those non-whites whose first language is not English, are particularly high. Within most schools we therefore find an exaggerated emphasis on outcomes (test scores) at the expense of understanding the validation process and the central role of dominant power in determining what goes on in schools (Kincheloe, 2005).

The Larger Context: Mechanical Functionalism as Social Organization

Ultimately, it can be argued that the mechanical approach to education, from leadership to classroom teaching, is designed to serve the interests of perpetu-ating an industrial model of capitalism. This hegemony continues, in large part, because people in these societies, such as the United States and Canada, at this stage in their development, from birth to death, are only ever exposed to social institutions organized hierarchically. Consequently reinforced is the idea that capitalism is the final and most advanced stage of human evolution *because* it most closely reflects an assumed objective hierarchy of intelligence measured by IQ and other high stakes test scores, caused by either genetics or culture, it is almost inconsequential that both are misconstrued.

The underlying assumption is that the small minority of elite leaders who make the majority of decisions concerning economic, military, educational, and other political affairs are better equipped to run *our* lives than *we* are. As a result of growing up in these institutions, schools in particular, students, from just *being* there, develop identities that connect them with a spectator approach to democratic participation and citizenship formation. In the schools where those who rely on a wage to survive attend, students are rewarded for *following direc-tions, paying attention, being quiet,* and remembering *the right answer* and punished for *talking too much, disrupting the teacher, not* remembering what you were told, and following your own internal interests and desires.

However, it is perhaps the social norms and sanctions *between* students that not only prevents them from fully engaging traditional *and* progressive instruc-tion but also prevents them from embracing student resistance that is transfor-mational, not just self-destructive. For example, consumer culture and popular commodities or products, such as sneakers and apparel, have influenced youth identity to such an extent that it is simply not *cool* to be critical or revolutionary because these approaches inevitably clash with the logic of capital and competitive, expansive consumption habits that signify social status and worth. One of the primary sources of bullying among students is not surprisingly being *out of fashion* and *poor* and ultimately, implicitly or explicitly *ignorant* or *stupid*.

The system, or the basic structures of power and class privilege, is self-perpetuating because it conditions its citizens through the mass media and education to equate wealth with intelligence. One only need rhetorically ask how many hundreds of movies follow the story line of the impoverished genius whose dedication and hard work eventually pay off financially, proving the legitimacy of the assumed meritocracy built into capitalism. We might also ask how many black and brown rap artists are packaged and marketed by large corporate advertising firms as proto-capitalist thugs whose sole motivation is material gain and access to elite consumer culture.

It is therefore the task of critical pedagogues to make social justice *cool* and positive, democratic transformation against neoliberalism *in style* and *hip*. The idea is not to re-indoctrinate or manipulate students but rather to foster a social culture where caring and being responsible to future unborn generations is not considered weak or unrealistic romanticism.

What follows is an outline of how conservative discourses have historically contributed to the philosophy or worldview that underlies the hegemony just outlined, focusing on the idea and practice of *leadership*. What we find, similar to what we have found above in the education leadership literature, is the advancement of a mechanical understanding of the world and its relationships. Put another way, the discussion below presents another influence on leadership practices in government, economics, and, inevitably, education.

***

Widely influential French sociologist, Emile Durkheim, is considered to be one of the "fathers" and founders of sociology and anthropology. Through the late 1800s Durkheim set out to demonstrate that the deep inequality between social classes that drew much attention from critics such as Marx—a central aspect of the Industrial Revolution that began in England—was a natural product of the development of human societies, and should therefore not be resisted, but encouraged through such sorting mechanisms as schools. Durkheim's educational leader here is the *grand sorter*, the overseer of the *educational factory* where *raw materials*, that is students, are *fed* in, and, after the pro-

duction process of school, the *output* consists of ranked groupings to fill the natural division of labor and consequently, the hierarchy of social classes, leaders
and laborers.

Essentially, what Durkheim (1893/2000) argues is that humanity (those natural followers relegated to the status of worker) would be wise to divest itself
of any illusions of maintaining an independent, democratic existence and
rather "equip yourself to fulfill usefully a specific function" (p. 39) because society and its leaders require it, that is, to bend ourselves to fit within the system
that exists, to submit ourselves to the labor it requires. What Durkheim suggests is that the bourgeoisie, rather than a ruling class that embodies its own
negation, represents the end of history and therefore the manifestation of the
final and most advanced stage of human social evolution. The educational
leader as *sorting manager*, from this ontological perspective, is therefore *not* contributing to a socially constructed system of oppression, but is only assisting society to come into greater balance with the natural, uneven order of the universe.

However, Durkheim could not ignore the intensity of the class antagonism
of his time and the recent memory of the workers' Paris Commune of 1871.
Acknowledging the human need of not being made a slave or being externally controlled, while maintaining his belief that inequality serves a necessary
function in *advanced* societies, Durkheim notes that "moral life, like that of body
and mind, responds to different needs which may even be contradictory. Thus
it is natural for it to be made up in part of opposing elements..." (p. 39). In
effect, Durkheim tells us that "progress" has a price—a price that tends to cause
distress within the individual—but that is the nature of the universe, and it is
not wise to challenge laws of nature. Building the foundation for this "functionalist" approach to sociology in his dissertation Durkheim (1893/2000) theorizes:

> We can no longer be under any illusion about the trends in modern industry. It
> involves increasingly powerful mechanisms, large-scale groupings of power and capi-
> tal, and consequently an extreme division of labor....This evolution occurs sponta-
> neously and unthinkingly. Those economists who study its causes and evaluate its
> results, far from condemning such diversification or attacking it, proclaim its necessi-
> ty. They perceive in it the higher law of human societies and the condition for
> progress. (pp. 37–38)

Again, Durkheim does not stop here in his analysis of *objective reality* as he
reaches ever deeper into the grandiose, going on to argue that the division of
labor does not just occur within the realm of economics but can be identified
within every aspect of life, and within all forms of life, rendering it a "biolog-

ical phenomenon," and therefore a law of nature. In the process Durkheim contributes to the theoretical foundation of the *systems theory* approach to leadership outlined above. This perspective is decidedly hegemonic as it claims that capitalism happened "spontaneously" and "unthinkingly," thereby effectively rewriting history, erasing the long struggle against the commodification of humanity that was anything but *spontaneous* or *without thought*.

This basic formula, with roots in Platonic epistemology that views intelligence as naturally and unevenly distributed, continues to exist in contemporary hegemonic discourses of the ruling elite—it is the presupposition informing the entire foundation of ruling class policy and practice including educational leadership. What follows is an analysis of how this framework of leadership has influenced policy in the United States situated in a more contemporary context from Lippmann to Friedman.

***

Beginning with Walter Lippmann we investigate how the idea of a natural hierarchy represented in the existence of rankable social classes informed his leadership ideas concerning both domestic and foreign affairs. Walter Lippmann was a highly influential architect of this discursive model contributing significantly to the implementation of its practice, a point world-renowned scholar/activist Noam Chomsky (1999) has consistently given much attention to. For more than fifty years Lippmann was perhaps the most respected political journalist in the United States "winning the attention of national political leaders from the era of Woodrow Wilson through that of Lyndon B. Johnson" (Wilentz, 2008, p. vii). However, it is important to note that Lippmann, however objectionable his work might be from a progressive perspective, as argued below, represents the progressive end of the elite political continuum of hierarchy. Lippmann's *moderate* elitism, in part, can be attributed to the influence of British liberal economist John Maynard Keynes (1936/1997), who paternalistically advocated for a series of restrictions and taxations placed on accumulated wealth in order to "get rid" of the "objectionable characteristics of capital," such as "instability" (p. 221). This was done not only on behalf of the ignorant masses too stupid to handle their own affairs but also to keep them placid and working (or waiting to work).

Lippmann (1937/2005) argued that taxing the rich was necessary in "relatively rich societies," such as the United States, because "there is a strong tendency for the supply of capital to become so large that the rate of interest falls to a level where there is little inducement to invest it in new enterprise" (p.

229). In other words, when the profit gained from investing x amount of cap-ital becomes so minimal that taking the economic risks that accompany spec-ulative enterprise leads to dramatic reductions in investment and the resulting economic instability, government intervention becomes a necessity for the per-petuation of capitalism. When capitalists hoard capital, Lippmann (1937/2005) reasons, substantial sums of "wealth" are "withheld from use," which slows down production, increases unemployment, and leads to "the extreme poverty of the marginal workers" (p. 229).

Lippmann (1937/2005) concludes that "under these circumstances" it is necessary to use "taxing power" to "pump the surplus funds of the rich out of the ordinary capital market and into public investments" (p. 229). This form of leadership presupposes an unequal relationship resembling a parent making decisions for their small children not mature or sophisticated enough to under-stand the world, let alone decide its fate. Within this discourse public leader-ship, from the role of principals, superintendents, and secretaries of education, is positioned as a neutral occupation necessary to ensure workers are not beat-en up too badly by their natural capitalist superiors. The government leader therefore regulates the balance of power by placing limits and restrictions on capital.

For example, Keynes (1936/1997) points to the "separation between own-ership and management" and "the development of organized investment mar-kets," that is, the *Stock Exchange* system, as contributing to both increased investment, which, from a capitalist perspective, is positive, but also to "great-ly" enhancing "the instability of the system" (pp. 150–151). For example, Keynes (1936/1997) observes that because the Stock Exchange is primarily designed to "facilitate transfers of old investments between one individual and another," there is a propensity to "spend on a new project what may seem an extravagant sum, if it can be floated off on the Stock Exchange at an imme-diate profit" (p. 151). As a solution Keynes (1936/1997) suggests that capital should be made "less scarce" to "diminish" the "excess yield" or profit, which can be done "without its having become less productive—at least in the phys-ical sense" (p. 213). This ability to stabilize markets through regulating "the competition of the rate of interest on money" led Keynes (1936/1997) to "sym-pathize" with the observation that all value "is produced by labor" (p. 213).

While John Maynard Keynes is responsible for developing the economic theory known as *social democratic liberalism*, which was harshly condemned during the 1950s and beyond by Friedman and other neoliberals as *socialist* or *collectivist* and therefore *misguided* (Hill & Kumar, 2009; Hursh, 2008; Porfilio

& Malott, 2008), Lippmann can be said to have situated the theory within a propagandist framework. Again, within the Western tradition of hegemonic philosophy and practice, Lippmann's ideas tended to fall on the liberal end of the spectrum. That is, while he believed it was the paternalistic responsibility of democratic governmental leadership, comprised of those endowed with a naturally superior intelligence, to mold "the will of the people," it must be for *the common good* and carried out without the conscious manipulation of propaganda. Set against what he believed to be the crude tactics of McCarthyism and the Red Scare, Lippmann was concerned with purifying "the rivers of opinion that fed public opinion" (Steel, 2008, p. xv).

Like Durkheim before him, Lippmann too, discounted the ideals of democracy (such as the notion that the will of the people does not need to be externally commanded through a hierarchical structure of leadership) as an "illusion" referring to it in *Public Opinion* (1922) as "the original dogma of democracy." As we will see, Lippmann constructed a theory of humanity, assumed to represent *objective reality*, as being too ignorant and steeped in prejudice and bias to be able to achieve the necessary competence to know what is best for themselves, rendering the theoretical idea of democracy a fantastic vision, but not conducive to the imperfect reality of human depravity. Lippmann biographer Ronald Steel (2008), in his foreword to the recently re-issued *Liberty and the News* (1920/2008), reasons that:

> The horrors of World War I had shattered his optimism about human nature. His propaganda work, reinforced by the repressive activities of the government's propaganda bureau, the Committee on Public Information, had made him realize how easily public opinion could be molded. He had always believed that a free press was the cornerstone of democracy. He still believed that, but with a new qualification. (pp. xii-xiii)

That "qualification" was his assertion that democracy itself is an unachievable ideal. Contributing to his belief in the inferior intelligence of the general public was his engagement with the emerging field of behaviorist psychology, as outlined above, that reinforced his beliefs about the nature of human perception rendering most people unfit to participate in the democratic process. For example, in *The Phantom Public* (1927) Lippmann argues that, "man's reflexes are, as the psychologists say, conditioned. And, therefore, he responds quite readily to a glass egg, a decoy duck, a stuffed shirt, or a political platform" (p. 30). Lippmann was clearly informed by the idea that the public is limited to perceiving the world only as it has been trained to. As a result, there tends to be a great gap between what is believed about the world and the actual world, or, *objec-*

tive reality. According to Lippmann (1927), not only is the public inherently limited in its sense of perception, but in its desire to know, commenting that "the citizen gives but a little of his time to public affairs, has but a casual interest in facts and but a poor appetite for theory" (p. 24–25).

Summarizing his position Lippmann (1927) concludes that it is false to "...assume that either the voters are inherently competent to direct the course of affairs or that they are making progress toward such an ideal. I think it is a false ideal. I do not mean an undesirable ideal. I mean an unattainable ideal..." (pp. 38–39). Lippmann therefore viewed education as no more suitable to foster the intelligence needed for democratic competence within average citizens than any other false sense of hope. Within this social universe of capital it is therefore the task of educational leaders to paternalistically create the conditions where students can avoid complete marginalization by acquiring the basic skills and dispositions demanded by capital. As it turns out then, the United States, which has long presented itself as *the* world's leading proponent of democracy, has a history of being influenced by thinkers who believe in hierarchy and supremacy and therefore view the theoretical context of democracy as not representative of the concrete context of human nature, and therefore an unwise leadership goal to pursue. However, not only was democracy portrayed as unwise but dangerous. Summarizing this point in classic prose Lippmann (1927) notes:

> A false ideal of democracy can lead only to disillusionment and to meddlesome tyranny. If democracy cannot direct affairs, then a philosophy which expects it to direct them will encourage the people to attempt the impossible; they will fail, but that will interfere outrageously with the productive liberties of the individual. The public must be put in its place, so that it may exercise its own powers, but no less and perhaps even more, so that each of us may live free of the trampling and the roar of a bewildered herd. (p. 145)

Of course men like Lippmann, armed with their superior capacities, do not suffer from the afflictions of inadequacy or the illusion that the public man is of the same mind as the public. From this perspective the division of labor is largely based on the naturally occurring unequal capacities of *men* rendering some more fit to lead and design the social structure, while the most useful function for the vast majority reside in their physical ability to follow direction and labor—as passive spectators rather than active participants. The responsibility of those most fit to lead, the responsible or capable men, is therefore to regiment the public mind as an army regiments its troops. This is the boss's moral and paternalistic "commitment," as Lippmann (1943) referred to it. Because Lippmann's conception of leadership was based on the assumption of a natural hierarchy, he was logically able to claim a moral relativism as well, which stands in stark contrast to critical pedagogy's privileging of democratic relations over the unjust relationship between labor and capital, that is, between the oppressed and their oppressors. In making this case—a case ultimately against democracy—Lippmann (1927) proclaims, "it requires intense partisanship and much self-deception to argue that some sort of peculiar righteousness adheres to…the employers' against the wage-earners,' the creditors' against the debtors,' or the other way around" (p. 34).

The peculiar nature of Lippmann's political relativism is further brought to the fore in his discourse on U.S. foreign policy and international leadrship where he draws on the notion of "justice" as it pertains to the use of force. Lippmann's analysis in *U.S. Foreign Policy* (1943), seems, in many ways, to be a direct response to the arguments presented in the highly publicized *War Is a Racket* (1935/2003) by anti-war activist, World War I veteran, and Brigadier General Smedley D. Butler. Summarizing his position on war Butler (1935/2003) comments:

> War is a racket. It always has been. It is possibly the oldest, easily the most profitable, surely the most vicious. It is the only one international in scope. It is the only one in which the profits are reckoned in dollars and the losses in lives. (p. 23)

Reflecting on the United States' involvement in the First World War, from a leadership perspective, Butler (1935/2003) notes that, "we forgot, or shunted aside, the advice of the Father of our country. We forgot Washington's warning about 'entangling alliances'" (p. 26). In *U.S. Foreign Policy: Shield of the Republic*, published eight years after *War Is a Racket*, Lippmann (1943) invests a significant amount of time making an argument against the pacifism alluded to in *War Is a Racket*, without, however, referring directly to Butler or his work. Like Butler, Lippmann too draws on the leadership legacy of General George Washington, but draws almost opposite conclusions. Consistent with his usual style, Lippmann (1943) paints a picture of the benevolent leader whose responsibility it is to protect the national interest—the interests of the rich—which *he* must have the military capacity to do. Otherwise, through his vulnerability, he is inviting his enemy's provocation, and therefore irresponsibly putting those who rely on his paternalistic protection at unnecessary risk.

Washington did not say that the nation should or could renounce war and seek only peace. For he knew that the national "interest, guided by justice" might bring the Republic into conflict with other nations. Since he knew that the conflict might be irreconcilable by negotiation and compromise, his primary concern was to make sure that the national interest was wisely and adequately supported with armaments, suitable frontiers, and the appropriate alliances." (Lippmann, 1943, p. 51)

Lippmann's reasoning here is simple enough: an empire, such as the United States, will not survive without room to grow and the muscle needed to protect its "interests," that is, the interests of the rich or responsible men which include the subjugation of their own population during crises of confidence and the extraction and concentration of wealth. The essence of his argumentation lies in the same age-old paternalistic guardianship and moral relativism that allows questions of justice to be freed from issues of domination and subjugation. In making his argument Lippmann cites the Monroe Doctrine of 1823 as evidence of the United States' "commitment" to extend its "protection…to the whole of the Western hemisphere" and that "at the risk of war, the United States would thereafter resist the creation of new European empires in this hemisphere" (Lippmann, 1943, p. 16). Monroe's doctrine has come to be interpreted as "professing a unilateral US 'right' to circumscribe the sovereignty of all other nations in the hemisphere" (Churchill, 2002, p. 335) influencing its aggressive dealings with Indigenous sovereigns within its boundaries and those within its hemisphere such as Cuba and Jamaica and all other Latin American and Caribbean nations (Malott, 2008, 2007; Malott & Malott, 2008).

The context Lippmann situates US foreign policy in provides a useful lens for understanding the nation's current leadership practices. After all, it is the responsibility of the more capable *men* to make decisions for less capable *men*, and any illusions concerning democratic principles only restrict the natural development of the division of labor worldwide. As we will see below, Milton Friedman (1962/2002) picks up on this line of reasoning, yet reflective of the more conservative and reactionary times of the contemporary era, arguing that restrictions on the extraction and accumulation of wealth and the further entrenchment of class antagonisms only threaten the freedom of "progress," that is, capitalism, and of men and women pursuing it.

***

Milton Friedman, pro-capital economist extraordinaire, received worldwide recognition in 1976, winning the Nobel Prize in Economic Sciences and has been touted as the world's most influential economist of the twentieth century. Friedman has drawn the attention of the likes of internationally-renowned political analyst and activist Noam Chomsky (1999) who referred to him as a "neoliberal guru" while vociferously critiquing his (1962/2002) *Capitalism and Freedom* for hegemonically equating "profit-making" with being "the essence of democracy" and that "any government that pursues antimarket policies is being anti-democratic, no matter how much informed popular support they might enjoy" (p. 9).

Friedman's supposition that the surest way to freedom is through capitalism is informed by the ancient hierarchy of intelligence paradigm that views economic competition the playing field most conducive to fostering the environment that will encourage and enable the superior individuals to rise to the top and assume their place as leaders and decision makers, that is, capitalists. Attempts to legislate against exploitation and abuse to ensure a functioning democracy, from this approach to knowledge production, is viewed as an attack on freedom because it prevents the naturally endowed masters from assuming their biologically determined place within the hierarchy. This construction is an unquestionable aspect of *objective reality*. Informed by this logic, the primary responsibility of government is therefore to "preserve the rules of the game by enforcing contracts, preventing coercion, and keeping markets free" (Friedman, 1955, p. 1). Connecting Friedman's philosophy to practice Chomsky (1999) observes:

> Equipped with this perverse understanding of democracy, neoliberals like Friedman had no qualms over the military overthrow of Chile's democratically elected Allende government in 1973, because Allende was interfering with business control of Chilean society. (p. 9)

This neoliberal approach to leadership, that places profit over people, can be understood as a recovery attempt against the social movements of the 1960s and 1970s made possible by economic policies and the advent of the internet, allowing large scale manufacturing to be broken up in small operations around the world following hot spots of cheap labor and the military dictatorships enforcing the necessary *stability* or consent. While *stability* tends to be achieved through force in the developing world where U.S. corporations have virtually eliminated the cost of labor, in the West it is achieved through the control of ideas. In this context educational leaders are charged with ensuring students have learned the proper way to understand the world and the importance of *following directions* and respecting authority.

For example, alluding to Western societies such as the U.S., Friedman (1955) reasons that in order for government, and society more generally, to fulfill their scripted functions they require *social stability*, which is not possible without "widespread acceptance of some common set of values" and "a minimum degree of literacy and knowledge" (p. 2). Friedman (1955) reasons that the government should subsidize these *basic* levels of education because it "adds to the economic value of the student" (p. 4) and capitalists should invest in their labor just as they invest in machinery. The public is therefore viewed as a resource to be manipulated by the natural leaders for the *common good*. Making this point Friedman (1955) argues that education "is a form of investment in human capital precisely analogous to investment in machinery, buildings, or other forms of non human capital" and can be justified as a necessary expenditure because "its function is to raise the economic productivity of the human being" (p. 13). For Friedman (1955) then, knowledge production as an actively engaged endeavor is reserved for the elite, the leaders, rendering the vast majority subject to the necessary "indoctrination" needed to ensure the widespread acceptance of "common social values required for a stable society" even if it means "inhibiting freedom of thought and belief" (p. 7).

As one of the world's leading theoreticians of free market capitalism, it should not be surprising that Friedman (1955) was a strong supporter of the privatization of, and thus the corporate control over, public education, masking it with a discourse of *choice*. In more recent times Milton Friedman acknowledged that the testing-based No Child Left Behind Act touted as the surest path to increasing achievement was really designed to lend weight to the *choice* and voucher movement by setting schools up to fail and then handing them over to private managing firms such as Edison Schools (Kohn, 2004). Critical educator Alfie Kohn (2004) has commented that "you don't have to be a conspiracy nut to understand the real purpose of NCLB" (p. 84). That is, NCLB is nothing more than a "backdoor maneuver" (Kohn, 2004, p. 84) constructed around conceptions of *choice* allowing private for-profit capitalists to take over public education. Friedman's theory paved the theoretical pathway for these *neoliberal* tendencies of the public realm being handed over to corporations to be realized.

Friedman's theory is based on the assumption that the competition for education dollars would push, out of the necessity to survive, education investors to offer superior products to attract customers. Schools that offered a substandard product would not be profitable and would therefore be forced to either improve or close. Again, The No Child Left Behind Act of George W. Bush has served as a standards-based approach to usher in Friedman's desire to privatize public education, which has had disastrous results on the knowledge production process. As a result, a major blow was leveled against the practice of education as an active engagement designed to understand the world and to transform it, taking aim specifically at the labor/capital relationship and its manifest hegemonies such as white supremacy and patriarchy.

These developments, however, are well documented. For the purposes of this discussion we will turn our attention to the larger Eurocentric vision of Friedman's discourse, which is equally relevant as we approach a potentially new era in knowledge production in North America. That is, the Democratic presidency of Barack Obama, while pro-neoliberal capitalist in principle, claims to "believe" that "teachers should not be forced to spend the academic year preparing students to fill in bubbles on standardized tests" (Obama and Biden). The manifestation of this desire would provide critical pedagogues much needed breathing room to engage in counter-hegemonic knowledge production and critical praxis after this long period of Friedman inspired privatization.

Friedman leaves little room for misinterpretation regarding his conceptualization of democracy and social class, which, we will see, is, in many ways, almost the exact opposite of critical pedagogy. Within his paradigm Friedman (1962/2002) situates capitalism as the central driving force behind human evolution and therefore responsible for the "great advances of civilization" such as Columbus "seeking a new route to China" (p. 3), which consequently led to the emergence of vast fortunes generated by Europe's colonialist empire building, slavery, genocide/depopulation and repopulation, and on a scale so massive, so horrendous and so utterly barbaric as to render comprehending its manifestation as a criminal act carried out by real living, breathing, feeling people almost unimaginable (Malott, 2008). Friedman, therefore, does not seem too different from his predecessors. That is, describing Columbus coming to the America's as one of the great advances in civilization can only be understood as callous and thoroughly Eurocentric. Educational leadership, from Friedman's point of view, can therefore be understood as the perpetuation of colonialist practices.

But again, Friedman draws on the example of Columbus for the "advances" that have resulted from the "freedom" to pursue private "economic interests," and therefore as evidence to support capitalism. Friedman (1962/2002) goes so far as to argue that free market "capitalism is a necessary condition for political freedom" (p. 10). Friedman's thesis can be understood as a direct response to the popular support for democratic leadership and nationalized economies designed to promote an equal distribution of the wealth generated by the productive apparatus, arguing that "collectivist economic planning has …interfered with individual freedom" (p. 11). Individual freedom, for Friedman, stems from unregulated market mechanisms "stabilized" by a limited government whose function is to "protect our freedom both from the enemies outside our gates and from our fellow citizens: to preserve law and order, to enforce private contracts, and to foster competitive markets" (p. 2). Friedman points to the Soviet Union as an example of what he argues is the coercive tendency of government intervention in economic affairs. It is not surprising that Friedman does not mention the infinitely more democratic and egalitarian nature of Cuba's centrally-planned economy compared to the U.S.-supported free-market systems in the Caribbean and Latin America (Malott, 2007, 2009; Malott & Malott, 2008).

The "law and order" referred to by Friedman can best be understood as the way in which "the descendents of European colonizers shaped...rules to seize title to indigenous lands" (Robertson, 2005, p. ix) and to "enforce" these "private contracts." Similarly, the Monroe Doctrine, touted by Lippmann (1927) as bounded by "law" and "custom," can be understood as extending the United States' "sphere of influence" to the entire Western Hemisphere. That is, to ensure that the resources and productive capacities of not only this region, but much of the world, would be controlled by U.S. interests. The minds of men and women are most certainly a very large part of these *U.S. interests.* Educational leadership, from the factory model of education for African Americans after the Civil War (see Chapter Three) to the Indian boarding schools after 1890 when the last of the *Indian Wars* were over (see Chapter Four) to working class schools for European immigrants, have always been informed by the logic of potential profitability and wealth extraction, which has resulted in attempts to replace the culture and knowledge of students with identities more conducive to the needs of business.

The goal of education for those deemed most suitable for manual labor (Native and African Americans and the vast majority of whites) was designed to replace any previous conception of self with "worker"—that is, to define oneself as a slave, a worker. If your identity is based on being a worker, then you will feel incomplete if not working or taking orders. This sense of dependency was and continues to be reinforced in public education through a model leadership based on a neoliberal, efficiency-driven behaviorism. In this model education is something that is done to you—you go to school to *be* educated. In this context student and teacher success is measured by how well he or she can follow directions and regurgitate prepackaged knowledge—often referred to as *the* "right" answer.

In response to this alienating education and oppressive mode of work, which should not be confused with a community employing their collective labor power to actively engage *with* the world and not merely *in* or *on* the world, that is, passively, many Native American communities have taken control of their schools and embarked on a campaign of cultural rejuvenation and economic development with an emphasis on traditional value systems, customs, and language (see Chapter Four).

From Hierarchy to Democracy in Educational Leadership: An Introduction

"When you have your boot on somebody's neck, you can't just say, 'I'm doing this because I'm a brute.' You have to say, 'I'm doing it because they deserve it. It's for their good. They're naughty children, who have to be disciplined.'" (Chomsky, 2007, p. 48)

In response to the growing criticism against the mechanical-behaviorist approaches to educational leadership for being cold, calculating and over-concerned with achieving the goals of the organization at the expense of the individual, James MacGregor Burns, in 1979, proposed the notion of a transformational leadership that was to engage both the needs of individuals and organizations rather than only the latter. Through this more progressive or liberal model, it is assumed that the educational leader will become an agent of social change and a proponent of social justice. However, from a critical pedagogy perspective this body of work has failed to fully challenge the hierarchy embedded within the very notion of *educational leadership*.

As a result, the *transformational leadership* model continues to follow a paternalistic framework where the primary concern of the leader is to act "on behalf of" the "disadvantaged and oppressed" (Tierney and Foster 1989, p. 2) rather than advancing the programs and policies of the oppressed themselves. Despite this criticism, leadership, since the post-civil rights Reagan years, has moved so far to the right and against those who depend on a wage to survive, for example, that the leadership promised by the Obama administration that follows a more *transformational* framework where the leader acts *on behalf of their constituency*, was received as a breath of fresh air. As we have seen in practice, however, it is far too easy for a leader promising to act on behalf of the people to refocus and act on behalf of the elite capitalists and investors. In the area of education, Obama's appointment of Arne Duncan as his Secretary of Education, demonstrates his acting on behalf of capital in this context.

It is therefore clear that a more democratic approach to leadership in general, and educational leadership in particular, is desperately needed in much of the world, especially in the Western world. Fortunately, such examples *do* exist; they are just not the norm, and are therefore rarely reported on, especially favorably, in the mainstream press. Cautious not to get lost in the decontextualized realm of romanticized images of Indigeneity, in North America, we can look to the example of the Zapatistas of Chiapas, Mexico.

The Zapatistas are Indigenous Mayans from the state of Chiapas in central Mexico, many from the Lacandón Jungle. By naming themselves *Zapatistas*, they invoke the memory of the famed, martyred, rebel-leader of the Mexican Revolution (1910–1917), Emiliano Zapata, himself a Zapoteca "Indio." Zapata led a group of Indigenous Mexicans in a struggle for land and the right to be land-based people. Connecting this history to neoliberal, global capitalist economic policy and the subsequent Zapatista uprising, Staughton Lynd and Andrej Grubacic (2008) note:

> The Mexican Revolution wrote into the national constitution the opportunity for a village to hold its land communally, in an ejido, so that no individual could alienate any portion of it. Chiapas pioneers fiercely defended these communal landholdings. When the United States insisted that, as a precondition for participation in the North American Free Trade Agreement (NAFTA), Mexico must delete this provision from its Constitution, it triggered the Zapatista uprising. (p. 5)

Essentially, the Zapatistas' decision to engage in armed rebellion against the Mexican government was informed by a deep-seated desire to defend their democratic approach to leadership and social organization, which requires a stable land base not for sale or open to the competition of market forces. Highlighting the central thread of traditional Mayan leadership, the notion of *leading by obeying*, Lynd and Grubacic (2008), once again, offer invaluable insight:

> The most intriguing component of Zapatismo, according to Teresa Ortiz, was the Mayan tradition of *mandar obediciendo*, "to lead by obeying." She explained what it meant at the village level. Imagine a village. To use her examples, we feel the need for a teacher and a storekeeper. But these two persons can be freed for those communal tasks only if we, as a community, undertake to cultivate their *milpas* (their corn fields). In the most literal sense their ability to take leadership roles depends on our willingness to provide their livelihoods. (p. 5)

In practice, Lynd and Grubacic (2008) note that "village functionaries (like the teacher and the storekeeper) meet regularly with the entire local population," where they are not "expected to talk, but to listen" (p. 6). The idea is that those who are chosen to *command do so by obeying those they represent*. While this insight might seem like an obvious *fact* of *common sense*, the chasm between policy and public opinion in North America could not be wider on most issues that affect the lives of millions. Chomsky, in fact, views this insight to be so important that he has devoted considerable energy drawing attention to it. For example, in *Imperial Ambitions: Conversations on the Post-9/11 World*, Chomsky (2005) cites recent public opinion polls as evidence, however grossly unreported, that policy is far to the right of public opinion, demonstrating the refusal of leadership to *listen* or *obey* the will of the people because it tends to be antagonistically related to the class interests of the capitalist class. Highlighting these and other points Chomsky (2005) elaborates:

> ...An overwhelming majority of the population, around 80 percent, are in favor of increased health care; around 70 percent want increased aid to education and social security...98 recent...want universal health care...What all these polls basically show is that the whole population is so far to the left of both parties that you can understand why the polls aren't published. (p. 137)

Because these polls tend not to be published, Chomsky (2005) speculates that if you were to ask people such questions as "What do you think the general mood of the country is?"—I'm sure most people would say, 'I'm the only person who believes this. I'm crazy.' They never hear any reinforcement for their views in popular discussion; or in either party platform, or in the media" (p. 138). If there is any validity to Chomsky's (2005) observations, then it can be read as *a call to action* to educational leaders who are interested in *obeying*, in the spirit of the Zapatistas, the society and communities they serve by practicing their trade with equality, social justice, and a fierce commitment against all forms of oppression and economic and military imperialism. The question is therefore what does this look like in practice in the twenty-first century? To begin this reflective process let us begin considering what social justice leadership currently looks like in the African American community.

African American Educational Leaders in the Twenty-First Century

Black mayors, black city executives, black legislators, and black police officials are more numerous now than at any other time since the Reconstruction era. This should be an African American renaissance. Why then is African American community life at such a low ebb?...There are many reasons...but only one will be addressed here—the critical crisis in confidence in black leadership. (Abu-Jamal, 2000, p. 130)

While Abu-Jamal's (2000) comments are nearly a decade old, he has, more recently, made similar observations regarding Barack Obama. Abu-Jamal (2000) refers to the cultural and political indoctrination that occurs as the result of black leaders being "trained by white peers" resulting in "black polls" mimicking "their trainers, rather than creatively acting to address the actual issues facing their black constituency" (p. 130). The irony, points out Abu-Jamal (2000), resides in the observation that today's black leaders, who, more often than not, serve the interests of the same ruling class the Black Power movement rebelled against in the 1960s to whom their positions are now owed. In other words, as Abu-Jamal (2000) observes, "all of today's black 'leaders' owe their position to the expressions of black discontent, rage, riot, and rebellion made by the nameless blacks, many of whom took to the streets in the 1960s" (p. 131).

Making a similar argument, while providing a deeper analysis, world-renowned professor of African American studies, Manning Marable (1996), argues that, "there have been three general approaches to the struggle for black empowerment in America…inclusion, black nationalism, and transformation" (p. 101). Defining these categories, Marable (1996) elaborates:

> An "inclusionist" approach toward black politics has relied on coalitions with white parties or organizations to achieve reforms; it seeks access and opportunities for blacks within the existing system and utilizes the courts to pursue legal challenges to end discrimination. Frequently, an inclusionist approach emphasizes cultural assimilation, the effort to be accepted within the American mainstream. A "black nationalist" approach to black empowerment favors the building of all-black institutions to provide goods, services, and education to African American people; it culturally rejects the values and ideals of white America and emphasizes our unity with other people of African descent throughout the Black Diaspora. A "transformationist" or multicultural democratic approach argues that institutional racism cannot be dismantled unless the power, privileges, and property of elite whites are redistributed more democratically to oppressed Americans. A transformationist strategy calls for an internationalist perspective linking black struggles for freedom with those of other people of color and oppressed people; it favors the construction of a dynamic coalition of the oppressed in American society to extend the principles of political democracy into economic and social relations. (p. 101)

We might observe that Abu-Jamal's (2000) critiques are leveled at those black leaders assuming an inclusionist approach that sidelines the struggles of working class African Americans for the interests of the white ruling class. Many of today's large black and Latino high schools in urban areas such as New York City tend to be run by black principals based on many of Marable's tenets of Black

Nationalism. Because many of these large urban school districts are facing severe challenges, such as increasing drop out/push out rates situated in a context of rising poverty, the African American principals and superintendents that are running them are often perceived by the communities they serve as either messiahs or scapegoats. That is, these educational leaders are expected to solve all the problems of the community, and when they do not, which is inevitable, they are turned into scapegoats not only within the black community, but within the mainstream white society as well.

While the tenets of Black Nationalism often make sense for educational leaders working in the trenches, as it were, we will examine Marable's (1996) notion of transformation as a possible model for educational leadership. Because principals tend to see their role as the facilitator who builds a bridge between their school and the community they serve, their work often takes the form of developing a strong black community. What we find is that the limits of the institution of education itself often prevent the implementation of a truly transformational agenda. That is, educational workers, from principals to teachers, are working in a highly structured institutional environment founded upon the unstated presupposition that employees will follow their predetermined roles within the hierarchy of command.

In urban high school settings, especially where *student bodies* are black, brown and poor, *student populations* are coded as *troubled youth*, predisposed for *violence*, and *at risk* for dropping out and being *left behind*. Viewing *urban* secondary *education* through this lens—the white, paternalistic lens of colonization—the role of the principal (i.e., educational leadership) is to *whip into shape* the school as *hellhole* where the students are *demons* and therefore demonized (Leistyna, 2002). In this context it is the principal who, endowed with the blessings and certification from the dominant society, saves the savage minority from himself and herself. This is portrayed as a gift done with the scientific efficiency of Taylor and the paternalistic manipulation of Skinner. Because these youth are viewed as either criminals or future criminals, it is assumed that a military-style approach to leadership is necessary, which is best executed by a strong man. It is thus assumed that women are too weak for this task and therefore better equipped to be coddling mothers *taking care of innocent children* at the elementary and childhood levels.

Conclusion

Critical pedagogy, on the other hand, calls for an approach to educational leadership that maintains high standards of rigor and criticality for both teachers and students, but without devaluing who the students are or viewing them as in need of being saved from themselves. This approach rejects the old hierarchy of power where the principal is on the top and the students are on the bottom by challenging students to take personal responsibility for their own learning as part of becoming critically self-actualized in the spirit of Marable's (1996) transformation approach. This critical pedagogical approach to educational leadership, which strives to achieve a more horizontal distribution of power, is based on a number of insights, including, but not limited to:

~ The best cure for discipline problems is an engaging curriculum.

~ Students are not empty vessels waiting to be filled with valuable knowledge, but come to the classroom with years of cultural experience and knowledge that informs how they read the world and construct new ideas.

~ Intelligence is not a rare quality, but is the human trait most widely distributed throughout the species, rendering democracy practically possible, as demonstrated by the Zapatistas (and countless others).

~ Students and teachers should therefore be actively engaged in democratic problem solving and not left up to the arbitrary decisions of principals and state and federal policy makers.

~ The European enslavement of Africans and native Americans and the ongoing imperial colonization of the Americas (and much of the world) created the conditions for the institutionalization of formal education to shape the ideas of the worker populations as a necessary process for manufacturing consent.

~ Education's focus on training people so they can compete in the workforce is not just about achieving the ability to perform some neutral task like teaching a kid how to do a math problem, but it is about learning the proper way to think about the world and how one fits into that world.

~ The goal is therefore to teach people that capitalism is good, it is inevitable, and our freedom depends on its perpetuation.

~ The goal or purpose of a critical pedagogical approach to educational leadership is therefore not only to ensure students have the best possible opportunity to survive within the world that exists, but to transform it as well.

Having explored some ideas regarding democratic examples and theories/philosophies of educational leadership, let us conclude by asking some questions that seem central to our quest to connect theory to practice and back again:

~   Because leaders, in the current system that exists, are conceptualized to be the thinking and directing force that moves practitioner-teachers, how have education workers made the work of educational leadership democratic, when, by definition, it is undemocratic? If leadership is undemocratic, why does it exist in that form?

~   Why are we to assume that social arrangements grounded in conceptions of democracy are more favorable than those grounded in authoritarianism?

~   Who decides what the goals and outcomes of education are to be?

~   What are the connections between student learning and leadership practices?

· 2 ·

THE RELATIONSHIP BETWEEN RESEARCH AND POLICY IN EDUCATION

An Introductory Outline

As we engage this study of the relationship between research and policy in education, we can begin by considering what we might call a *common sense understanding*. That is, we would expect for *research* to drive and inform *policy* because we know from our high school science courses that conclusions and recommendations come at the end of the experiment, study, or investigation, not at the beginning before we have learned anything. However, when we examine the cutting edge research on pedagogy, learning theories, and curriculum development, we find few significant similarities with educational policy. If educational research, or science, is not guiding policy, then what power or force is directing it?

When we review the social context that education is situated in, we want to hone in on all the possible sources of influence that could be acting upon educational policy. In our examination we uncover four primary sources of power in addition to the power of science, which has already been identified. The first two sources of power, corporate/private power and state and federal governmental power, have tended to work together toward shared visions of social control and the accumulation of wealth. The third source of power, the power of the corporate, mainstream media to shape public perception regarding education tends to serve the interests of the first two sources of power, corporate and governmental power. The fourth and final source of power, the collective power of labor power, or the public's will, tends to be antagonistically related to the first three sources of ruling class, elite power.

While this web of power and influence is highly complex, and, at times, overwhelmingly contradictory, the distinguishable and consistent patterns of relationship mentioned above are useful for understanding historical events and tendencies. Further reducing the above analysis we might observe that there are really just *two* primary sources of power in society, the power of those who rely on a wage to survive, the vast majority, and the ruling class power of the elite few, which are antagonistically related to one another. These two sources of power, or these two social classes with competing interests, to employ Marxist terminology, have therefore been historically engaged in a struggle over the purpose and outcome of education. In this struggle the dissemination of ideas, or *agenda setting* and *framing*, has been central.

For example, from a ruling class perspective, education can be defined as a branch of government charged with the task of socializing individuals to become *law-abiding, contributing* (i.e., consenting) members of society, that is, citizenship formation. From a working class perspective, on the other hand, education can be defined as an important vehicle in the struggle for liberation against ruling class subjugation and exploitation. Each opposing force vies for the power of science and government to serve its respective ends. The winner tends to be the competitor with the greatest control over the power to socially construct reality, and therefore, the power of knowledge (i.e., science), and the power to set the agenda.

In this chapter we explore the relationship between research and policy in education and the intervening role the media have played in manufacturing the necessary consent to advance the corporate, neo-liberal model of education. In our discussion we also celebrate the many creative ways students, teachers, administrators and others have resisted the neoliberalization of education through embracing more democratic approaches to educational leadership.

The Relationship Between Research and Policy: The No Child Left Behind Act (NCLB)

While NCLB was accompanied by much rhetorical emphasis on "research-based" education policy, the breath of this research is narrow, largely settled on specific pedagogies and curricula that are "measurable." Compelling research on larger themes—

the social reasons for school dropouts…the misdesign of many schools, the evidence
of growing inequalities among population groups and communities…find no place in
the act. (Sizer, 2004, p. xxi)

Theodore Sizer, in the above quote, draws attention to the *political* relationship
between policy and research we are interested in. That is, when educational legislation *invokes the authority of science*, such as NCLB's "emphatic call for education policy and practice to be based on *scientifically based research*" (Hess &
Petrilli, 2008, pp. 20–21) but fails to demonstrate an honest attempt to respect
the norms of the scientific community, serious alarms and signals of distress should
emanate from the professional education community in colleges, universities,
and public schools. While such critiques have been made, we argue that educational leaders, researchers and practitioners have been far too complicit.

This passivity can be explained, in part, by the tendency to reduce the acts
of leading, researching, and practicing (i.e., teaching), as separate and distinct
tasks engaged in by separate and distinct *experts*. These dichotomies between
leaders and *the led*, and between researchers/knowledge producers *and* practition-
ers/knowledge implementers set up a hierarchy where policy makers construct
educational programs that supposedly are informed by the work of the expert
researchers, which are then to be implemented by teachers and enforced by
principals and superintendents. As a result, when teaching is reduced to the
technical and mechanical act of carrying out orders, practitioners are more vulnerable to be *led* to implement unsound curriculum and pedagogy. Critical pedagogues therefore argue that teachers should be researchers, curriculum
developers, *and* leaders (see the concluding chapter).

Again, a critical pedagogical approach to educational leadership would
challenge mandates to implement programs and educational strategies founded upon questionable science and scholarship. As a place of departure we can
approach an examination of NCLB based on the criteria it claims to be based
upon, which, again, are the norms of the scientific community. As a demonstration let's take the norm that is arguably the most widely cited and hotly con-
tested—disinterestedness. In addition to disinterestedness let us also examine
honesty. According to Laurence Neuman (1994) in *Social Research Methods:
Qualitative and Quantitative Approaches*, the notion of *disinterestedness* poses
the following challenges:

> Scientists must be neutral, impartial, receptive, and open to unexpected observations
> or new ideas. Scientists should not be rigidly wedded to a particular idea or point of
> view. They should accept, even look for, evidence that runs against their position and
> should honestly accept all findings based on high-quality research. (p. 8)

In the same volume Neuman (1994) defines honesty, the fifth norm of the scientific community, as "especially strong in scientific research" (p. 8). Ensuring his point is not missed, Neuman continues, noting that, "scientists demand honesty in all research, and dishonesty or cheating in scientific research is a major taboo" (p. 8).

While we are highly skeptical of such scientific claims of objectivity and neutrality found within these norms of the scientific community, especially within the notion of disinterestedness because they have been historically employed to normalize Euro-centric, capitalistic, and colonizing forms of knowledge production, we can nevertheless examine *how* scientific NCLB actually is based upon the norms of the scientific community, as previously suggested. In "Learning to Read 'Scientifically'" Gerald Coles (2003) holds NCLB up to these standards of the scientific community. That is, Coles (2003) takes a close look at the discourse of *scientific research* and the methodologies used in selecting the approach to reading instruction endorsed by NCLB.

As Bush geared up to sell his education initiative to the nation he promised to eradicate the growing threat of illiteracy in the country, ensuring every child would learn to read by grade three. Bush pointed to the work of the National Reading Panel (NRP) who, it was argued, reviewed 100,000, studies on reading instruction, and had identified, through scientific analysis, the most effective strategies for teaching children how to read. This number, 100,000 was often cited in the media as a panacea for the nation's *reading deficit*. However, as demonstrated below, this number is far higher than the 300 studies that were actually analyzed. As we see in the following excerpt Coles (2003) clearly concludes that NCLB does *not* follow the norms of the scientific community, especially the concept of disinterestedness, as defined above by Neuman (1994). Because of the relevancy of Coles' (2003) analysis, a sizable segment is provided:

> The panel did begin by looking at the research studies on reading and found that approximately 100,000 had been published since 1966. however, the panel used several criteria for extensive pruning of this number. For example, the studies had to deal with reading development from preschool through high school, and therefore excluded studies on many reading topics such as literacy skills in occupations or brain functioning and literacy activity. The studies also had to meet the panel's definition of "scientific research," which was limited almost entirely—and narrowly—to quantitative, experimental studies.
>
> Perhaps most important, the panel used only studies relating to the instructional topics which the panel majority had decided were key areas of good reading instruction....This questionable procedure eliminated a variety of important instructional

issues contained in the research literature, such as the relationship between reading
and writing, meaning-emphasis instruction....This panel of experts had no qualms
about exercising a priori its judgment on what is central to successful reading instruction, and ignoring contrary views of other leading reading researchers on what com-
prises the best way to learn to read. (pp. 184–187)

Coles goes on to argue that "there were members of Bush's education adviso-
ry committee who were familiar with the NRP report and knew the 100,000
figure was a misrepresentation" (p. 187), but, as we know, Bush and his
Department of Education continued to misinform the public. However, not only
did they misinform the public, but they charged educational leaders with
enforcing teaching strategies based on what they knew were inaccurate scientific conclusions. In the end it was a phonics-centered approach that emerged
as the dominant perspective. Consequently, the NRP included "52 studies on
phonemic awareness, 38 studies for phonics, 14 for fluency, and 203 for 16 categories of comprehension instruction" (Coles, 2003, p. 184). Based on the conclusions made by Coles, NCLB has no right invoking the authority of science
because its methods were not *honest* or *disinterested*. What is worse, schools,
teachers, and students have been punished for mandates founded upon this
pseudo-science. However, in some respects this should be of little surprise to those
who follow trends in academic research.

That is, many research methodologists had long concluded that there was
little connection between academic, peer-reviewed research and the construction of educational policies. For example, in 1998, three years before NCLB was
signed into official existence, Ray Rist, in "Influencing the Policy Process with
Qualitative Research," notes that:

> Research can contribute to informed decision making, but the manner in which this
> is done needs to be reformulated. We are past the time when it is possible to argue that
> good research will, because it is good, influence the policy process. That kind of lin-
> ear relation of research to action simply is not a viable way in which to think about
> how knowledge can inform decision-making....Research is but one (and often minor
> at that) among the number of frequently contradictory and competing sources that seek
> to influence what is an ongoing and constantly evolving process. (pp. 403–404)

These insights could have been the result of an analysis of the more recent
NCLB reinforcing the conclusion that in today's educational context where
schooling is an increasingly corporate affair. Rist's (1998) observations therefore continue to hold relevancy. *That research should have an impact on decision
making seems to have become more and more an article of faith*, unfortunately,

remains true. Again, we must therefore strive to understand policy and practice in a larger social, historical, geographical context. In so doing, we must look at where power lies and how it operates.

Other qualitative research methodologies have made similar observations. Elliot Eisner (1998) in *The Enlightened Eye*, noted that "in educational matters the proliferation of policies based upon limited and sometimes erroneous conceptions is particularly egregious" (p. 118). As previously mentioned, the reasons have remained relatively consistent. Stan Karp (2004), commenting on NCLB, observed that "external agendas are often imposed without developing any shared assessment of a school's problems or the common priorities needed to make reform credible" (p. 260). What this line of reasoning suggests is that careful analysis of many sources of knowledge provides more valid and reliable conclusions, and, as a result, produces better science.

Informed by this spirit of accuracy we must be careful not to fall victim to being "rigidly wedded to a particular idea or point of view" (Neuman, 1994, p. 8) as the creators of NCLB seem to have been. In practice, this means we exercise *organized skepticism*, which Neuman (1994) describes as not accepting "new ideas or evidence in a carefree, uncritical manner," ensuring that "the research can stand up to close examination" (p. 8). Based upon our review of the literature, our examination of NCLB, and informal interviews with a number of teachers, professors, and public school administrators, we not only found similar critiques as those made by Coles (2003), but we found even more scathing repudiations. For example, many scholars and educators argue that NCLB is not only scientifically unsound, but it is, essentially, a way to set schools up for failure, paving the way for private management companies to come in and turn public education into a for-profit enterprise, which is part of a larger trend dubbed neoliberal capitalism (for an introduction to this vast body of work, see, for example, Hess & Petrilli, 2008; Kohn, 2004; Kozol, 2005; Meier & Wood, 2004; Sizer, 2004).

This analysis begins to explain the reasons *why* NCLB is not grounded in a more genuine engagement with the literature/research. For example, some critical scholars have suggested that NCLB is not really designed to increase learning and understanding, but to guarantee that schools will be *graded* as *failing* through a federally mandated system of high stakes testing. That is, the testing would document students' failure, which would be ensured by selecting the least relevant, least contextualized approach to literacy development available, phonics. A phonics-based approach is only concerned with decoding words or sounding them out devoid of meaning or context. This vulgar reductionism is so intense that many phonics-based curricula use nonsense words to teach subjects how to decode sounds, such as *thop jop gack*. Part of what was excluded by the NRP through their *pruning of the 100,000 studies on how students learn to read* was a long and rich tradition of qualitative research teeming with highly effective, engaging, contextualized, rigorous, complex, critical approaches to reading the word and the world. These methods, many of which are philosophical anti-methods, have proven highly engaging and conducive to fostering high-level, life-long learners actively engaged in knowledge production as political praxis. It is therefore not surprising that the media have played a central role in perpetuating this fraudulent system by serving a propaganda function and setting the parameters of the debate.

The Hegemonic Role of the Media

Focusing specifically on the role the media play in educational policy development Kathleen Rhoades (2008) examines "'policy elite's' use of the media to embed semi-overt messages about the institution of public schools in order to achieve public support for a set of pro-business initiatives, predominately large-scale testing reforms, the deprofessionalization of teaching, and the privatization of public schools" (p. 179), all of which are represented within NCLB. Rhoades (2008) identifies three "media devices" elites employ to alter public perception, "agenda setting, news framing, and propaganda" (p. 180). These devices or hegemonic tools, situated in the context of educational policy and leadership, can be conceived of in the following ways:

~   Rhoades (2008) defines *agenda setting* as "the use of repetitious news content" (p. 180), which the media's repeating the *100,000 studies* NCLB message is an example of. The media's handling of NCLB, as an educational policy event, can also be described as *news framing* and *propaganda*.

~   Rhoades (2008) defines "news framing" as "the promotion or adoption of an intentional and cohesive narrative structure in news reports. The frame presents a particular perspective on an issue, replete with a set of identified problems, solutions, and guilty parties" (p. 180). Of particular importance for the context of NCLB is that framing "sets parameters around the facts admissible to the discussion" (Rhoades, 2008, p. 180).

~   Perhaps the most inflammatory charge is that of *propaganda*, which

Rhoades (2008) describes as "the generation of deceptive, inaccurate news coverage…used to deliberately misrepresent an issue in order to influence policy" (p. 180).

What this analysis overwhelmingly suggests is that because educational policy is not founded upon the science and objective methodologies policy elites claim it is, a series of *media devices* are needed to manufacture the public consent needed to push these overwhelmingly pro-business initiatives forward. What we find in many of these discussions is no mention of the hierarchical structure of leadership and therefore no challenges to it. The emphasis, rather, is on the decisions of leaders and who the leaders are. In other words, when our focus is on how policy was created—through the direction of scientific research or by the demands of capital—we fail to disrupt the assumption that teachers need to be told what to teach and how to teach it. What this analysis alludes to the presence of a series of hierarchical assumptions embedded within the social structure of capitalist society. After we briefly re-explore some of these perspectives, we turn to an introductory exploration of some of the work that offers an alternative to the current capitalist, Euro-centric structure of education with special emphasis on leadership.

Hierarchical Assumptions within Capitalist Society

The dominant perspective regarding the division of labor or the difference between capitalists (i.e., the bosses) and workers (i.e., those who rely on wages to survive) is that workers need capitalists because the bosses have the money and therefore the jobs to offer those with no money. This is the boss's perspective, which, again, sets up the relationship between labor and capital as mutually beneficial, yet, naturally imbalanced with the intellectually or culturally inferior *poor people* as dependent on the biologically and culturally superior capitalist class.

From the perspective of labor, on the other hand, it is the bosses who are dependent on labor because it is the power of physical labor that produces all wealth, or transforms the Earth, a living entity, into lifeless commodities and byproducts. Capitalists, from this point of view, are therefore not a source of livelihood, but a life extractor, a leech, or a vampire.

Consequently, it has been the historical struggle of labor to relieve itself of this multi-pronged burden. Capitalist accumulation not only extracts wealth generated through one's labor power by paying a wage far less than the value it produces, but it does so by suppressing human creativity and community building by externally controlling the labor power of those relegated to the status of worker as the result of primitive accumulation (the process by which peasants, first in England, were disconnected from the land, the source of their personal livelihood, leaving them with nothing but their ability to work, or labor, to sell for a wage so that they might consume the commodities produced by others to survive. Feudalism was therefore not replaced with something more free and democratic but with something just as oppressive, capitalism).

Because critical pedagogy is a way to approach education from the perspective of democracy or what is in the best interest of the vast majority (according to the insights of the vast majority), it values the epistemologies or knowledges that have been belittled and disrespected as primitive by the dominant Western approach to science, such as those coming from Indigenous communities all over the world and Marxist and other Western counter-hegemonic views.

Miner's article is therefore written from the perspective of the vast majority or critical pedagogy. Friedman's, on the other hand, is written from the perspective of capital or the bosses. Friedman's is a neoliberal view that sees the world as naturally unequal, rendering any attempt to legislate equality an attack on freedom because it prevents the natural superiors from rising to their predetermined place of leadership. Critical pedagogy rejects this hierarchy, arguing that everyone, with the exception of those who have serious cognitive disabilities, use critical thinking every day. Because of the narrow way schools teach and measure intelligence, very few of the mental abilities of students, especially those most dissimilar to the white male, middle-class, unstated norm, are recognized.

> The role of pedagogical researchers is to discover the laws of education, while the role of educational leaders is to make sure that everyone acts in accordance with them. Such educational laws would include universal statements regarding how students learn and how they should be taught. (Thomas and Kincheloe 2006, p. 3)

What conclusions does one seem compelled to come to regarding the public K-12 education system in North America after considering the anti-intellectualism that plagues its institutional culture? The idea that *theory is nothing more than a luxurious foray into a non-existent fantasy land that real teachers and administrators cannot afford to waste their valuable time with* speaks to the dogmatic nature of policy formation that too easily dismisses cutting edge research.

This analysis leads us to ask the following questions:

~ What role has research played in educational policy formation?
~ Who has traditionally been included and excluded in the development of the goals and means of educational policy?
~ Whose interests are supported (and excluded) in contemporary educational policy?
~ 80% of political contributions come from 1% of the population.
~ How might philosophy assist in better understanding these issues?
~ Example: Every educational policy presupposes a philosophy

It seems that the nation has tended to "ignore" what McNeil (2003) identifies as "a broad and sophisticated research base on the teaching of reading" (p. 218) that has stressed the importance of understanding literature from multiple perspectives, including, and perhaps especially, *dissident voices.*

Reconnecting Research and Policy: An Introduction to Educational Leadership

> Viewing policy research as serving an enlightenment function suggests that policy researchers work with policy makers and their staffs over time to create a contextual understanding about an issue, build linkages that will exist over time, and strive constantly to educate about new developments and research findings in the area. (Rist, 1998, p. 403)

We can begin our investigation here by observing that our new paradigm for educational leadership would fundamentally transform it to such an extent that it would, for all intents and purposes, be abolished. That is, when you take the vertical hierarchy of leadership, with the administrators and policy makers on top, and make it horizontal, there is no longer anyone with an unequal distribution of power, and therefore no longer anyone with power to command another, and, consequently, no leadership positions. Another way to phrase it would be to argue that a horizontal structure of power creates a situation where everyone is a leader with equal weight behind his or her voice. The democratic leadership structures of new social movements (discussed in the Introduction) become indispensable here as we envision alternative ways to engage with knowledge and social arrangements or relationships. Before we continue our journey into the world of democratic leadership practices in education, we first briefly outline the characteristics of mobilizations deemed to be *new social movements* (NSM) by leading scholars in the field:

~ First, NSMs "do not bear a clear relation to structural roles of participants. There is a tendency for the social base of new social movements
to transcend class structure" (Johnston, Laraña, & Gusfield, 1994, p.
6)

~ "The ideological characteristics of NSMs stand in sharp contrast to the
working-class movement and to the Marxist conception of ideology as
a unifying and totalizing element for collective action....The new
social movements are more difficult to characterize in such terms.
They exhibit a pluralism of ideas and values, and they tend to have
pragmatic orientations and search for institutional reforms that enlarge
the systems of members' participation in decision making" (Johnston,
Laraña, & Gusfield, 1994, p. 6).

~ Consequently, these new movements signify the democratization of
civil society in the Western world.

~ "NSMs often involve the emergence of new or formerly weak dimen-
sions of identity....They are associated with a set of beliefs, symbols,
values, and meanings related to sentiments of belonging to a differen-
tiated social group" (Johnston, Laraña, & Gusfield, 1994, p. 7).

~ "Another common feature of NSMs is the use of radical mobilization
tactics of disruption and resistance that differ from those practiced by
the working-class movement" (Johnston, Laraña, & Gusfield, 1994, p.
8).

~ "The organization and proliferation of new social movement groups are
related to the credibility crisis of the conventional channels for participation in Western democracies" (Johnston, Laraña, & Gusfield, 1994,
p. 8).

~ NSM identity is largely based on maintaining autonomy of the large
mass movement with a hierarchical leadership structure.

~ Consequently, NSMs tend to be "segmented, diffuse, and decentralized"
(Johnston, Laraña, & Gusfield, 1994, p. 8).

With this context for new social movements in mind, we can begin to image
what a NSM approach to educational leadership might look like in practice.
Movement toward educational policy for a democratic society, fortunately,
does have a long and generous history as underscored in Chapters Three and
Four specifically. However, we can also explore the critical pedagogical work
being done in many diverse contexts. For example, in *Rethinking School Reform:
Views from the Classroom* edited by Linda Christensen and Stan Karp (2003),

a number of democratic, teacher-led initiatives to curriculum development and, by implication, educational leadership, are explored, offering a number of possible places of departure for interested leaders, practitioners, and researchers:

~ In "Teacher Councils: Tools for Change," Bob Peterson (2003a) reflects on "a network of teacher-led, district wide councils" that operated within the Milwaukee Public Schools (MPS) during the 1990s having a "significant impact on reform in MPS" (p. 287). Peterson (2003a) describes this initiative and the resulting councils as significant because they "provided a way for progressive teachers to promote student-centered, anti-racist curricular reform" (p. 8). Conducive to our democratic choice for educational leadership Peterson (2003a) describes the structure of these *teacher councils*—including, among many others, the *Multicultural Curriculum Council*, the *Whole Language Council*, the *Humanities Council*, and the *Bilingual Council*—as representing "a strategy that contrasts sharply with the top-down approaches that characterize many school reform initiatives" (p. 287). That is, "instead of imposing an external agenda developed far from classroom life, the teacher councils represented an opportunity for teachers to help shape the reform agenda and to bring credibility and leadership to the effort" (Peterson, 2003a, pp. 287–288) for school improvement.

~ The power of this *movement of councils* resided within the fact that it had been "integrated into a district wide curriculum reform effort with explicitly anti-racist goals" (Peterson, 2003a, p. 288). Also contributing to their effectiveness was the promotion of unity and solidarity through encouraging classroom teachers to "share their best practices" (Peterson, 2003a, p. 288), which stands in stark contrast to many school cultures where teachers view themselves as in competition with one another, and therefore never share teaching strategies or curriculum ideas. Peterson (2003a) also points to the model of formalizing "teacher collaboration, mobilization, and training" which transcends the limited reach of "one-time-in services" (p. 288) creating the necessary spaces for long-term transformation, which many educational leaders would argue are cultural changes, that is, changes to the culture of the school, the district, the state, the country, and so on.

~ Because the model of professional development embraced by the councils required such a large time commitment on the part of teachers, the success of the councils was based on the district's decision to allocate funds to pay for substitute teachers. Again, adopting a teacher-led *pol-icy* proved to be an effective way for the councils to work as peer-review structures ensuring that new practices were informed by sound research.

~ Peterson (2003a) offers a number of factors that contributed to the demise of the councils "including budget cuts, the push for radical, school-based decentralization, a shift away from the K-12 curriculum effort towards a school-to-work-focus, a national reform effort driven by standardized test scores, and some weaknesses within the councils themselves" (p. 294).

~ In "'Summer Camp' for Teachers: Alternative Staff Development," S.J. Childs (2003) provides another example of an educational reform effort informed by a democratic approach to leadership and a rigorous engagement with research. In this model of professional development the traditional top-down approach guided by outside *experts* is reject-ed for a teacher-led initiative. The rotating leadership method adopt-ed by this Portland, Oregon-based Summer Literacy Institute, and the fact that it is fully funded by the district, has resulted in the fact that "the majority of Portland Public School's 175 high school language arts teachers" have been through the program and many have "led work-shops during the year" (Childs, 2003, p. 297). The institute consists of "one week of intensive collaboration among teachers to develop cur-riculum units and workshops around multicultural texts" (Childs, 2003, p. 297). Childs reports that it has also been an effective way to train new teachers as they are paired with veteran expert multicultur-al, critical pedagogues.

~ This model was grew out of the dissatisfaction of being subjected to tra-ditional in-service lecture formats where the experiences and profes-sional knowledge of teachers tend to be ignored. The vision and goal of the Summer Literacy Institute, according to Childs (2003) are to achieve district wide reform, which, it is believed, will provide safety to progressive educators who stand out and are therefore often target-ed for harassment and demotion in uncritical Euro-centric contexts.

~ Providing a more detailed picture of what these institutes look like in practice, Childs (2003) notes that "teachers engage in three main activities. First, they read research articles on literacy, language, and achievement. Second, mornings are devoted to teachers sharing lessons" (p. 298). There is a third activity, which is designed to bring it all together, "in the afternoon teams of teachers meet to develop units filled with literacy lessons and strategies around a book or theme that are available for other teachers to use throughout the year" (Childs, 2003, p. 299). As an example of something created out of this democratic approach to curriculum development Childs (2003) reflects on their desire to encourage teacher-facilitators to adopt books that "put traditionally marginalized groups at the center" (p. 300). As a result, during the first year of the Institute, the organizers adapted a set of guidelines for text selection, including, "reflect high literary quality, have cross-cultural themes, actively challenge stereotypes, raise issues of class, race, gender, and justice, move beyond victimization and show resistance and empowerment, provide historical context and deepen cultural knowledge, and have the potential for use across the curriculum" (Childs, 2003, p. 300).

~ Here, in "Survival and Justice: Twin Goals for Teacher Unions," Peterson (2003b) makes a case for a social justice-oriented approach to teacher unionism, which, again, is conducive to our radically democratic call for educational leadership as critical pedagogy. Peterson describes two models of traditional unionism, *industrial* and *professional*, which he argues could better serve their constituencies and the communities in which they are situated by adopting "a new vision of unionism" (p. 309) he calls *social justice unionism*. However, Peterson (2003b) notes that, "these are somewhat arbitrary distinctions, most useful in helping to frame discussion. In practice, the models often overlap, blending into one another depending on circumstances" (p. 305). In general though, Peterson (2003b) defines the *industrial* model as primarily concerned with "defending the working conditions and rights of teachers" (p. 305). The *professional* model, according to Peterson (2003b), "incorporates, yet moves beyond, the industrial model and suggests that unions also play a leading role in professional issues, such as teacher accountability and quality of school programs" (pp. 305–306). The social justice model, while incorporating the practices of the industrial and professional models, "is linked to a tradition that views unions as part of a broader movement for social progress. It calls for participatory union membership; education reform focused on serving all children, with special attention to collaboration with parents and community organizations; and a concern for broader issues of equity throughout society" (p. 306).

These examples of what we might call new social movement approaches to educational reform and leadership all share common values associated with democracy, understood as not just an *unrealistic ideal*, but as an *achievable goal* conducive to the human condition. These examples and analysis highlight common principles, which begin to paint a picture of what a critical pedagogical approach to educational leadership might look like in practice. What follows is a brief sketch of some conclusions regarding teaching, learning, and curriculum informed by these general principles of social justice and democratic practice:

~ One size fits all approach to policy development and implementation is flawed. It ignores the existence of multiple intelligences/learning styles and the ways colonizing and capitalizing forces Euro-centrically belittle and exclude particular epistemologies. Policy must therefore be context specific.

~ Knowers construct meaning as cultural, social, historical beings.

~ Positionality determines relationship to dominant forms of power: Schools serving working class versus elite populations; Columbian versus Indigenous perspective on conquest.

~ These democratic approaches to educational reform and leadership reject the assumption that brilliant intelligence is a rare quality.

~ They reject invalid constructions such as hierarchy of intelligence in favor of postformal approach that appreciates the higher order, critical thinking skills equally distributed throughout the species.

~ Simultaneously, they acknowledge that humans have demonstrated a vulnerability to hegemonic indoctrination, but not without feeling oppressed, resisting external control, and advancing democracy (social movements of 1960s and 1970s and solidarity movements of the 1980s, 1990s, and on, for example). This history is therefore complex and riddled with *curious alliances*.

~ Nevertheless, they continue to support the conclusion that people are endowed with the capacity to act as free thinkers democratically working together toward common goals.

~ They also assume that the best policy makers are those most affected by particular policies. That is, the *public's will*, or the *collective unconsciousness*, as it were, has demonstrated a propensity for fairness, or a *leveling effect* highly suspicious of concentrated power (and wealth).

~ Within the realm of epistemology or knowledge production, the notion of celebrating and learning from epistemological diversity tends to be widespread.

~ Toward these ends there is an awareness that curriculum is not objective but tends to be informed by a Euro-centric manifestation of Western philosophy.

~ As a result, when we study education, we situate official curriculum within the *social history of philosophy* context.

~ We therefore approach curriculum development from the perspective of the non-European influences of Western Civilization. For example, we can look at the role of ancient *Black* Egypt that made many early contributions to the foundation of science, philosophy, writing, modern commerce, etc. We can also acknowledge that as a result of the Islamic *Moors'* conquest and occupation of Spain between 500–1492, the knowledge from antiquity, such as Aristotle, and new knowledge such as algebra, were reintroduced to Europe leading to The Enlightenment and their emergence from their own Age of Darkness. Finally, Native North American democracy has provided the world with the notions of equality, justice, peace, and unity, for example, providing the possibility for increasingly democratic social arrangements.

~ As a result, producing knowledge about and within the world non-Eurocentrically will produce a particular kind of democratic identity, and, hopefully, a particular kind of democracy free from human suffering and exploitation.

~ The idea is to move from spectator democracy to an engaged democracy where programs and policies come from the organized population who elect leaders from their own ranks.

~ Learning and growth, as a result, occur not through transmission, but through an active engagement with ideas situated in a social, historical cultural context.

~ Group comprehension of a text occurs as different points of view become exposed to each other.

~ Reading as dialectical process where text transforms readers and readers re-write text without betraying its spirit. Learning is therefore a full body experience, which suggests an ontology of interconnectedness.

What these principles and conclusions suggest is that a critical pedagogical approach to educational leadership not only results in a more honest relationship between policy and research, but it suggests that teachers should not be viewed as mere consumers of research, but researchers/knowledge producers themselves. However, this is not a new observation. In 1991, for example, Joe L. Kincheloe's *Teachers as Researchers: Qualitative Inquiry as a Path to Empowerment* offered a postmodern critique of Western Enlightenment, Cartesian reductionistic science and a complete conceptual framework for what a critical pedagogical approach to *doing research* has and could look like in practice. Since the publication of *Teachers as Researchers*, a whole tradition of critical pedagogical research methodology has emerged. For example, *Doing Teacher-Research: A Handbook for Perplexed Practitioners* by W.-M. Roth (2007) was written from the perspective that "teachers who research their own practice are and become better practitioners" (p. 1). Roth (2007) sets out to answer the question, "How does one do research as a teacher?" (p. 1), and, in the process, offers an invaluable tool to educators interested in becoming more effective contributors to the democratization of education in the twenty-first century.

Conclusion

As we transition into the next sections of this volume we need to refocus our thinking to the internal structure of schools that are organized hierarchically depending largely upon the social class and racial identities of the students. Elite children, for example, tend to position themselves as superior to their teachers and administrators because they occupy a higher social position within the larger society. However, most of us do not teach these children. Most of us work in schools and teacher education programs that serve the working and middle classes, that is, those who rely on a wage to survive. As we continue to engage this text and listen to the voices of educational leaders and how they understand their positions, keep these larger class structures in mind because they speak to the purpose of education in a colonialist, Euro-centric, neoliberal, capitalist society.

EDUCATIONAL LEADERSHIP CRITICALLY EXAMINED

Two Historical Examples

· 3 ·

HEGEMONIC TRENDS IN POLICY

The Contested History of Post-Civil War African American Education

Embarking on this study of African Americans and education, examined from a leadership perspective, we must begin by providing a concrete context from which our analysis can be grounded. As the African experience in the Americas after 1492 is marked by the tragedy and suffering of the African physical and cultural genocides that were the byproducts of the trans-Atlantic slave-trade carried out by European enslavers, we must understand that socialization, in the plantation context, and later education, in the post-Civil-War context, have always been a tool for the social control of Africans in America who have consistently, in various complex, and at times contradictory, forms, resisted their subjugation, threatening the mode of production and thus the basic structure of power and leadership (Abu-Jamal, 2003; Kincheloe, 2008; Shawki, 2006; Watkins, 2001).

By focusing our attention on the long legacy of abuse afflicted by ruling class whites on Africans and other people of color for the sole purpose of amassing vast fortunes, beginning with slavery, which laid the economic and social foundation for industrial capitalism, that eventually saw the system of slavery as an "impediment to capitalist development" (Shawki, 2006, p. 54), we provide a conceptual framework for whites to understand why and how we are privileged, therefore creating an opportunity for taking responsibility for what we have participated in. However, there is a paradox here: this important work simultaneously runs the risk of perpetuating "the white person's need for self-display in relation to nonwhite persons" (Gresson, 2004, p. 13), and therefore keeping whiteness at the center of attention.

In other words, this study of abuse, while a necessary component of anti-racist education, alone, is not enough because it misses one of the most important aspects of both colonialism and neo-colonialism—that is, human agency. In other words, while the legacy of abuse emerging from the African slave trade, and now global neoliberal capitalism, is important to study because it helps us better understand contemporary manifestations of this history of Euro-centrically-justified profiteering, alone, it does not *fully* disrupt the hierarchy of intelligence paradigm that positions white people, or more recently, *white culture*, as inherently superior or important, and, in the process, further obscuring the primary purpose of the basic structures of power, and that is the accumulation of vast fortunes at whatever human or environmental cost. To more fully disrupt the institutionalization of a Euro-centric history curriculum, we must re-examine the role of Black Africa as a world leader in culture, science, philosophy, and social organization, however imperialistic, in the pre-Columbian context (Malott, Waukau, & Waukau-Villagomez, 2009).

For example, von Wuthenau (1992/2002) argues that it is not enough to document the genocidal cruelties of Europeans engaged in the West African, trans-Atlantic slave trade, but scholars should also work to re-write the official curriculum to include detailed accounts of "the nobility of Black rulers who had their portraits carved in colossal stone monuments on American soil" which underscores "the glorious past of African lords in Ancient America" (pp. 82–83) hundreds, and perhaps even thousands, of years before the arrival of Columbus. While it has become increasingly acceptable in academic circles to discuss "the enslavement of Black people in the New world" since the birth of the Columbian pedagogy of conquest and plunder (Malott, 2008), it remains bitterly unacceptable to examine "the role of Blacks in the Americas prior to the slave-trade" (Clegg, 1992/2002, p. 231). It is equally unpopular to discuss the role *Black* Egypt played in the development of ancient Greece (Bernal, 1987; Diop, 1955/1974; Malott, Waukau, Waukau-Villagomez, 2009).

Even leading figures in multicultural education, such as James Banks (2003), downplay the significance of the African presence in pre-Columbian America. In the seventh edition of his widely read, *Teaching Strategies for Ethnic Studies*, Banks (2003), without sharing even one example, concludes that the "evidence" that Africans had "established a colony in Mexico long before Columbus's voyage in 1492" is "inconclusive" (p. 187). However, when we examine the mountains of evidence and the conclusions many archeologists have come to in regards to Africans in ancient America, "inconclusive" does not seem to be a popular response. For example, the presence of Egyptian hieroglyphs, that is script or writing, found in the late 1950s on a number of seals excavated in Chiapas, Mexico and carbon-14 dated to be as old as 1000 B.C., for some anthropological scientists, is perhaps the strongest piece of evidence that has been unearthed. For Wayne Chandler (1992/2002), "writing can be used to identify a culture" (p. 251) as accurately as DNA evidence can identify an individual.

From a critical constructivist perspective, we might therefore observe that under the current hegemony it is acceptable to produce knowledge that critiques Europe's atrocities, if their victims, in this case Africans, are presented as inferior. In the contemporary context the Black victims of white superiority are discursively positioned as *at risk* because of their *inferior culture* and, at times, their biologically determined cognitive deficiencies, although behaviorist, cultural racism is far more popular in the twenty-first century. At the same time, it is not acceptable to produce knowledge informed by schema grounded in the evidence that highlights the African role as a world leader in science and technology since the beginning of human civilization (Malott, Waukau, & Wakau-Villagomenz, 2009). It is therefore not widely permissible to critique the assumed superiority of authorized, dogmatic versions of Western science.

In our examination of the *struggle* over the education of African Americans in post-Civil War United States we therefore pay particular attention to the activist role of Black educational and religious leaders' (although these domains, historically, in the Black community, have often been indistinguishable) efforts to ensure their students' self-esteems are not damaged by a Euro-centric curriculum and an uncaring pedagogy of domination. We then examine the challenges faced by today's Black leaders in education, such as challenging capitalist exploitation and redundancy. This focus is crucial to our critical pedagogy because agency and self-determination are the hallmarks of social justice education, based not on the values of competition and domination, but on community and the democratic distribution of social, cultural, and economic power.

However, in our examination, we attempt to avoid the pitfalls of oversimplification indicative of *romanticization*, for example. What we do, however, is look for complexity, contradiction, and conditioning, while rejecting predetermination, and thus embracing the capacity for critical consciousness because critical, higher order thinking appears to be a biological trait of the human species (Chomsky, 2002), just as Canadian geese, for example, are genetically encoded with internal navigation systems.

Situated within this spirit of critical pedagogy what follows is an analysis of the education of African Americans since the Civil War as Northern industrial capitalists sought to mold the Black labor force of the South into consenting low-level, wage workers. Basing our critical pedagogy here on von Wuthenau's (1992/2002) emphasis on African leadership on the world stage, we also focus on the ways formerly enslaved Africans and the descendents of formerly enslaved Africans fought back and became a world-leading force against an indoctrinating, capitalist education with a critical education against subjugation by the late 1960s. In our investigation we find that African history has been a consistent tool used by liberatory pedagogues to counter the low self-esteem engendered by white supremacy. We end our investigation considering the ways this analysis might further inform our critical pedagogical choice for teaching and learning in the twenty-first century.

African Americans and Education: A Brief History

After the Civil War, or after the completion of the bourgeois revolution of 1776, from a Marxist perspective, when "northern corporate industrialists emerged as the undisputed power brokers of the period" (Watkins, 2001, p. 14), the newly empowered capitalists became highly interested in education because of their need for social stability, and thus social control, which education is particularly conducive for manufacturing. After the war, many uncertainties loomed large, such as how to subdue an emancipated African population who fought passionately for their freedom in the Civil War?

To assist in this transition, from chattel slavery to wage slavery, in 1865 the federal government legislated the Freedman's Bureau to "provide rudimentary education and social services" to African Americans (Watkins, 2001, p. 46). Understanding the significance of the Freedman's Bureau, W.E.B. Du Bois (1989) describes it as "one of the most singular and interesting of the attempts made by a great nation to grapple with the vast problems of race and social condition" (p. 14). The education was designed to incorporate freed Africans into wage labor society. The leadership of the Bureau was assigned to General Oliver Howard because, after the war, bands of unruly poor whites roved about and small groups of Africans had fled into the countryside, beginning the slow process of building a functioning society growing food and running small schools. Howard's white supremacist perspective informed his paternalistic objective of subduing the population with the assistance of humanistic mission-aries and an industrial style education with an emphasis on discipline, behav-ior, taking orders, and role memorization. While some argued for deportation, genocide, or re-enslavement, the official policy was to paternalistically civilize and train the assumed inferior ex-slave (and poor white) as low-level wage earners.

The goal of capitalist education has always been twofold: first, to train com-munity "leaders" (including teachers) in the application of "law" (as it pertains to every aspect of capitalist society) to serve the interests, even if by default, of the rich and powerful, and simultaneously, to mold those who are slated to be wage earners or the working class, such as recent immigrants, those being colonized on their own land, that is, Native Americans, and recently freed slaves after the Civil War, into accepting the "law" of the capitalist class as legit-imate, as just, as inevitable, and at times, divine (i.e., "in God we trust"). This is achieved by institutionalizing a Euro-centric one answer and one approach formula to knowledge production, rendering the Northern industrial capital-ists the only legitimate possessors of truth and knowledge. The framework on which this approach to the social structure is based is hierarchical and is there-fore represented in unequal educational practices, giving way to the normal-ization of white supremacy and social class.

During slavery, however, "most states had no provisions for educating slaves prior to the Civil War" (Watkins, 2001, p. 12). In fact, many states passed "compulsory ignorance laws prohibiting the schooling of blacks," which were not "declared illegal" until 1868 (Menchaca, 1997, p. 36). Enslavers therefore relied on a plantation system of divide and rule, and force, for perpetuating the economic and social system of slavery. Because capitalism is presented as a *nat-ural* system and thus in need of no coercion, its perpetuation relies heavily on consent and thus ideological indoctrination, with special emphasis placed on education. Again, the form of education the *White Architects of Black Education* offered Black Americans during Reconstruction was spearheaded by humanis-tic missionaries who tended to embrace "notions of altruism, free expression, salvation, and the unfettered development of the individual" (Watkins, 2001, p. 14).

However, as previously mentioned, the missionaries' *progressive* vision of progress and social justice *for* Blacks was situated within the context of an unquestioned industrial capitalism that "espoused the paternal social and racial relations of the South" (Watkins, 2001, p. 15). What this meant was keeping poor whites and poor blacks separate because a divided working class is far more

manageable and controllable than a united one. These segregationist relations were formally institutionalized in 1896 when the Supreme Court passed
Plessy v. Ferguson, which "officially gave the states the right to segregate racial
minorities in separate schools" (Menchaca, 1997, p. 37). While the states had
already been practicing segregation, the significance of *Plessy*, according to
Menchaca (1997), was that it sent the message "to non-whites that they did
not have any legal recourse to protest against the educational policies of the
states" (p. 37).

Shedding considerable light on what emerged as a white-supremacist
approach to industrial education for Blacks are the psychological assumptions
behind its construction. That is, the North's industrial education for African
Americans might be described as being informed by a combination of behaviorist and mentalist perspectives. That is, mentalist because the hierarchy of
intelligence was assumed to be biologically determined based on race, and
behaviorist because the assumed low level of intelligence of Blacks rendered
them not fit to make important decisions and thus in need of external conditioning and control. The rudimentary industrial education offered to Blacks by
Northern industrialists was therefore presented as not only a good intellectual match, but as their destiny due to inherently inferior cognitive abilities
(Kincheloe, 2005; Menchaca, 1997; Watkins, 2001).

However, while the Northern capitalist ruling class was busy constructing
a domesticating education for African Americans, the undercover agency of the
Black Church in the South had already a long established history of subversive
educational and liberatory practices despite the compulsory *ignorance laws*
mentioned above. After the Civil War one of the only available official leadership roles for African Americans was as teachers and principals, which afforded them a special position of esteem and respect within the Black community
(Loder, 2006; Tyler, 2006). Underscoring the significance of the Black Church
as a pivotal vehicle for Black liberation, Eric C. Lincoln (1984) has commented that, "by the end of the Civil War, to belong to an African church was the
clearest statement about how one felt about freedom" (p. 64). "God's challenge," from the perspective of the Black Church, was for "every man [sic] to
realize the highest potential of his humanity by being a living testament of the
divine image in which he was cast. Since God himself was free, and was created free in his image, then man's struggle must ever be to maintain or recover the freedom with which he was endowed by his Creator" (Lincoln, 1984, p.
63). Leading Black liberation theologian, James Cone (2003), in the context
of Mumia Abu-Jamal's (2003) *Faith of Our fathers: An Examination of the*

Spiritual Life of African and African American People, reiterates the instrumental role of the Black church noting:

> *Faith of Our Fathers* tells the story of an African people who in the midst of the most devastating circumstance held themselves together and fought back—refusing to let 244 years of legal servitude in America define their humanity. How did they do that? How could enslaved Africans know that they were human beings in a land that only recognized them as chattel? Mumia Abu-Jamal correctly locates the answer in the cultural and religious life that slaves created through an affirmation of their African past and a radical reinterpretation of the Christian religion of white missionaries. (p. vii)

The African American liberation struggles that have emerged from this legacy of the Black Church have always been rooted, as Cone underscores, at various levels of complexity and sophistication, in the African cultural and spiritual heritage because slavery, through the process of cultural genocide (Malott, 2008), required its African subjects to abandon their indigenous cultures and religions in the creation of an enslaved subjectivity. The significance of this African culture and history, situated in the context of white supremacist America, lies in the evidence that overwhelmingly suggests that ancient *Black* Egypt provided ancient Greece with the model of civilization that the West would later attribute to European sources and therefore the basis of white supremacy (Bernal, 1987; Diop, 1955/1974; Malott, Waukau, Waukau-Villagomez, 2009). This history therefore disrupts the paternalistic white supremacy that portrays Africans as primitive, underdeveloped savages whose salvation resides within the hands of their white, naturally superior masters. Consequently, liberation, for many enslaved Africans, meant not only freeing oneself and one's community from chattel slavery and later wage-slavery (i.e., industrial capitalism), but recovering one's African cultural heritage.

For example, William Edward Burghardt Du Bois (1868–1963), who had been under FBI surveillance for more than forty years by the age of ninety-three in 1961 (O'Reilly, 1994), argued that far too many African Americans had been robbed of their cultural consciousness and in 1946 wrote that a truly liberating African American education must be firmly grounded in African history and social development based on the awareness that African epistemologies and ontologies represented some of the most sophisticated perspectives ever developed by humankind. In practice, it has, and in many instances continues to be, the Black religious leader who serves the function of the organic intellectual, the cultural workers, the political leaders, the respected men and women of ideas that lead and direct the community, either toward accommodation through the boss's religion, or through a deeper interpretation of religious texts that identify with Jesus as a figure of the oppressed, a freedom fighter. Summarizing this view of the Black religious leader as revolutionary, Du Bois (1989) comments:

> The free Negro leader early arose and his chief characteristic was intense earnestness and deep feeling on the slavery question. Freedom became to him a real thing and not a dream. His religion became darker and more intense, and into his ethics crept a note of revenge, into his songs a day of reckoning close at hand. The "Coming of the Lord" swept this side of Death, and came to be a thing to be hoped for in this day....For fifty years Negro religion thus transformed itself and identified itself with the dream of Abolition. (pp. 121–122)

For Du Bois then, religious leaders, and by implication the Black leaders of Black education, should serve the interests of the students, and therefore work to subvert the basic structures of power within white supremacist society. Within the context of Du Bois' approach, formal education is highly desirable to the extent that it is presented as an indispensable tool in the project of humanization. In other words, humanity's struggle to free itself from all forms of oppression is portrayed as not possible without a revolutionary form of mass education and an empowering conception of the divine or the spirit that views the "deliverance from bondage as a divine act" (Abu-Jamal, 2003, p. 53).

Consequently, for many Africans in America "the political was deeply infused with the spiritual" (Abu-Jamal, 2003, p. 53). Making this connection crystal clear, Abu-Jamal (2003) rhetorically asks, "Wasn't their most fervent hope, for freedom, a prayer for the transformation of a political reality" (p. 53)? To deny people a transformative education and religion is therefore an act of oppression or subjugation. The struggle for liberation, or the "passage from slavery to freedom," situated within this spiritual context, is therefore not so much "the work of man as it was the work of God (Abu-Jamal, 2003, p. 51). Unlike the boss's religion marked by an obsession with other-worldliness, Abu-Jamal (2003) highlights Du Bois' recognition that black religious institutions were firmly grounded in the affairs of *this world* "given the hellish temporal experiences of most black congregates held in bondage (p. 103).

Du Bois' work can therefore be understood within the context of the liberation theology of the Black Church that places special emphasis on achieving one's highest God-given potential. The low-level industrial education of Northern industrialists and a domesticating religion that commanded its flock to accommodate the basic structures of power, subjected Blacks to the development of a dependent relationship where capitalists are not viewed as a barrier to self-actualization, but as a necessity of life. Through this process, those conditioned to be workers are trained to view *the paycheck* as an inevitable requirement of survival, locking struggle within the confines of the labor/capital relationship. Du Bois' pedagogy, on the other hand, offers students a way to view the world not as deterministically fixed, but as a place of possibility and critical transformation. As we see below, this racially mediated struggle between labor and capital has continued to inform the politics of education into the twenty-first century.

***

Education, especially higher education, in post-WWII America, has been touted within the settler community as evidence of the existence of meritocracy, that is, if you work hard, are a "good" (i.e., obedient) citizen, and (have access to the material and cultural capital needed to) go to college, then it is expected that you will be rewarded with "success" within the system that exists. Education has therefore been held up in the West as a key to full democratic participation (within the limitations of capitalism). Because of the social power and privilege afforded those with a formal education in Western societies, it has been used as a tool of oppression, as previously mentioned, by denying it to certain people such as African Americans.

Much of the civil rights movement of the 1960s and 1970s in the United States, after *Brown v. Board of Education* reversed *Plessy* in 1954, and after the 1964 Civil Rights Act was ratified, was focused on achieving equal access to educational opportunities for historically oppressed peoples in the self-actualizing spirit of the Black Church. Demanding the right to an education has not only been implicated in accommodating the system that exists, that is, attempting to "succeed" within it as wage earners, but, as argued above, it has also been advocated for as a means of becoming critically conscious and politically active, that is, transformative or liberatory. The symbolic and material significance of the struggle to bring equality to the nation's public schools, especially to the seventeen states in the South that mandated segregation by law, resides within the notion that, "it was an integral part of a much broader movement for racial and economic justice supported by a unique alliance of major civil rights organizations, churches, students, and leaders of both national political parties" (Orfield, 2003, p. 155).

At the same time, however, after *Brown v. Board of Education*, "more than 30,000 black teachers lost their jobs" (Tyler, 2006, p. 132). As black students began to be placed in white schools (very rarely were white students ever placed in traditionally all black schools), black teachers were replaced by white teachers because "African-American teachers were restricted from teaching white students because of the belief that African-American teachers were inferior to white teachers" (p. 132). As a result, much of the black community feared that their children "would not be taught racial pride" (Tyler, 2006, p. 132). Reflecting on her own experiences as a black student in the south during this time of turmoil, bell hooks (1994) compares her education in all black schools to the white schools she was *desegregated* into. Her insights are instructive:

> Almost all our teachers at Booker T. Washington were black women. They were committed to nurturing intellect so that we could become scholars, thinkers, and cultural workers—black folks who used our "minds." We learned early that our devotion to learning, to a life of the mind, was a counter-hegemonic act, a fundamental way to resist every strategy of white racist colonization....My teachers were on a mission. To fulfill that mission, my teachers made sure they "knew" us. They knew our parents, our economic status, where we worshipped, what our homes were like, and how we were treated in the family....Attending school then was sheer joy....School was the place of ecstasy—pleasure and danger. (pp. 2–3)

Comparing this enlightening and empowering experience with education after desegregation, hooks (1994) continues:

> School changed utterly with racial integration. Gone was the messianic zeal to transform our minds and beings that had characterized teachers and their pedagogical practices in our all-black schools. Knowledge was suddenly about information only. It had no relation to how one lived, behaved. It was no longer connected to anti-racist struggle. Bussed to white schools, we soon learned that obedience, and not a zealous will to learn, was what was expected of us. (p. 3)

The Contemporary Neoliberal Context

However, between 1954 and 1964 little had changed in Southern schools as mandated desegregation was met with almost universal state and local racist resistance. In 1964 a civil rights empowered Congress considered withholding funding for programs that operated with discrimination, such as education. Consequently, between 1964 and 1970, Southern schools went from being the most segregated in the Nation to the least segregated. After the social movements of the 1960s and 1970s realized these and other economic and cultural gains and achievements, such as the advancement of multicultural education (MCE), the capitalist class moved swiftly to recover all it perceived itself to have lost. As a result, by the 1990s this trend was beginning to reverse and by 2001 schools were as segregated as they were three decades earlier (Orfield, 2003; Watkins, 2001).

The election of Richard Nixon in 1968 was the turning point, signaling a shift in policy and practice with the elimination of the desegregation enforcement machinery and eventually the slowing down, and, in some instances, the reversing of desegregation requirements. These trends continued with President Jimmy Carter and intensified under President Reagan with a new discourse of *crisis* painting the civil rights movement and desegregation as a failure, which posed a serious danger to whites as a form of reverse discrimination. As a result, there has been no serious attempt to integrate schools since the 1970s (Orfield, 2003).

The legacy of Reagan's conservative discourse can be found within his famous education report, *A Nation at Risk*. In the report, Reagan appeals to people's sense of fear, employing the language of crisis or urgency, in which he blames multicultural education and the civil rights movement for watering down the curriculum, reducing academic rigor, and eventually leading to the decline of the United States as a world power. Employing militaristic language the report argues that if the nation's schools do not return to *the basics* (i.e., math, science, and reading), then the Communist threat of the Soviet Union will jeopardize American freedom embodied in free market capitalism (Kincheloe, Slattery, and Steinberg, 2000).

This brings us to another layer of analysis that is central to our investigation here. Part of the ruling elite's effort to regain control over those who rely on a wage to survive, and simultaneously increase their profit margin, has been the neoliberalization of capital, which represents the real cause of people's economic suffering or the decrease in real wages, not multicultural education and the civil rights movement. It is widely accepted among critical economists that the dismantling of the Bretton Woods system in 1971 signaled the beginning of this most recent neoliberal era of capitalism. Bretton Woods was established in 1944 to limit the power of capital to externalize the costs of not only normal production, but the high costs of the stock market crash and Great Depression of 1929, on labor, especially African American labor.

However, this was not a generous gesture made by benevolent leaders, but rather, an attempt to save the system because the working class's level of resistance and rebellion was reaching critical levels threatening the basic structure of power. Something had to be done, workers had to be appeased, but real and permanent change in the relationship between labor and capital was not an option, from the perspective of elite interests (Malott, Waukau, Waukau-Villagomez, 2009). It is therefore not surprising that the time before and during the Great Depression is characterized by the Harlem Renaissance as the migration of African Americans from the South realized relatively significant income gains as Northern manufacturers had a shortage of labor—a favorable position for collective bargaining. Consequently, the African American community had the income to fund an African and African American cultural rejuvenation movement that would inspire Malcolm X and later the revolutions of the 1960s and beyond.

Given this context it is not surprising that Bretton Woods was dismantled and capital was once again free to move with limited restrictions on where and how it could function. International trade laws, such as the North American Free Trade Agreement (NAFTA), have removed tariffs on international trade, allowing capital to move more freely across borders, limiting the effectiveness of unions as corporations can much more easily relocate to areas with the least powerful working classes. Consequently, the wages of working people, globally, have decreased in the past thirty years. At the same time, the earnings of the richest capitalists have exploded. For example, of the world's six billion people, the poorest forty percent receive only five percent of the world's income whereas the richest twenty percent receive seventy-five percent.

Neoliberalism has also enabled capital to *move* into more areas of public and social life from hospitals, libraries, prisons, and schools. As a result, the control of public schools, in many instances, has been handed over to private, for-profit management companies, such as Edison—the hidden agenda of George W. Bush's No Child Left Behind Act. It is argued that schools are intentionally set up to fail by imposing Adequate Yearly Progress goals set by NCLB guidelines that the schools cannot meet because the program is severely underfunded and the phonics-based approach to literacy endorsed by the Act is not engaging for students. The testing-based No Child Left Behind Act touted as the surest path to increasing achievement was therefore really designed to lend weight to privatization and the neoliberal agenda represented by the *choice* and voucher movement. Critical educator Alfie Kohn (2004) has commented that "you don't have to be a conspiracy nut to understand the real purpose of NCLB" (p. 84). That is, NCLB is nothing more than a "backdoor maneuver" (Kohn, 2004, p. 84) constructed around conceptions of *choice* allowing private for-profit capitalists to take over public education. The increasing role that high stakes standardized testing has played through NCLB in determining what students and what schools are effective, disproportionately affecting the educational achievement of traditionally oppressed peoples, such as African Americans. Arne Duncan, the current Secretary of Education, was frequently protested for supporting NCLB's privatization agenda when he ran Chicago's school system. In recent speeches Duncan has continued the legacy of Reagan's discourse of urgency or crisis as a justification for neoliberal NCLB-style programs.

Consequently, the largely segregated schools Black and Latino students attend in the twenty-first century present a host of problems to educational leaders unfathomable just thirty years ago. Summarizing this context Tondra L. Loder (2006) in "Dilemmas Confronting Urban Principals in the Post-Civil Rights Era," comments:

> Fifty years after the landmark *Brown v. Board of Education of Topeka, Kansas* Supreme Court case declared legalized racial segregation in public education unconstitutional, African American principals in urban schools confront leadership dilemmas unlike any others they have faced in United States history. As student bodies become increasingly ethnically and economically diverse, and as social and technological changes render the principal's role more complex, urban principals today confront problems and crises that did not exist for principals fifty years ago. (p. 70)

Loder (2006) finds this turn of events "ironic" because the desegregation policies allowing African Americans to enter the ranks of public school administration also signaled "the loss of middle-class white and African American students and families who were formerly invested in urban schools" and the "shrinking financial commitments from state and federal governments," rendering this new generation of Black principals "at the helm of extremely troubled urban schools" (p. 70). Black educational leaders in the post-civil rights era have therefore been portrayed as both messiahs and scapegoats. That is, working class Black communities throughout the United States have looked to their Black educational leaders holding "unrealistic expectations and unusually high hopes that significant improvements in public education could be gained solely through their empowerment" (p. 71). At the same time, it has been predicted that many of these new Black leaders would be viewed by the Black community as representatives of the white power structure and therefore with suspicion. At the same time the Black educational leadership community has been blamed by "white politicians and members of the business community" for "proliferating societal ills" (Loder, 2006, p. 71).

Critical Pedagogy and Educational Leadership

> The career and martyrdom of M.L. King ushered in an extraordinary era of American life, but like the ebb and flow of nature's mighty oceans, it might fairly be said that the movement he led and energized is on the wane. This is due, in no small part, to conservative counter movements in the United States… Conservative judicial and political actors have responded to this countermovement by a policy of retrenchment on issues (such as affirmative action) that are seen as supportive of Black interests. In some respects, then, it would be fair to call this period a post-civil rights era. (Abu-Jamal, 2003, p. 123–124)

Situated within this atmosphere of repression and right-wing white supremacist resurgence are glimpses of African American agency and transformative cultural rejuvenation. Of course there are many Black teachers who have internalized the dominant paradigm and work in the interests of the Eurocentric capitalist class as part of the dominant society with white, Latina/o and others who have been similarly indoctrinated. However, it seems the more one looks, the more examples and instances there of Black teachers (and whites, Chinese, Chicana/o and countless others) working for peace and democracy taking inspiration from many sources, such as the Black theology of liberation.

For example, twenty-year veteran New York City public school teacher, Winthrop Holder (2007), demonstrates that doing critical pedagogy with traditionally oppressed students is something that can be done *now* and it can be done successfully as he, and many others, have built vast communities of subversive producers and engagers of subjugated knowledges. Holder (2007) stands as a steadfast example of a high school social studies critical pedagogue who has been "giving voice to the voiceless" for decades, publishing, and in the process empowering, the critical insights of the hundreds upon hundreds of students he has worked with over the years. Holder began reproducing student work in a series of self-produced and student-run journals, such as *Crossing Swords*, which quickly gained the support of parents, university professors, school districts, school janitors and schoolteachers.

These critical approaches to education deserve much celebration and reflection because they successfully embrace diverse ways of knowing, allowing educators and students to "hang out in the epistemological bazaar listening to and picking up on articulations of subjugated knowledges" (Kincheloe, 2005, p. 127). It is therefore not saying too much that restructuring the curriculum (at least within our own classrooms) for social justice (however defined) is within our *immediate grasp*. Aware of these possibilities an increasing number of African American principals who lead traditionally Black schools have found ways to allow spaces for teachers to explore ways to incorporate Afro-centric content into the state-mandated content standards. In the language arts, for example, teachers frequently use African American writers to teach literary terms such as metaphor and irony.

For example, Bernard Gassaway, the new principal of one of the nation's largest public high schools, Boys and Girls High School in Brooklyn, NY (a "failing" school according to NCLB guidelines), was a guest on Gill Noble's television program, *Like It Is*, where he argued that the curriculum of the NYC public school system, in general, is Euro-centric. Consequently, Gassaway supports efforts made by individual teachers in his school to incorporate content from African and African American history and studies in their curricula. He sees his role as principal as the ambassador to the Black community his school and students are an intimate part of. He wants the working class families of his student body to see the school not as an external imposition designed to white-wash or *de-Blackify* their children, but a partner in the struggle for a better life. Consequently, there is a feeling of not only increased rigor among the predominantly Black teachers, but also a sense of cultural pride and mission. It is therefore becoming increasingly more common to observe groups of teachers working together developing Afro-centric curricula. These efforts, in the spirit of Du Bois, are not only assisting students in seeing themselves through their own eyes rather than through the colonialist gaze of white eyes, but they are fostering a passion to know the skills of language arts, science, and mathematics, as these disciplines have deep roots in the ancient Black world.

Conclusion: Revisiting Critical Pedagogy

If our critical pedagogies are to take as their place of departure the concrete context in which they are situated, then the analyses presented here are of particular importance, and, by implication, counter-hegemonic. Because these histories are controversial in mainstream academia, as critical pedagogues, we should make it one of our primary objectives to challenge this tendency. That is, it would serve us well to treat engaging with the subjugated knowledges of African Americans and ancient African civilizations, for example, not as a *radical* endeavor, but as the practice of rationally expanding our epistemological parameters and therefore conducive to the ideals of justice and equality that our democracies are based on. This approach is designed to celebrate the multiple epistemological perspectives characteristic of all peoples and all backgrounds, and is therefore substantially more revolutionary than any one perspective by itself, such as the many critical pedagogies associated with critical theories (Kincheloe, 2008).

This unified approach is not just a liberal attempt to *lend equal weight to all ideas*, as it were, but rather, it represents a conclusion we have arrived at after a thorough investigation of the evidence. What we have seen is that the history of the many peoples and epistemologies of the earth is not a series of *isolated histories* where each individual locale represents a distinct and unrelated march toward the same universal standard for advanced civilization. The history of humanity, according to science, on the other hand, is a complex story of convergence, passive diffusion, and compulsory diffusion. Such historical understandings make crystal clear that the epistemologies of the world's peoples are closely related and share long, complex relationships as ancient as human civilization itself. Following Du Bois, when we study world history non-Euro-centrically, we are left with a much more African-influenced understanding of human culture and civilization (see Malott, Waukau, and Waukau-Villagomez, 2009).

Again, this Afro-centrism should not be conceived of as controversial, and it should not make *white* people, or anyone else who relies on a wage to survive, uncomfortable (which is nearly all of humanity because capitalists are a very small minority of the world's population) because there is only one species, even if at the present moment those of European descent happen to be the current beneficiaries of hegemonic prejudice and oppression. For example, white people in the United States, and throughout much of the contemporary world, who currently possess racial privilege because of the long legacy of the racializing that accompanied the African trans-Atlantic genocidal slave trade and the genocide of ninety-eight percent of all Native American peoples since 1492, can become change-agents by choosing to denounce racial privilege, working as labor organizers, and opposing all forms of undemocratic hierarchy. For schools, this means that the curriculum needs to be de-Euro-cenricized.

The content presented here is an example of one such attempt. Of course, as critical pedagogues, we encourage all educators and all students to be actively engaged in this work. Reformulating the curriculum should not just be the act of replacing the subject matter that is to be deposited by teachers into students but should question the very basis of the knowledge-producing process. This is the task of the socially just educator because it is the responsibility of schools to provide a positive and nurturing environment for all students taking special care to ensure their self-esteems are not damaged in any way by the learning experience.

Our approach to critical praxis here is informed by a refusal to accept the mainstream proposition that one often hears in the parroted echo of the dominant discourse—*there will always be inequality and exploitation because it is human nature*—rendering any struggle waged against such tendencies counterproductive. Our critical pedagogies, which consciously strive for universal democracy, however, are based on the evidence that overwhelmingly suggests that social hierarchy is not an inherited biological trait universal among the species. Inequality, where the few dominate the many, is not determined by genetics, but by the combined use of force, consent, and divide and rule, and can therefore be resisted and transformed. This is the objective of critical pedagogy, and our collective histories offer many invaluable insights and sources of empowerment, as demonstrated thus far from the Black Church to the Black school.

But our attention to detail does not end here. In our critical examinations of Euro-centric curriculum and the subsequent explorations of subjugated knowledges, we must continuously challenge ourselves and the students we work with to always bring to the fore the contexts such perspectives are constructed in. Similarly, Joe Kincheloe (2005), in his *Critical Constructivism Primer*, notes that critical constructivist educators are "concerned with the processes through which certain information becomes validated knowledge" as well as "the processes through which certain information was not deemed to be worthy or validated knowledge" (p. 3). In the end then, to reiterate, from this critical pedagogical perspective, the goal "is not to transmit a body of validated truths to students for memorization," but rather, "to engage students in the knowledge production process" (Kincheloe, 2005, p. 3). Teachers who are successful at this show a great capacity to create the conditions where students can spark their own epistemological curiosities which tends to be marked by the creation of a classroom "where students' personal experience intersects with academic knowledges" (Kincheloe, 2005, p. 4). Kincheloe (2005) offers some insight into what this might look like in practice noting that "in their search for ways to produce democratic and evocative knowledges, critical constructivists become detectives of new ways of seeing and constructing the world" (p. 4). Put another way, critical scholars, dedicated to not only understanding the world but contributing to uplifting its democratic imperatives, tend to be perpetually searching for new interpretative frameworks (philosophies) or "ways of seeing" that can better serve these ends.

· 4 ·

EDUCATIONAL LEADERSHIP AND THE CULTURAL GENOCIDE OF NATIVE AMERICANS

The Boarding School Experience and Beyond

In this chapter we examine the utterly destructive nature of America's model of education for the continent's Indigenous peoples—peoples consisting of 500 different tribes and nations and hundreds of distinct languages and cultures. We begin with an analysis of the founding architect and leader of this externally imposed form of education, Captain Richard Pratt. After reviewing the magnitude of loss inflicted by the boarding school project, we explore more recent Indigenous efforts to transform what was once a destructive force, the Western model of schooling, into a space of cultural rejuvenation. Through this investigation we begin to notice the emergence of more Indigenous approaches to educational leadership conducive to our critical pedagogical project for educational leadership.

***

One is hard pressed to recollect an example of educational policy that more centrally locates schooling outside the realm of scientific inquiry regarding the learning and development of the human being than *Indian Boarding Schools*. Underscoring this point, we can begin by considering the fact that in 1879 a man of military training and experience was chosen by the U.S. to construct and lead the system of *educating Indians*, Captain Richard Henry Pratt, not a person with expertise in the science of teaching and learning. It is therefore not surprising that the underlying philosophy informing his purpose as an educational leader comes from a military source, General Phil Sheridan, who was known for his statement, *the only good Indian is a dead one* (Churchill, 2004, p. 14). Reflecting this belief in 1892 in a public address Pratt opines "a great general has said that the only good Indian is a dead one…In a sense, I agree with the sentiment, but only in this: that all the Indian there is in the race should be dead. Kill the Indian in him, and save the man" (p. 1).

Pratt's approach, keep in mind, from a ruling-elite, settler-state perspective, was considered to be the humane *solution* to *the Indian problem*—which was *the problem* of what to do with multiple communities of thousands of people occupying lands west of the Mississippi, after militarily defeating them through the combined use of force and divide and conquer. Rather than continue the policy of *outright physical slaughter*, Pratt believed Indigenous peoples could be relieved of their cultural baggage and learn to become part of what he considered to be a far superior model of civilization—the Western model. Pratt therefore saw the boarding school project as *doing Indians a favor*.

> It is a sad day for the Indians when they fall under the assaults of our troops…as in the massacre of Old Black Kettle and his Cheyenne…and hundreds of other like places in the history of our dealings with them; but a far sadder day is it for them when they fall under the baneful influences of a treaty agreement with the United States whereby they are to receive large annuities, and to be protected on reservations, and held apart from all association with the best of our civilization. (Pratt, 1892, p. 1)

The obvious value of considering this text is the honesty and matter-of-factness within which Pratt proclaims his belief in white supremacy. Pratt's paternalistic, Euro-centric approach is so all-encompassing that he reminds his audience that his work will not be complete "until there is throughout all of our communities the most unequivocal and complete acceptance of our own doctrines, both national and religious" (p. 2). Making his point crystal clear Pratt draws on the example of "the black man," who, he argues, was of "the lowest savagery" until "we" (I assume here he means other white leaders like himself), became even wiser and *allowed* them to come into intelligence and attain "industrial value," therefore contributing to the ruling class' accumulation of wealth.

It is this ideology—the ideology of *the white man's burden*—that positions slavery and colonization as painful favors embodied in the sentiment, *you may hate me now for what I am doing to you, but you will thank me in the long run*—

that informed Pratt's own justification for cultural genocide. For example, Pratt, reasoning from this white supremacist point of view, argues that while slavery was horrible, it contained a hidden benefit, which he described as "the greatest blessing that ever came to the Negro race" (p. 2). That is, to have the opportunity to be around white people and assimilate into their capitalist civilization, which, from this white supremacist perspective, represents the most, advanced stage of human cultural development. Again, Pratt draws on this example to argue that it was only by associating with people of the superior race, Europeans, that Africans were able to so readily become somewhat industrious and aware of the basic tenets of citizenship, which he argued would never have happened if they had been left in Africa and "surrounded by fellow savages" (p. 2). Making this point, Pratt argues that Native Americans too will continue their savage ways and remain a burden unless they have the opportunity to benefit from the presence of *the master race*, hence, the boarding school project.

Making his case Pratt challenges the assumption that Native Americans had not previously been *civilized* and *absorbed* into the settler society because they did not possess the cognitive ability to comprehend the complex ideas of civilization. Because of the central significance of the following excerpt to the connection between Pratt's theory of learning and approach to educational leadership, a sizable quote is provided:

> It is a great mistake to think that the Indian is born an inevitable savage. He is born a blank, like all the rest of us. Left in the surroundings of savagery, he grows to possess a savage language, superstition, and life. We, left in the surroundings of civilization, grow to possess a civilized language, life, and purpose. Transfer the infant white to the savage surroundings, he will grow to possess a savage language, superstition, and habit. Transfer the savage-born infant to the surroundings of civilization, and he will grow to possess a civilized language and habit. These results have been established over and over again beyond all question; and it is also well established that those advanced in life, even to maturity, of either class, lose already acquired qualities belonging to the side of their birth, and gradually take on those of the side to which they have been transferred. (p. 5)

While it is true that culture, language, and other beliefs, value systems, and worldviews are not biologically determined but are learned from a very young age on, as Pratt argues, the civil-savage scale he uses to position the West above all that is not European is not an *objective* measure as he and other proponents of dominant power would lead us to believe. Rather, the civil-savage scale is informed by a set of subjective values that privilege domination, competition, and the accumulation of vast fortunes, regardless of human or environmental costs, over community, balance, cooperation, and peace.

Consequently, the cleverness of Pratt's discourse resides within its partial truthfulness. As a result, Pratt's thoroughly colonial, Euro-centric, white supremacist, industrial-capitalistic, blank slate approach to learning has been so ingrained and absorbed into the nation's school culture, it remains apparent despite the emergence of highly influential constructivist and critical competing approaches. That is, constructivist science teacher educators have long since disproved the blank slate theory by demonstrating that students have *minds of their own*. In other words, it is impossible to passively deposit a new idea into someone's mind because every new idea we are presented with gets filtered through our preexisting schema or interpretive frameworks, which are always informed by a particular political interest because *you cannot be neutral on a moving train*—that is, society is moving in a particular direction, supporting particular kinds of relationships, arrangements, and interests, and therefore the position of neutrality is really one of acceptance of that which already exists, which is more often than not reproduced unconsciously through the process of hegemony.

The external imposed banking model also continues to hold political sway because it is conducive to manufacturing obedience and passivity among those slated to be wageworkers, the vast majority. Again, the unstated political interest that persistently informs the institutions of the dominant society, such as schools, continues to be for an industrial, capitalist society assumed to represent evidence of the supremacy of Western civilization. This is why Pratt himself was so adamant about removing Indian children from their own cultural context at the youngest possible age before they fully developed Indigenous schema and interpretive frameworks, which represent a barrier to the adoption of the industrial, hierarchical, human-centric Western philosophy.

In other words, the offensiveness of the *environmental* (not to be confused with environmentalism) approach resides within its dehumanizing tendencies. For example, assuming students are empty vessels reduces them to the most rudimentary and unexciting forms of cognition, and in the process, ignores the vast potential within their cultural and biological inheritances. In the case of Pratt, his adoption of the blank slate formula belittled the most special gift of his Native students—their Indigeneity, that is, their worldview, their language, and all the unique cultural sophistication embodied in distinct human languages. While Pratt portrayed himself as a progressive reformer, for many critical scholars, he was just another of Columbus' heirs.

David Daily (2004), in his *Battle for the BIA: G.E.E. Lindquist and the*

Missionary Crusade against John Collier, invokes the memory of Pratt in the context of his support for radical assimilation and immediate land allotment and his subsequent disdain for the gradual assimilation approach of missionaries, whose perspective was largely informed by the *rigid determinism* of *scientific racism* emerging around the early years of the twentieth century (Daily, 2004). In this context Pratt was able to portray his *paternalistic favor* (i.e., civilizing the savage) as more socially just than the missionarie's form of *paternalistic protectionism* because the latter was based on the assumption that, compared to *Caucasians*, Native Americans occupied a subservient place on the racial ladder. Connecting his *progressive* environmental theory of learning to his support for radical assimilation, and his support for land allotment to an economic motive, Daily (2004) comments:

> Because they believed racial differences were merely the product of environmental factors, they set out to transform the next generation of Indians into citizens fully capable of participating as equals in American society. In social terms, they proposed a process of rapid immersion in the dominant society—a sink-or-swim approach that involved removing Indian children from their homes and educating them in distant boarding schools where they were forbidden to use Native languages. Economically, radical assimilation entailed breaking up tribal landholdings in reservations and allotting the lands to individual Indians. In theory, land allotments—the mere possession of valuable private property—would instill a healthy self-interest in individual Indians, prompting them toward industrious habits and respect for the laws that protected their own property as well as that of others. (p. 25)

Within this excerpt Daily eloquently connects all of the dots underscoring the connection between education and the process of value production, which requires that all subjects within its sphere of influence embody the values and beliefs of Western, capitalist hegemony, private property in particular. Underscored here is the political nature of education itself—schooling has never been purely technical or mechanical. The schoolhouse itself is an industrial tool designed to prepare the individual for citizenship, which requires fitting into the existing productive apparatus for the harvest of one's physical and cognitive abilities. Our critical pedagogical choice for educational leadership rejects both the cultural Euro-centric paternalism of Pratt and the biologically racist paternalism of the coddling missionaries.

While we agree with Pratt that there exists no biologically or genetically predetermined hierarchy of intelligence, especially across racial lines because the socially-constructed concept of race is not a scientifically supported or validated property, we do not endorse or adopt his conviction that Western civilization represents the highest stage of human, cultural evolution. First, we reject outright the notion that there exists, objectively, and therefore independent of human thought, a civilization hierarchy. That is, we are not saying that the Western model should be replaced with something more authentic or romantic, but we should challenge and abandon the ontology of hierarchy outright.

This cognitive shift is significant because it leads to different questions and ultimately different knowledges and practices. Rather than asking, *In what order should the hierarchy be arranged?* We should ask, *What kind of social arrangements might best serve our most cherished values, such as, dignity, respect, social justice, individual freedom, equal protection under the law, etc.?* What we see below is that once Native communities began obtaining control of their own schools around the 1970s, there began a concerted effort on the part of tribal leaders and educators to place Indigenous knowledge at the center of curriculum and pedagogy in order to begin recovering what was lost under the paternalistic educational leadership of Pratt *and* the missionaries. These efforts continue to thrive despite recent setbacks due to No Child Left Behind (NCLB) standardized testing mandates, which have worked to displace Indigeneity and everything else that is *not on the test*.

***

What this discussion of Pratt underscores is the *purpose* for education regarding America's indigenous peoples, and the extent to which it was carried out (Adams, 1995; Churchill, 2004). Churchill (2004) lists 129 Indian boarding schools operating within the United States between 1880 and 1980. Similarly, he lists 87 such institutions operating in Canada within the same time period. The Canadian model was designed to achieve the same results as their U.S. counterparts where children were forcibly removed from resistant parents and taken sometimes thousands of miles from home for years on end and prohibited from speaking their native tongue or practicing any of their other cultural traditions. In other words, they were prohibited from being "Indian" and made, sometimes with deadly force, to be something else, that is, a low-level, manual laborer with white values and worldview. Consequently, viewing the world as white people do, they were conditioned to despise, ridicule, and reject their indigenous background.

In other words, education has been used by the United States and Canadian governments to exterminate what it is about Native Americans, beyond genetic composition, that is characteristically Native American, and that is, in two words, culture and land. Children, as young as four years old, were physically removed from their communities, from the love and nurturance of their mothers and grandmothers by "coercing" (violently if needed) families into allowing their children to be taken away to schools far from their communities and for years on end. Roughly between the late 1800s and the mid 1900s more than half of all Native American children had been removed from their homes to be forced to act and think like white children (Churchill, 2004) and therefore become something other than what they formerly were through the boarding school project. This compulsory assimilation was put into practice in the classroom by beating Native children over the head with ideas like the U.S. and Canadian governments and white society in general represented everything good and civilized and that "Indian" ways were shameful and savage. The "unhappy history" (colonization and genocide) of Indigenous peoples was rarely discussed, and if it was, it was to be contrasted with the superior future that is now within their grasp thanks to the generous gift of "Western civilization."

In addition to manipulating the curriculum, Native American children were indoctrinated by severely controlling their actions and very closely monitoring their behavior. The "teachers" accomplished their objectives through a number of means: changing the children's dress and hairstyles from their individualized traditional tribal attire to institutionalized military-style uniforms; destroying all of the cultural materials they brought with them from their home communities, that is everything they brought with them from their home communities; banning all cultural practices and severely punishing "students" for engaging in their Indigenous cultures such as speaking their native tongues, even outside of "class"; and by only allowing English to be spoken while spending the majority of their time toiling in boarding school factories.

In 2001 the Truth Commission on Genocide in Canada found that mainstream churches and government were directly responsible for the deaths of at least 50,000 children as a result of this process of compulsory assimilation. The list of crimes these institutions were found to be guilty of includes murder through beating, poisoning, hanging, starvation, strangulation, medical experimentation and forced sterilization (Smith, 2005). The report also found that "…clergy, police and business and government officials were involved in maintaining pedophile rings using children from residential schools" (Smith, 2005, p. 40). Indigenous children were so thoroughly dehumanized and commodified through the predatory process of value production that they became frequent victims of sexual predators who flocked to boarding schools under the false titles of "priest" and "teacher." In other words, while cultural genocide both damages the soul and deters the mind from reaching enlightenment, physical and sexual abuse provides the final attack on one's sense of self, giving way to the creation of a slave.

It was an openly expressed policy among Indian boarding schools that the students would contribute to the funding of their own cultural destruction through their collective labor power expended at "school." Some girls toiled in sweatshops sewing linens and garments while others worked in laundries or bakeries producing an abundance of food sold to the surrounding white communities while they themselves were malnourished. The labor power of boys was put to the task of turning out commercial items in wood, metal and leather shops. Churchill (2004) cited a 1928 US investigating commission that determined that most of what went on at Indian boarding schools would be illegal in most settler communities because of child labor laws. Native American children were forced to work long hours often for no wages at all, but in some instances were "paid" between one and three cents an hour as an "incentive." These "wages" were often put in a fund and then typically mismanaged and squandered by the BIA (Bureau of Indian Affairs).

As a result, many Native American children, when they returned to their communities, were not only traumatized from years of abuse, but in many ways they were cultural outsiders, that is, for all intents and purposes, non-"Indian," and haters-of-self. Many Indigenous boarding school "students" were therefore not only lonely, scared, and preyed upon at "school," but they found themselves with dangerously damaged self-esteems in whatever context they found themselves in, giving way to an epidemic of suicide and drug and alcohol abuse. In response, the Boarding School Healing Project (BSHP) was established in 2000 informed by a multi-pronged approach to activism. First and foremost the BSHP provides an invaluable source of support for the victims of abuse while simultaneously documenting abuses and educating the general public. The BSHP is also dedicated to holding those responsible accountable through national and international courts (Smith, 2005).

As should be expected, and alluded to by the BSHP, amid the atmosphere of boarding school repression emerged a culture of resistance because our humanity, while it can be limited, can never be fully destroyed. Regardless of how harmful our conditioning has been we always retain the ability to become conscious of our own consciousness (Freire, 1998, 2005). Put another way, despite how hopeless a situation appears, there is always hope, it is an ontological need of the human condition (Freire, 1999). Summarizing the frequency and ways Native American children fought back Churchill (2004) notes:

> ....Native children were not merely the passive victims of all that was being done to
> them. Virtually without exception, survivor narratives include accounts of subversion,
> both individual and collective, most commonly involving such activities as 'stealing'
> and/or foraging food, possessing other 'contraband,' persistence in the speaking of
> native languages and running away. In many—perhaps most—residential schools,
> such activities were so common and sustained as to comprise outright 'cultures of resis-
> tance.' (p. 51)

The primary goal of replacing the Indigenous culture with the foreign settler
culture was to transform the peoples' relationship to the land, making them willing accomplices in their own subjugation rendering the process of colonization
that much easier for the oppressor. Native children were to internalize the same
white supremacy and support for the system that other people slated to be workers in the settler communities were to incorporate into their consciousnesses.
The tendency for white people is to hate the other, while the tendency for people of color, such as Native Americans, as we have seen, is to hate the self.
Consumed by their own guilt, however, many white people wind up hating
themselves too (see Introduction). While white supremacy is obviously more
harmful to people of color, white people would also be better served by a system based on positivism rather than the very negative order that exists. Once
again, this is one of those intersections for radical solidarity against whiteness.

The educational goal for Native children and the majority of Europeans and
Africans brought to North America to be put to work for the investors was to
instill a fear of God, that is, the ruling authority, and a commitment to sacri-
fice and hard work because it would appease the fearful God and lead to salvation. While the schoolhouse was often used for Europeans and Native
Americans, the classroom for Africans was more often the plantation. While
white laborers, often flogged or whipped for falling victim to Satan, that is,
showing any signs of free thinking, they were nevertheless born into the
Western world and therefore tended not to possess worldviews that challenged
the occupier's use and control of the land. This, in part, helps to explain the
harsher measures the U.S. and Canadian governments have taken against
Native children, reaching genocidal proportions. In other words, those raised
in the settler communities were born and bred to be wage earners, to be externally controlled, which essentially, is to be a slave. Native American communities with an independent existence from the settler-states socialize themselves
to be free and not externally commanded. The true goal of boarding schools was

therefore to colonize the mind and enslave the body.

The goal of education for those deemed most suitable for manual labor (Native and African Americans and the vast majority of whites) was designed to replace any previous conception of self with "worker." That is, to define one-self as a slave, a worker. If the only thing your identity is based on is being a worker, then you will feel incomplete if not working or taking orders. This sense of dependency was and continues to be reinforced in the schools through a banking model of education where the teacher and/or the creators of curriculum are deemed to be the sole possessors of valuable knowledge and the students therefore as void of useful information and understandings. In this model education is something that is done to you—you go to school to *be* educated. In this context the students' success is measured by how well he or she can follow directions and regurgitate prepackaged knowledge—often referred to as *the* "right" answer (Freire, 1998).

In response to this alienating education and oppressive mode of work, which should not be confused with a community employing their collective labor power to actively engage *with* the world and not merely *in* or *on* the world, that is, passively, many Native American communities have taken control of their schools and embarked on a campaign of cultural rejuvenation with an emphasis on traditional value systems, customs and language.

Indigenous Philosophy in North American Settler Education

Again, the focus of tribally conceived and controlled education has been on countering the deleterious effects of the boarding school experience. However, the ideological damage inflicted by boarding schools has, at times, impeded the process of putting formal education in the hands of tribal communities as advocated for in the federal government's Great Society programs of the 1960s. For example, in 1969 Gerald Vizenor (1990) reported that Commissioner Bennett of the Bureau of Indian Affairs, himself a Native American graduate of federal boarding school, defended the BIA, arguing that all the decisions of the past were the best that could be made at the time and in so doing apologized for every imaginable atrocity committed by the federal, settler-state government, including genocide. Bennett was put under fire for not taking a more active role in fulfilling President Johnson's mandate that Native communities establish "Indian school boards," thereby partially relieving the BIA from administrative control of their local schools. Despite the BIA's foot-dragging by May of 1969 one hundred and seventy-four of the BIA's 222 schools had Native American elected school boards (Tippeconnic III, 1999). The first fully tribally controlled school was the highly acclaimed Arizona-based Rough Rock, which was turned over to the Navajo in 1966 just prior to its opening (Vizenor, 1990). Rough Rock was the first school to have elected a completely Native American school board.

From its inception Rough Rock placed special emphasis on their bilingual program, providing students with instruction in both English and Navajo. Many of the teachers at Rough Rock are Navajo, and there has been special care taken to ensure a culturally appropriate curriculum with Navajo mothers in every classroom weaving on traditional Navajo looms while telling the children stories in the customary oral tradition. The Navajo administration has stressed the importance of having philosophy taught by medicine men. These efforts have resulted in greater community and parental involvement, which has been challenging given the bad reputation of education in Indian country, due primarily to the horrors of the boarding school era. Rather than experiencing punishment and discipline for being "Indian," students at Rough Rock are rewarded and encouraged to explore their indigeneity and develop culturally as Indigenous people. President Johnson pointed to Rough Rock as a model for other reservation schools to follow. However, driving the push for tribally controlled schools has not been the benevolence of Congress or Parliament or any particular presidency or prime minister, but a movement of dedicated and persistent Native American educators, institutions, organizations, tribes, and other community-based power blocs. The legislation this pushback has been responsible for has included:

1972—*Indian Education Act*—Committed funds to making Native American education culturally relevant

1975—Indian Self-Determination and Education Assistance Act—Enabled the federal government to create 638 contracts between the BIA and tribes for tribal control of schools and health services

1988—Tribally Controlled School Act—Allowed tribal boards to move from "contracting" to "direct granting" which was intended to institutionalize tribal control of schools contributing to the sense of permanency

1990-present—The Vanishing Money Situation—Since the 1990s and the ascendancy of neo-liberal policies in the capitalist world, we have seen an attack on the public sphere marked by sharp cuts in funding for public programs such as education. While tribes control more "Indian" schools than ever before, more than half as of 1994–95, the resources and federal support for such programs seem to be drying up, despite the efforts of the grassroots pushback (Tippeconnic III 1999)

Despite the fading support for Native American education by the federal government of the United States, the hopeful spirit of determination seems to be alive and well within many Native American communities—these neglected communities which some Native Americans have alluded to are essentially refugee camps (Neihardt, 1932/2004), suffer from the highest unemployment, poverty and alcoholism rates in North America. The teacher training texts developed in the interest of facilitating the manifestation of such culturally relevant educational practices and collaborations tend to focus on challenging prospective teachers to develop cultural competence within themselves, which is especially relevant because it is mostly white teachers who teach Native American youth, both on and off the reservation.

On reservations white teachers continue to work in both tribally controlled schools and even more often in BIA-controlled facilities. What is more, 90% of all Indigenous youth within the United States attend public state-controlled and run schools, and 90% of the teachers within these institutions throughout North America are white. It is therefore not surprising that in texts such as Collected Wisdom: American Indian Education by Linda Miller Cleary and Thomas D. Peacock (1998), which is essentially a teacher-training manual for future and current teachers of Native American students, white teachers are highlighted who have developed sophisticated levels of cultural competence and are therefore successful in their work with Native American students. One such "white" teacher of Native American students highlighted in Collected Wisdom (1998), "Ketron," stressed the importance of listening because of all the cultural knowledge he had to learn to become a teacher respected in the community. Such examples provide future white teachers with role models they can learn from in their struggles to become anti-racist educators who are part of the solution and not part of the problem. Also instructive to their approach to Indian education are their "profiles" on Native American teachers.

These Indigenous teachers are presented in Collected Wisdom as role models or examples alluding to what the authors believe are positive manifestations of culturally appropriate and practical Indian education. In Chapter Four,

"Creating a Two-Way Bridge: Being Indian in a Non-Indian World," Wayne Newell is "profiled" and in the process described as "...a successful individual who has found balance between his Passamaquoddy culture and the school in which he is a teacher" (p. 100). Cleary and Peacock (1998) go on to praise Newell for being a respected traditional person in his Indigenous community, an accomplished Passamaquoddy language teacher at Indian Township School in northern Maine, as well as having "lived successfully in the non-Indian work and academic environment" (p. 100) having earned an MA from Harvard University.

The vision for Indian education that emerges from *Collected Wisdom* is similar to that put forth by the progressive educator collective, Rethinking Schools. For example, in the Introduction to the second volume of *Rethinking Our Classrooms*, Bill Bigelow, Brenda Harvey, Stan Karp and Larry Miller (2001), making the case for how schools should be "laboratories for a more just society" (p. 1), argue that educators have two primary responsibilities to their students—to help them survive within the world that exists and to transform it—and if either of the two are neglected, the teacher has not fulfilled her or his obligations.

Cleary and Peacock's (1998) example of Wayne Newell, the Native American teacher, is presented as someone who has survived within the world that exists and simultaneously is engaged in transforming it as a Passamaquoddy language teacher assisting his predominantly Passamaquoddy students in following a similar path to higher education and thus to surviving within the world that exists. Newell's work as a language teacher, in the context of the United States with its long history of cultural genocide, is in itself transformative. In other words, teaching Native children their Indigenous culture, if successful, is to change the world that exists because it would be a beginning in countering the many generations of cultural loss. Reflecting on the transformative nature of his work as a teacher of native language Newell is quoted by Cleary and Peacock (1998) passionately arguing,

> What people didn't understand is that those boarding school terrorists thought that culture could disappear in a generation, and they would have white-thinking children. They couldn't erase it, and therein lies the hope…And when that spirit is reawakened, and it's within our own language, you've become a whole new person; you're alive again. (p. 102)

While acknowledging the harmful impact of the boarding schools, noting that "we became like the conquerors" and "the biggest helpers" of cultural genocide,

Newell simultaneously satisfies our ontological needs in the profound sense of hope he expresses when reflecting on his endeavors as a Native American cultural worker/teacher. Cleary and Peacock (1998) situate Newell's hope in the context of the ability to "successfully" live in two worlds, in an "Indian" world and in a "white" world. One of the struggles highlighted by Cleary and Peacock in teaching Native American students about their culture is developing programs that successfully engage their interests—interests that tend to be heavily influenced by the dominant society's consumer culture. As evidence for their position that many Native students are not interested in their culture, Cleary and Peacock (1998) cite a teacher of Native American students, Kay Lasagna. Consider her words:

> I gave a pretest on Sioux culture to my students, and 94 percent of them failed it; they knew little or nothing about their culture. I was given some federal money to start a culture center, and I couldn't get any of them interested in a culture center or participating in it. They were interested in the same things other kids were interested in; they were interested in cars, in dating, in the school dance that was coming up, in the basketball game on Friday night. And their background just wasn't that important to them. (p. 107)

While the deleterious effects of cultural genocide and cultural imposition are obvious, all hope is not lost as previously alluded to in the discussion on Newell, the Native American teacher from present-day Maine. Perhaps Lasagna's failure to engage her Lakota students in cultural work is because her "culture center" romantically situated Lakota culture in the past and was therefore viewed as irrelevant by her students who live in the concrete context of the present moment. In other words, maybe this educator's approach did not demonstrate the relevance of traditional values for negotiating the challenges and struggles of the here-and-now. Lasagna clearly has an idea about her students' interests—cars, dating, the school dance, and basketball—the question is, how could she draw on their interests to spark a passion within them to know and own their Lakota culture (i.e., Lakota philosophy and language)? That is the challenge of the critical educator—to be in a perpetual state of self-reflection as part of the process of continually bettering one's practice. Similarly, in the following discussion centered on the text *The Seventh Generation* we see that the conclusion the authors come to is that the ways in which Native students draw on their traditional values to inform their lives is not something that can be dictated from above, or externally controlled, especially in the context of the dominant society that is marked by deception and trickery.

After publishing *Collected Wisdom*, Cleary and Peacock realized that they "should have included the voices of young people" because students are the best equipped to "tell us about education" due to the fact that they are "experiencing it at the moment" (p. 3). To fill this void Cleary and Peacock joined forces with Amy Bergstrom, "a young Ojibwe teacher," and wrote *The Seventh Generation* after interviewing 120 Native American students, some in the author's own communities in the northern Midwest of the United States and others they traveled to interview whose Indigenous identities include Abenaki, Aleut, Choctaw, Cree, Dakota, Hoopa, Inuit, Karuk, Lakota, Mohawk, Navajo, Oneida, Penobscot, Seneca, Ute, Wampanoag and Yurok. Collectively, the students in their sample attended public, tribal, federal and alternative schools off reservations in cities, on reservations, and near reservations.

The Seventh Generation: Native Students Speak About Finding the Good Path by Amy Bergstrom, Linda Miller Cleary and Thomas D. Peacock (2003) is written for not only Native American students, but teachers of Native American students as well. For students *The Seventh Generation* is a source of self-affirmation, and therefore a potentially empowering inspiration, while simultaneously providing advice from one's peers on matters of central importance such as how to successfully negotiate life in two worlds. A re-emerging theme throughout the beautifully illustrated and laid-out volume, *The Seventh Generation*, is the racism Native students have to contend with in mainstream schools dominated by Eurocentric curriculum and teachers that subsequently do not understand that students who come from "more traditional homes" have to "accommodate" their "learning style to...the ways in which the teachers and curriculum expect [them] to learn," which is difficult, frustrating, and oppressive because it tends to take Native American students out of their "natural ways of being and learning" (p. 40).

The authors of *The Seventh Generation* privilege these voices of Native youth because they offer current and future Indigenous students insights on resisting being transformed into something other than Native American while simultaneously succeeding within the world that exists. While the implications of *The Seventh Generation* tend to point to the goal of surviving in two worlds clearly articulated in *Collected Wisdom*, there is more of an emphasis on students' ability to find "the good path" on their own, which is left open for the students and therefore not necessarily defined for them as negotiating two worlds. The good path is defined in *The Seventh Generation* as "a set of traditional values" that "are universal to Indigenous people, indeed, to all humankind," which are given special attention because "the solutions to many of the problems in

Native communities, including education, lie within the values of our tribal cultures, or ways of being" (pp. 129–130). This perspective is instructive for not only Native American students but for teachers of Native American students as well.

For educators, *The Seventh Generation* (2003) provides considerable insight into the worldviews, hopes, fears and desires of these 120 Native American students, and is therefore a valuable tool for non-Native and Native educators alike in developing geographical and generational-specific cultural competence. Towards these ends in many such curricula pre-service teachers are introduced to relevant cultural differences such as the different ways "…majority and minority students interact linguistically and cognitively" (Yazzie 1999. p. 87) because misunderstandings due to interaction styles can lead to distrust and therefore hinder teaching and learning. Such work contributes to what tribally controlled schools tend to be good at: that is, fostering a sense of self-respect within Native students. As a result, some of these schools have drastically reduced push-out rates from 70–80% down to 20–30% (Tippeconnic, 1999). These trends serve as an affirmation of the prophecy of the seventh Indigenous generation of the current post-freedom (see the discussion of Crazy Horse below) stage of colonialism. It was predicted by many Native peoples that a long period of cultural loss and hardship would be followed by a resurgence in Native languages, culture and traditional values by the seventh generation. For example, after the massacre at Wounded Knee in 1889 where the Minneconjou Lakota leader Big Foot (Mohawk, 2000) and other teachers of ancient philosophy were lost, a number of Lakota medicine men had visions and made such predictions of great loss and rebirth. Bergstrom, Cleary and Peacock's (2003) *The Seventh Generation* stands as a powerful source of hope for the seventh generation offering valuable contributions towards healing the deep wounds that have been, and continue to be, inflicted over the past 500 years of intense, persistent and extremely deadly predation.

However, despite the many benefits of this important work in Native American education, from a critical pedagogical perspective, these efforts could be enhanced by a critical engagement with critical pedagogy. That is, while Native approaches to education have been praised for their efforts at cultural rejuvenation, they have simultaneously been criticized for neglecting to consciously develop within their Native students a critical vision for dealing with the global encroachment of capitalist hegemony. Contrary to Native philosophy that understands everything to be interrelated, much of the collaborative work Native and non-Native teacher educators are developing for teachers of Native Americans dichotomizes individual cultural development and the skills needed to survive in the world that exists as if there is no relationship between the two; that they are mutually exclusive. What this false dichotomy seems to be intended to hide is the contradiction between advancing an educational program designed to strengthen students' Indigeneity and therefore their existence as land-based peoples while uncritically gaining the skills to be employable within the very system responsible for genocide, exploitation and the destruction of land. In other words, presenting this false dichotomy covers up the fact that, while Native American education is much better today than it was just 30 years ago, it has not yet completely been relieved of coddling the aggressor. Until the project of cultural rejuvenation is connected to transforming the basic structures of power within dominant society, Native education will have room for improvement. Critical pedagogy provides invaluable insight here.

What follows is a careful consideration of what that might look like for us, as future and current educators, in practice. At the heart of this discussion are the many insights offered by critical pedagogy that have been scattered throughout this book. Critical pedagogy is an approach to education designed to preserve the *wildness* of the human creative spirit, that is, the very essence of human nature—freedom and democracy. A truly contextualized, and thus "wild," education begins with the very ground underneath one's feet. What is the indigenous philosophy under your feet? That is our place of departure. How have those Indigenous knowledges been suppressed and defended, and how are they connected to other indigenous cultures? In this spirit of critical contextualization we begin our discussion of critical pedagogy with Crazy Horse, one of the last great "wild" Lakota leaders. Within this discussion we begin to see how the values of an ancient Indigenous ontology combined with critical pedagogy can offer ways to approach cultural rejuvenation that are revolutionary, that is, that are transformative because they challenge us to consider the need for real system-wide change, not just tinkering, but complete *destruction* and total *reconstruction*.

Critical Pedagogy in Native North America

Before we continue this sub-section warrants another brief pause. In *Recovering the Sacred: The Power of Naming and Claiming* Winona LaDuke (2005) beautifully documents, and in the process celebrates, Native North Americans' recent strides in recovering and revitalizing the intimate relationship between land and culture that has been so severely degraded in the process of predation. In her book LaDuke (2005) dedicates a chapter to Native Americans efforts at challenging the settlers' unjust practice of "naming that which he has no right to own" (p. 149). Not only does LaDuke retell the stories of a few of the many successful campaigns against the white supremacist "Indian" mascots of colleges and universities, but she also documents one of the victories opposing the corporate, for-profit use of names such as Crazy Horse to sell beer. For example, Stroh Brewing Company released "Crazy Horse Malt Liquor" in 1992, resulting in the Lakota Tribal Court filing a legal defamation complaint that resulted in a formal apology from the manufacturer and the discontinuation of the offensive labeling (the beer was renamed "Crazy Stallion"). The Lakota's statement makes perfectly clear the historical and cultural insensitivity embedded within the product Stroh Brewing Company was setting out to profit from:

> The purposeful use and appropriation of another ascertainable person's name or likeness in an insulting and disparaging manner, without consent or permission of the lawful owner of said name or his heirs and especially in the commercial exploitation for financial gain in association with a product that has proved so deadly to Indian people, are despicable and disparaging invasions of privacy and are egregious violations of Lakota customary law protecting the spiritual, personal, social and cultural importance of an individual's name to an individual and his family during his life and his spirit and reputation, along with those of his relations, after his life so as to amount to disparagement and defamation of both the individual and the group. (Lakota Tribal Court complaint against Crazy Horse Malt Liquor quoted in LaDuke, 2005, p. 145)

It has been my intention in the following sub-section to draw on the legacy of Crazy Horse not disrespectfully or disparagingly, as settlers have done in the past in their quest to commodify and exploit everything "Native," but as a way of honoring his commitment and dedication to social justice, which continues to hold great contemporary relevance. In this way I hope to contribute to the proper education of the settler-community about the history of Native North American resistance and the colonialist attempt to destroy it and its peoples. In other words, this is my effort to not contribute to maintaining but rather contribute to, in however small a way, ending the process of predation. That is, by saying "no" to predation and searching for ways to connect that commitment to my practice, as an educator, I invite students, as future teachers, to also say "no" to predation and to creatively find ways to live that choice both individually and collectively. LaDuke's (2005) *Recovering the Sacred* offers invaluable insight here by providing many examples of the roles some settlers have been playing in returning ancestral lands to Native peoples as conscious acts against predation—that is, in one word, solidarity, which has always been humanity's most powerful weapon against oppression and injustice. With this spirit of solidarity in mind let us return to our discussion of Crazy Horse considering the many ways his story can inform our critical pedagogies.

We therefore begin this section by considering the critical pedagogy embodied within *The Journey of Crazy Horse* (Marshall, 2004) as told by the community from which the legendary Lakota leader came. Within this story is embedded Lakota philosophy and how it informed their struggle against settler-state oppression, and thus to remain free, that is, not colonized. Crazy Horse is represented by Marshall (2004) as the epitome of the traditional Lakota way, because he uncompromisingly defended it through resisting the subjugation of his people, which meant holding onto the ability to humanize the world informed by Lakota culture. This meant not surrendering the natural right of all life to be self-determined and self-sufficient and not dependent on external power for survival such as government annuities, which was an enslaving pacification and therefore represented war on the people. This war on the people had to be resisted, which proved difficult for Crazy Horse and his people because the U.S., using deceit, divisiveness, and genocide as military tactics, did not prove to be an honorable enemy unlike their traditional rivals the Crow and the Snake (Shoshone) people. The colonial enemy against humanity during Crazy Horse's day is still with us today, that is, the spirit of Columbus (outlined in Chapter One). There is therefore much to be learned from his example. The purpose here is not to romantically long for the days of old, but rather, to consider what might be learned from yesterday, to help us better understand and fight today and therefore more effectively organize for the future. As suggested above, this requires a revolutionary approach to cultural rejuvenation for all people.

Putting this general sentiment forward in "MindFuck," *The Coup*, in a verse reflecting on the state's deadly war on political dissidents from the perspective of an African American woman searching for the strength and guidance to resist the oppressive present in the leaders of the past, such as Malcolm X and Dr. Huey P. Newton, lead vocalist Boots Riley, notes, "she wish the great leaders wasn't always dead. She could resurrect 'em inside of her instead." It is readily apparent from Marshall's (2004) account that, for the Lakota, contrary to Euro-centric historians, Crazy Horse is considered one of these "great leaders" and one of the last great "wild" Lakota leaders with lessons that remain relevant in the contemporary context of global capitalism. "Wild" because he was part of a widespread refusal, along with Sitting Bull's contingency, longer than any of the other Lakota bands, to give up their freedom and relocate to one of the "soldier forts" built against the will of the Lakota on Lakota territory. Also "wild" because he was educated to be a warrior and hunter in the traditional Lakota way, that is, he was raised by the women of the community for the first four to five years of his life and then weaned into the world of the men and mentored in a one-on-one relationship for ten to twelve years resulting in a very sophisticated knowledge of self situated in community and geography.

Crazy Horse witnessed, with much frustration and heartache, other Lakota leaders, such as Red Cloud and Spotted Tail, and their bands, slowly giving in to settler-state oppression and thus the occupation of their lands, despite the Lakota outnumbering white soldiers. What Crazy Horse observed was therefore the Lakota trickling down to live on U.S. agencies by the soldier forts thereby giving up their freedom for "white things" such as the power over their people divisively *given* to them by the U.S., which represented the status they were not able to obtain within their own societies. With hegemony and therefore the manipulation of ideas it is not always necessary to have greater numbers, a lesson most bitterly learned (and still being learned). As more and more bands gave into the U.S., therefore weakening their ability to militarily resist, and consequently suffering many horrific atrocities at the hands of the U.S. military, such as the butchering of women and children, Crazy Horse and the other Lakota headmen and their councils struggled to know what was best for the future of their people: should they continue to resist and face extermination, or give up their freedom and the ability to fully live as free sovereign people on reservations? Commenting on these difficulties and the necessary qualities they demand in a leader Marshall (2004) explains:

> Facing the overall problems of life…especially as the one to whom the people looked for answers—was far more difficult [than making quick, effective decisions leading his warriors in the heat of battle]. People were constantly coming to his home to talk and the old men called him frequently to the council lodge….He [therefore] sought out the solitude of the prairies or the mountain slopes….In such places, he could gather his thoughts and pile them up like stones and examine them, one by one. His friends and relatives thought he shouldn't wander off alone as much as he did….A leader's place was with the people….When a man belonged to the people, he no longer belonged to himself. (Marshall, 2004, pp. 175–176)

From Marshall's (2004) account, what this required, more than anything else, was discipline—it was, and remains, an indispensable quality of a true servant of the people because a true leader teaches by example as she or he leads. Similarly, Freire (2005) argues that because we are teachers and therefore have the responsibility to serve the best interests of our students against oppression and dehumanization, we are political militants, which demands a well-developed, theoretically sophisticated discipline—needed, for example, because it is a life-long struggle to put aside personal desires for the larger benefit of one's community, most radically defined as "all that exists." As long as the need to resist exists, this discipline will be necessary because it is human to look inward, which is important but we have to safeguard against allowing our self-reflections to be dominated by our ego and personal desires. For example, after successful raids on the enemy, rather than build up his own wealth and status, Crazy Horse is said to have distributed captured horses to those most in need, such as "the old ones." In so doing Crazy Horse demonstrated his commitment to Lakota values such as generosity and community, which earned him a place of high regard within his society. As leaders are teachers and therefore not only responsible for making wise decisions while leading, they educate the people by demonstrating what values support critical participation and therefore the best interests of the whole. Teachers, as leaders, thus forfeit the right to squander their lives away with bad decisions that detract from the work of revolution. At the same time, our lives (our labor power) are not ours to allow to be externally controlled by ruling elite interests—it would be irresponsible for us to coddle the aggressor in any way—our labor power belongs to the humanization and therefore liberation of ourselves and the world in which we are situated. This demands that, as the first line of defense, we be extremely conscious of our own weaknesses. While these internal struggles remain the same today as they did in Crazy Horse's day, the external concrete context of resistance is in a perpetuate state of flux/transformation therefore requiring constant reflection on and revision of the tactics of insurrection. Marx, in a sense, describes this as the historical development of competing interests or internal relations.

Signaling this change in context, on his deathbed, Crazy Horse told his father Worm (the name he humbly gave to himself after giving his name, Crazy Horse, to his son, before then, known among his people as Light Hair) "tell the people they should not depend on me any longer." Crazy Horse and his Lakota community acknowledged this need for flexibility and change early on in their resistance against white encroachment as they had to re-adjust their military tactics because whites did not care about courage, they only cared about killing, it was their only measurement of military success because the goal was not to demonstrate courage, but to dominate and oppress. Crazy Horse taught the importance of adjusting the theoretical context of armed resistance to the concrete context of the battlefield because if theory does not match reality, then tactics will be ineffective. While the specifics of Crazy Horse's context are relevant, I will not focus on them here. Rather, I want to draw attention to the current relevance of maintaining a dialectical relationship between theory and practice. The goal of the occupying force is essentially the same today as it was in the mid- to late eighteen hundreds, that is, to maintain total control of the productive and creative capacities of the people because within this capacity to labor and humanize the world, lies the greatest strength of the people, our ability to labor, without which, the oppressors have nothing. It is therefore capital's weakest link because we can resist it being externally commanded and put it, and thus ourselves, to work fighting against being externally commanded and fight against the destruction of our only home, the Earth, our common mother. Again, while the enemy of the "wild" Lakota, and humanity and all life generally, is currently the same, the concrete context is different.

Crazy Horse operated from the position of pre-defeat and pre-colonialist indoctrination. Today, unfortunately, we are all more fully engaging the world from the position of post-defeat, and therefore from being indoctrinated with the oppressor's values, ideas and beliefs. The good thing is that there is only one model of domination, so we all share a common enemy, and therefore have no other option but to unite as one while celebrating and drawing on the strengths of our differences. Now, more than ever, we need the pedagogical example of Crazy Horse's discipline and his uncompromising selfless commitment to the people to most effectively utilize and build upon pedagogies of counter-indoctrination famously represented in Paulo Freire's *Pedagogy of the Oppressed* (1998), to best resist the concrete context of the capitalist present. This is a revolutionary approach to cultural rejuvenation. If this theoretical marriage were represented in a movie, we might creatively write the script with Crazy Horse and Paulo Freire leaving an engagement with Marx and Gramsci on their way to Chiapas to create democratic community in dialogue with the Zapatistas (as we will see in the final chapter of this book).

Because the concrete context of the contemporary moment so thunderously demands a well disciplined, fully-committed-to-the-people critical pedagogy, we will now take a look at critical pedagogy, which, again, we have been doing throughout this entire book. While actively engaging with the following section reflect on the case you could make for why your adoption of a critical pedagogical approach to curriculum and pedagogy would be in the best interests of the current or future students you have the responsibility of educating. Also, reflect on the relevance of Crazy Horse's example of discipline, courage and commitment as it pertains to the struggles you might face in becoming a critical pedagogue and therefore a teacher of critical consciousness.

IN THEIR WORDS
Educational Leadership in K-12

· 5 ·

AN ACTION RESEARCH APPROACH
TO EDUCATIONAL LEADERSHIP

An Interview with Frank Brathwaite

Can you talk a little about yourself and how you came to be an educational leader?

I started teaching in 1967 at the age of twenty in Ontario at an elementary school. I did not have a degree because, at the time, it was not a requirement. I did go to teachers' college. I was fortunate because the school I was in was large with six hundred and fifty kids situated in a resource town, Espanola, Ontario, a lumber, resource-based, working class community. The town was constructed around the lumber mill and a nearby mine as well. I decided to work there because I did not want to live in Toronto.

After about a year or two, I realized that the principal of the school had a lot of influence because he can say, "we can try these programs," or "we can try *this* program." Because I always thought curricular issues were important and I was interested in having students doing things beyond the classroom, but still meeting the standards. I thought the more engaging the curriculum is, the better it will be. Consequently, after two years of teaching, I decided to go back to the University of Toronto and get a degree. I made a decision to continue to study curriculum and ended up with a Bachelor's and Master's degree in it. The reason why I chose curriculum over educational leadership is because leadership deals with tasks and curriculum deals with learning and people. I figured that if you have a degree in curriculum development, then you would be significantly more effective in the longer term in regards to making changes in schools that support every student learning.

After receiving my Master's, I taught in a gifted program for two years and I wanted to be a vice principal at Holton, which is a large system, but I was told that I had to wait my turn as a relatively new teacher. However, I am not a patient person. Within four weeks I got a job as a vice principal north of Lake Superior. There I was given the school responsibilities at a large public institution; I also taught for grades seven and eight, *and* I was given the system role of being responsible for all PD activities. After two years of being a vice principal, and in the process, organizing many field trips, doing a lot of outdoor education, and organizing some action research projects, people were beginning to respond well to me as an educational leader. As a result, I accepted the position of principal, which provided me even more opportunities for doing action research supporting libraries, for example, because libraries are essential in providing all students opportunities to explore their academic interests and learn.

Because action research has been such a central part of my practice as an educational leader, it is worth taking a minute to offer a bit of elaboration defining what I mean by the concept. For me, action research includes many variables, including:

~ An idea that you want to try or a question you want to answer
~ A thorough review of the literature to gain the conceptual tools needed to understand the phenomena in question
~ A trial stage of intervention where new strategies are implemented
~ The accumulation of a significant amount of data
~ A rigorous approach to data analysis to determine if there is any validity to the teaching practices you are interested in
~ A reflection stage coupled with a refined approach to intervention and data collection
~ A persuasive presentation/proposal that should appeal to peoples' emotions by employing such tactics as bringing a child and teacher in to demonstrate the effectiveness of whatever program. The proposal is always intended to make roughly four arguments:
~ We can run this program
~ We think we can save some people, which beats the politicians
~ We think we can improve performance
~ We can show that this will have an impact on the whole school

One example of action research began with the question, "Why are we having ten to thirty percent of the students failing to learn to read at the elementary level no matter how good the teacher is?" We were concerned because those children unable to read after grade one or two would be sent off to special education where they would remain throughout the remainder of their time in school because it is extremely difficult to get out once you are in. Consequently, at my school, we had a mushrooming special education program, and it was always the same percent of children (between 10 and 30 percent) irrespective of gender or socioeconomic status. We therefore asked, "What can we do differently," and "If we are going to do something differently, what do we need to *learn* to do something differently?" We began by setting up study groups, which took about four years of research before we were ready to implement a pilot program and begin collecting raw data.

We started out with six teachers using Reading recovery. We tracked their results, we tracked how they were doing, and when our report came back—we always issued an annual report showing what we had done—we presented the results to the Board of Trustees. During such presentations we always brought a child in. I tended to be a bit of a showman at times. If you have a child to read to a Board of Trustees, you are providing them with visible evidence that the program is working. Then you would ask the mother to speak about what her child was doing. The teacher would then be called on to discuss what the student was like at the beginning of the program. You would also ask the child to describe their skill level at the start of the program, and if they said they could not read, that is powerful testimony. That is, when you have six-year-old children know they cannot read, and then are given an intervention, and, as a result, develop the ability to read, you will have made a solid case for your program. In short, this is an example of successful *action research*. It is research where the *results* immediately translate into *practical changes*.

Through all of these experiences I learned that, as a leader, you can do everything by yourself, *on your own*, as it were, *or*, you can choose to involve people to help you. I learned quickly that if you choose to involve people to help you, you end up with better ideas, greater buy in, more opportunities to reflect on your practice, and deeper analyses on the way we are doing things to make it better, that is, are our new approaches actually improving student learning? In other words, including others provides insightful program evaluations.

As a result, some of the initiatives that I started in 1976 and 1977 were still operating well into the 1990s and into the year 2000 because we worked at building alliances of support. A central aspect of this was providing financial resources to facilitate new teacher learning because without the opportunity for ongoing growth and professional development, teachers will burn out and cease to be productive. We understood that people *do* want to change and they do *not* want to burn out because of an internal need to be happy and fulfilled, and the state of being burned out is in fact the state of misery and unhappiness. To serve all educators you therefore always have groups of teachers rotating through building new skills and competencies. Another important part of the model is perpetually talking and building positive relationships with parents. Leaders therefore have to have a communication plan, they have to have a philosophy informing their programs, and they have to have a well-laid out program with clearly defined goals and strategies.

Another important strategy of mine—and a useful aspect of action research—was making a point to always work on *pilot projects*. Once we began to experience some successes trying out our new ideas, we would share our results with teachers and other administrators to gain further support for implementing our ideas for curricular reform. This is how I began my career as an educational leader. However, I was not content with being a principal at just an elementary school, so I pursued a position being a principal at a high school.

I therefore pursued and obtained a position in Alberta in a community called Oil Fields. The community was Black Diamond Turner Valley, southwest of Calgary. I became the fourth principal in four years. During that time there were behaviors that were inappropriate. For example, from the community I had heard that the vice principal was known for bouncing kids off lockers. I therefore told that particular vice principal that that was not acceptable, professional behavior. While I was principal there he never bounced any students off the lockers. I told teachers that they needed to engage students and make their classes interesting. However, not only did I tell them what was expected of them, I showed them how to engage students with an interesting curriculum. If they told me "I do not know how to engage students and develop interesting curricula," I would physically go in and teach their classes as a demonstration. I believe that if you cannot model what you want to happen, as an educational leader, positively or negatively, then you are wasting your time.

Modeling was part of transforming and making changes, but action research was also a big part of it because it engaged teachers in the decision making process. W would start by saying, "if we are working with these students, and they need to think about becoming more physically active and improve their attitudes," for example, "then why don't we try a different program?" We would then ask the teachers "What kind of projects could you do in your classrooms?" One grade six teacher, Mr. Taylor, said, "I like to do physical education every day." I therefore said, "Let's do that." Placing responsibility back on the teacher I asked, "what kinds of research can you find?" Mr. Taylor then gathered information conducting sort of a literature review on similar programs. We eventually selected a program that was a hybrid of a project started in France with an art curriculum because Mr. Taylor also had an interest in art as it related to academic achievement. I was also interested in physical fitness, so we got the Israeli Army handbook and Canada's official exercise program, and we spent a year developing and planning out the program.

The following year, the students who did the regular program from a sixth grade class were observed. They received physical education the standard three times a week. Mr. Taylor's class, on the other hand, received quarter day physical education and art every day using the Israeli Army handbook. We did a pretest to document how both groups were functioning in terms of blood pressure, levels of body fat, and fitness levels. At the end of the year we tested the students again and found that they had done a whole range of activities. They had done snowshoeing, cross-country skiing, downhill skiing, hiking, lots of art, all for our experimental program. These students' achievement, in not only physical fitness, but in academics as well, far exceeded what it normally would have been.

I was wondering if we were witnessing the Hawthorne Effect, so we mapped it out over another two years and expanded the program to grades seven and eight. Our findings remained consistent over those next two years. As a result, it meant that teachers had to become more focused in terms of considering what was important and what was not. After I left the school, the principal after me continued the program, and it continues to operate today, twenty-six years later. The success can be attributed to all of the players that were involved because they become personally motivated and ensure it operates smoothly and constantly improves. We therefore ask the teachers to interview parents about what they and their children liked and did not like about the program. The reports that come back become invaluable data and feedback for making curricular changes and adjustments. Perhaps most important is that it was fun to do. When learning is fun teachers and students excel and thrive.

While in Alberta I also realized that art ended in grade nine. There was nothing for high school students, just academics. I therefore suggested we start a grade ten, a grade eleven, and a grade twelve art program. Further reflecting, I said, "If we have art, why not have drama?" This decision was based on the perspective from cognitive science that looks at what kids need for healthy growth and development, which happens to be what appeals to them, and also addresses the diversity of learning styles within human populations. We were also concerned with appealing to parents, and parents want to see their children happy, healthy, and smart.

Part of my own practice that I modeled for teachers was being a life-long learner. That is, I was always reading the academic journals and gathering ideas and insights from cutting edge curriculum research. I paid attention to what was happening in Australia for example because they were known for innovations in education, and they used the English language so I did not have to struggle with that. I also had studied at the University of Toronto, which was supposed to be one of the premiere institutions to study curriculum, so I stayed in touch with scholars I met there, which was another way I remained familiar with the literature and the ideas that assisted in my own perpetual state of improvement as a teacher and educational leader.

Staying on top of the curriculum literature, however, is only part of the challenge of educational leaders. That is, from a leadership perspective, there are always teachers that do not want to do anything. There are people who watch what happens and say, "maybe I can participate," or "maybe I do not have to participate." There are also the *early adaptors to change*, and the *early adaptors* are the ones who eagerly volunteer early on. Once teachers realize that the principal supports their initiatives through the commitment of resources, encouragement, and protection—by protection I mean when other teachers, parents, and others complain, the principal is there with some research to support the initiative and deflect criticisms—they will readily embrace change because your pilot research demonstrates student and parent support. That is, if successful and well received, you will be able to discuss how students and parents like the program or initiative and how and why they want more. For example, after implementing the art program, teachers reported how students, who excelled in art, began to excel in other areas like math and science, for example.

All of these things helped me to sharpen my focus and come to the realization that being the principal is the best job. However, I wanted to be able to influence other principals. I therefore returned to Ontario as the principal of a highly multicultural school. I was then given the chance to be the Assistant Superintendent of Human Resources. This position gave me the responsibility of recruiting and evaluating teachers, and based on my evaluation, supporting them in appropriate staff development. As Assistant Superintendent of

Human Resources I also worked in the area of recruiting vice principals. I looked for new leaders who shared some of my views on leadership and collective change. After eighteen months in this position, I became a full superintendent for three years overseeing the learning of fourteen thousand students covering twenty-three schools from kindergarten to grade twelve. After undergoing some restructuring, I began working with another superintendent rather than alone. I always focused on the curriculum pieces and how you support principals.

Part of being an educational leader in a system is that you try to advocate for program changes. That is, if something is not working, why continue to do it? One of the programs I was fortunate enough to have led and implemented, and which is still going now, is the Reading Recovery program. It started out with three teachers in one geographical area. We got a person trained to be a teacher leader. That was in 1993. Now, in 2009, that program is fully implemented in one hundred and ninety-two elementary schools; it has a staff of seven teacher leaders; it has influenced many teachers to become better teachers, primarily in the primary division. These teacher leaders rotate in and out and become vice principals and principals. What I do is look at the long-term vision and depth of changes.

This long-term vision has best translated into practice for me by operating on a volunteer basis. Principals, if they chose, could learn to engage their profession from an action research perspective. People could learn to do this, and that meant principals who were interested could say that they would try. Because we often lacked the institutional resources to staff our action research, we depended on volunteers. To get teachers into our leadership training program principals and vice principals had to agree to teach for a semester or two in order to free up their time. Consequently, you begin to build a critical mass; the data are shared; the data are peer-reviewed by people within the system. Because of how the Reading Recovery program works, we would have people from different countries, such as the United States and New Zealand, come look at what we were doing.

Again, the action research perspective would offer alternative approaches to failing programs. My role was to organize people to work as a team. I was responsible, but there were four teams with two teacher-leaders, a trainer who would come to assist, and at least one or two principals who would give feedback, as well as a teacher to perform the same function. The teacher was not specially trained, but was a regular grade one or two teacher who could offer insight from that point of view. As mentioned above, this is part of the on-going process of gathering data and making changes.

Of course there were people who were not interested in participating and we would not bother them. We would just let the critical mass build. After starting with just six teachers in the late seventies, by the early nineteen nineties, we were about seventy-five percent of the schools. In the areas where schools were opposed to our changes, the parents eventually forced the principals to implement Reading Recovery because they had heard of the successes in the rest of the district. We therefore did not have to impose our ideas on anybody. We introduced the idea, and if it was a good idea, and we properly nurtured and advocated for it, it would eventually take on a life of its own. All of this program development work is based on the idea that if you want to make improvements, you have to invest some resources, that is, money and time.

Where and how money is spent seems to always cause tension. For example, parents of special education became critical of Reading Recovery when they realized special education funds were being transferred to our program. What we had to let them know is that special education students were not being neglected, but that Reading Recovery was so successful, the number of students placed in special education was declining, which is a good thing. Most students in special education were placed there because they could not use language.

What is your philosophy of leadership? That is, what philosophies, theories, ideas, or ways of viewing the world inform your practice as a leader?

My philosophy is based on the work of many theorists and scholars, whom I have drawn on and pieced together over the years as I engaged my practice. Some of the researchers and approaches that have proven to be the most important to my work can be summarized in the following format:

~   The framework of cooperative learning, especially the work of David Johnson and Robert Johnson at the University of Minnesota, has been particularly important to my practice because it provides a framework for developing a culture of cooperation where teachers help each other. This is fundamental for doing action research.

~   In addition to cooperative learning, I also draw on the work of Thomas Sergiovanni (2007, 1979) out of Trinity University who advocates for an approach to leadership as stewardship, which highlights the nature of community building and the role principals, for example, can play in fostering it.

~ The third person who has really influenced my work is Peter Rucker, particularly his scholarship on the management of abandonment. If you really want to do something, you have to remove the things that are not helpful to the action. This will help you determine what it is that you really want to accomplish. By doing this you are then able to put together the evidence, effort, focus, energy, and enthusiasm into accomplishing the tasks.

~ The fourth approach that has influenced my practice deals with issues of community and resistance because they fit in nicely with the pieces I had already built upon intellectually and practically.

~ Then when I was doing my Ph.D. work in educational leadership, I was introduced to the notion of transformative leadership in the work of William Foster (1989), for example. Noel Tiechy and Warren Bennice have also done work in transformative leadership that has influenced me—specifically, their work on Judgment—which is that critical component of what you try to do. You can learn it, but you also have to draw on the intuitive.

The second part of my philosophy is informed by the fact that I am interested in results. I do not want to waste people's time. I do not want to have people engaging in something just for the sake of engaging in something that might be a simple process that does not move anything. That is, it does not produce results or an improvement in student learning. I am therefore task oriented in that process. What is key here is the balance between *task* and *people*. I am *people* first.

The role of the leader here is to take the people you have with you—and this is based on the recent work of Collins (2007) on why good companies survive—and examine their qualifications in relation to the positions they are in, and if they are not good for the task they are charged with performing, then you need to replace them. If you do not replace those workers who are not performing at expected levels, then nothing is going to move forward. When searching for a group of people to hire and bring together, there are certain attributes that I look for. I look for someone who has vision. I look for someone who has a sense of humor. I look for someone who is a problem solver. I always look for someone who is negative because they will point out the details that you would not always identify. I look for someone who is a *team player*, but who can also show some initiative. You therefore assemble a group of people who, collectively, hold these qualities and characteristics.

As a leader, you can then introduce them to a problem and engage them in actively solving it. To ensure harmony and the establishment of a healthy community of cooperative learning, as the leader, you cannot show your workers that you are overly concerned with taking the credit of whatever successes you may realize. Credit should be shared collectively, just as the problem was solved through collective effort. The teachers, especially, should be recognized because it is through their labor that programs are implemented and student learning is realized. The committee who came together and made it happen should also receive a fair amount of notoriety. Lastly, the educational leader gets some credit and praise for their role. This is based on the idea that the leader who seeks all of the credit is a waste of time because nobody will want to deal with him or her.

What I am pointing to here, yet again, is the central importance of community building. Without community and some sense of unity with those you work with, there is no hope for genuine improvement. Susanne Bailey played a significant part in teaching me about this point of view. She is from California and an external consultant for Kraft Foods in the United States. She did some work on schools and school systems. I did my first course with her in 1989 and then came back and did another class with her. We then invited her to come and help with a couple of our staff development projects.

What I learned from her is the importance of getting people to develop a sense of community because in every school there is a culture, which is positive, negative, or neutral. In many schools the culture is negative because we let the negative forces overpower the positive aspects. What all of these ideas and experiences taught me was how to engage teachers, parents, faculty groups, and departments in focusing on being clear about *what* we want to accomplish, *how* we want to accomplish it, and how we will change our negative behavior. This is where the concept of the gardener comes into play.

The primary objective of the gardener is to plant a seed and nurture it until it reaches maturity. In schools there are always new tasks that need to be accomplished. The beginning of every year is marked by a new agenda. Consequently, many of the gardener's seeds never reach maturity. Most projects never develop past the budding stage. The effective gardener, or educational leader, takes the initiative and says, "Let's limit what we focus on and make sure our initiatives get the care and attention they need to grow and develop into the programs they were designed to be." I am a big believer in the metaphorical compost pile, which encourages us to ask, "what can we draw from what already exists that will not waste our time and will help us move forward toward higher student achievement?"

When you actually ask people, it is surprising because they will tell you. Most people know what needs to be done and why certain things do not work, but they have been so alienated that they become frustrated and disengaged. Consequently, there is a lot of wasted and unrealized talent and ideas within teachers, due, primarily, to ineffective leaders. To be an effective leader therefore requires you to build a reputation over time as someone who is a fair shooter, someone who does not enforce rules arbitrarily. This is at the heart of my philosophy of leadership. To summarize, my philosophy includes the following components and ideas:

~ We have tasks to achieve, which can only be accomplished through people
~ Expand the credit for good work done
~ Make the timeline reasonable
~ Provide all the appropriate resources for success
~ People will therefore, over time, feel like they can make a change
~ Pressure towards goals gets results

What is the purpose of leadership?

Based on my own experiences as an educational leader it seems to me that leadership has many interrelated purposes. What follows is a brief outline and discussion of some of those *purposes*:

Sometimes the leader can play a visionary role articulating what is possible. That visionary role is a very important role, especially for those worker teachers who feel pressured and get lost in the backwater of educational experiences. These leaders can see ahead and articulate possibilities for what *could be* that can be empowering and motivating for those who have lost faith in the system. The visionary leader is able to identify possibilities that offer opportunities for teachers to find hope and purpose within their practice. Such possibilities arise out of many different educational foci, from learning technologies to multiculturalism to literacy. Whatever it is, you need someone who can articulate the ideas and hopefully build a cohort of people who are interested. The leader therefore needs to have a vision.

Second, the purpose of leadership is to communicate. What I mean by *to communicate* has this message: you have two ears and one mouth, use them proportionally.

The third variable or purpose is to master the acquisition of resources, people, political skills, and assessment procedures. As a result, whatever project you are working on, you are meeting these tasks and doing it with the support of others. It does not mean that you do not make tough choices; it just means that you have got some of those things in place.

Educational leaders must also know how to celebrate, which, for me, has always been really important. Whenever a task is accomplished, you do something to recognize the hard work of the people. This recognition takes multiple forms. First, there is the public recognition, sometimes there is financial recognition, but more importantly is the personal recognition that comes from notes that are given to people. While effective strategies are certificates, plaques, and charts, people want to be told on an ongoing basis that they are making a contribution. It does not matter if it is the caretaker or the parents, the principal, or the teachers you need to celebrate those things.

Educational leaders must also be able to plan and strategize for the future, especially in the context for policy changes you know will not be received well by the community. One of these examples, for me, was when the district was planning to redraw the school boundaries for individual facilities. Many people with children hold this romantic vision of walking their child to the local school on the first day. In the York region we were growing so fast, we did not have the space to accommodate all the new students, so we had to change boundaries. This process included holding consultation meetings with seven hundred to one thousand people who were not happy that we were going to change the boundaries and disrupt their romantic idea of walking their child to school. These groups of mostly parents would have already received the information—that because you were one of the parents between this number and that number, your child would not be going to the school they would have gone to under the old boundaries. Many people were not happy with this. What I would do to help diffuse the situation was to work with a group of parents who we shared all the data with. We would work with these parents before the problem came up. Knowing that in four years we would have to move a group of students somewhere unexpected, we did the planning and pre-work first. The parents had the perspective we needed to come up with solutions people would be happy with. For example, parents would say, "You want to have your child walk to the local school? This school does not have it." But you would want the majority of your family to be here, so we would work on the basis that if you have two siblings in a school, your child would always be accommodated. Whereas if you are starting off in a new school and are a new family, and you just moved in and bought this nice house for three hundred thousand dollars and want your child to go to this school, because you do not have a connection with the community yet, other than the fact that you are a tax payer, we will provide you with a bus to move your child over to another school, and eventually they will come back for grade one.

In doing these things I would use humor. I would tell the audience of angry parents, "ladies and gentlmen, I hope you like my new suit, it is made out of the latest in Kevlar technology," and they would laugh, lightening the atmosphere and diffusing the situation. I would say, "I do not expect people to be giving us a lot of accolades for what we are doing tonight, but I am relaying a message, and I am willing to listen. We also have members of the community here who have been helping us who will speak as well." To summarize, these things are part of the leadership where you have to think about things in the future. That is, you have to be able to anticipate what will happen rather than playing reaction. *Reaction* is such a painful process because you cannot ever meet the needs of people.

One thing I learned from a *major* sales and marketing person from Dallas, Texas who I heard in Calgary—and I was one of the only education people there—is that when you help enough people get what they want, you will have solved the problems. To do this you have to keep saying yes, and when someone comes to you with a problem that you cannot say yes to, you remind them of what you can say yes to, and that you really appreciate their concerns, and then you give them feedback on the areas where they need to improve in order for you to be able to continue to say yes. The idea is to figure out how to help people and remember that things happen in stages. After this kind of feedback, you have to give people time to process, which includes active listening, communicating, clarifying, providing details, and keeping things transparent. Finally, if you ever make mistakes in this process, learn to apologize.

Leaders must always deal with *concerns*. That is, if you are a leader and you have a concern, you have to deal with it because it will not go away or disappear. This is based on the concept that you can either pay for it now, or pay for it later. For example, if you see a practice going on that is not acceptable, and is hurtful to someone, like the unintended sexual harassment, racial slurs, or humiliating children, you must confront them because in so doing, you will resolve many of the causes of your stress.

I remember when I was a new principal. It was decades ago. I was coming from Alberta to Ontario to a school of seven hundred and fifty children. I used to wander the halls because I believed in the Effective Schools research of Ron

Edmonds, which argued that principals have to have a presence in the schools. I would therefore wander into teachers' classrooms and talk to students. I would observe practices and behaviors and write the teachers notes. Early on in the school year, in September, I saw a grade one student outside of a grade one classroom in the hall with his nose to the wall. I walked over to him, crouched down, and ask him why he was there and what he had done wrong. Of course he said that he did not know because that is what they always say. So I asked him which person sent him out. He pointed through the door to his teacher. I turned the young lad around and told him to wait there while I go investigate.

I went down to the office and asked the secretary about the practice, and she confirmed that with the previous principal it had been standard practice to place students in the hall with their nose touching the wall. I asked her if she would like that done to her, and she confirmed my own feeling that it would be embarrassing.

At the end of the day I therefore went back down the hall to talk with his teacher. I was very upset because I do not believe we should treat people that way. This particular teacher was a primary special education teacher with a lot of experience and respect. In short, she was *the queen* of the school. Every school has people who are the informal leaders who everybody relies on. I therefore had to approach her with the respect she consciously knew she deserved. I therefore asked her to help me understand the instructional benefits of putting a kid's nose to the wall. She said that she did not know if there were any benefits, but that they had always disciplined students in that manner. I commented that *tradition* is an interesting phenomenon to look at. I then invited her to reframe her thinking so that we only engage in practices that have instructional benefits. If a practice does not have any instructional benefits, then we will not engage in that practice. She readily agreed and thought that she could do that. I then told her that I was not going to be making an announcement in a staff meeting because that is irrelevant. I said that I was sure people would pick up the message. I told her that if she still thought putting the noses of children to the wall makes sense, I would sit there and listen. She said that she agreed with me. To make absolutely clear to her how serious I thought the issue was, I told her that if I saw her doing it again, I would write her up. This, I ensured her, was not a threat, but a statement of fact.

Three or four days later in her division, the primary division—and the primary division is the division with the youngest and most developmentally vulnerable children—another teacher began to bring two students at the same time out into the hallway and put their noses up to the wall, one hand on each of their shoulders. Before she could go back into her classroom, the teacher I had previously disciplined, came up to her and told her that they do not engage in that practice anymore. From that day forward the culture in that school began to change. The school became more humane, which was my message that was heard and embraced because my tactics were just as humane as the justice I demanded from the teachers.

Can you talk about your own approach in the context of competing ideas or purposes of leadership?

The existence of competition is very evident on school boards and in organizations. To demonstrate, I am going to revisit the issue with Reading Recovery. When we were studying the phenomena of reading acquisition in school, we were consistently finding that between ten and thirty percent of students were not learning or achieving. There were some people on the school board, like the Superintendent of Programs, who were trained in the field of curriculum. I was the Superintendent of Field Operations. I was talking about things like Reading Recovery, and they were talking about things like Jolly Phonics and Accelerated Reading. We therefore had competing demands that stemmed from a difference in our theories of learning and our relationship to teaching. The Director, the Chief Superintendent, even commented that *anybody could teach someone to read if they took them for thirty minutes a day. I could teach a monkey how to read.* This was said at a project meeting that I was leading. I responded by noting that he was *presenting an interesting perspective* in an attempt to regain control and preserve the dignity of our work.

My philosophy is that you have to use guerrilla tactics. What I mean by that is you have to work incessantly gathering resources; you talk to as many people as you can, and you build a coalition of like-minded individuals who are willing to try and do action research. That is, you talk to principals and teachers, and tell them that you are looking for volunteers who might be interested. You let them know that it will require more work, and you inform them of the things you can do to reduce their other obligations to make it happen. The key here to this approach, and the power of action research, is in the *pilot project* you conduct before implementing the program and changing the entire curriculum. The pilot project allows you to test your ideas before it is too late. In other words, you can try it and end it, and the investment is not large.

A competing approach to curricular reform is investing in commercial programs because there is a *huge* investment of dollars. Challenging this method I suggested we employ Reading Recovery eventhough the Curriculum Department was pushing Jolly Phonics, which the parents liked because they had seen it on television. Challenging this phonics-based hegemony I argued that if you are going to implement this then you need to do a pilot project. I worked with the Curriculum Department and convinced them to run pilot projects for both approaches, Jolly Phonics and Reading Recovery. When the preliminary data came back, Reading Recovery proved to be more effective.

However, I did not want a decision to be made too quickly, so I argued that we should continue to collect data for two more years before any final curricular decisions were made. If the decision was going to be based on data collected over just six months, the competition is going to be really high and you do not get accurate data. If you collect data for two years that high intensity competition fades away and you have a better chance of gathering more reliable data. The goal is always figuring out how to work together despite competing ideas. Usually, as a leader, you can negotiate and get something everyone is happy with. Put another way, from a long-term point of view, you get more with cooperation than you do with competition.

However, most people on school boards have Type A personalities, that is, they are very competitive. I know that I am competitive because I like to win, and most of my colleagues like to win also. That is why we are where we are. We worked our way up through the ranks driven by our competitive edge. In short, we are all basically hybrids of Type A, egotistical behaviors. Given this context, if the system to work, we have to acknowledge that we will fight like cats and dogs, but what is stated and agreed upon in public will be respected by all parties. Oftentimes the competitiveness is reserved for private meetings and when in public we portray an image of unity and agreement. If the public does not view the school board—the administration—as a unified force, then the system might experience a crisis in confidence and community support, which is fundamental to the smooth running of schools, will be jeopardized.

Consequently, there is not a clearly defined line between competition and cooperation within the educational leadership context. In my own approach, based on my own experiences, I attempt to achieve a balance between the two ends of this imaginary continuum with competition on one end and cooperation on the other. To realize this balance, as previously stated, requires the development of many important skills, such as listening, communicating, articulating, and coalition building.

How does educational research regarding teaching and learning inform your own personal approach to policy as an educational leader?

As a teacher I thought I knew some things, but I also realized that there was a lot that I did not know. I was therefore consciously competent, but I also knew that there were certain aspects of my practice as a teacher that I did not know enough about. As a result, I was also consciously incompetent in some areas. Similarly, when I became a principal, I was also consciously incompetent in some areas. For example, I hate timetabling and am therefore not very good at it. Instead of me doing time tabling and screwing it up, I would ask, "Who in the school likes to do timetabling?" I would thus arrange for someone to do timetabling, which we would post. Going back to the cooperative learning research, the work of an educational leader is like putting together a jigsaw, except in this puzzle, the characteristics of the pieces are constantly changing and the challenge is never over. The on-going goal is therefore to find a way to draw on the strengths of everyone you work with so all the tasks get accomplished and because people feel like they are doing what they want to be doing based on what they are good at, workers (i.e., teachers and staff) will tend to be happy (or more happy than when the system does not consider the individual).

In a school setting the principal will find that she or he will need people with specific kinds of dispositions and skills. For example, if you are a principal, you will need, what we might call:

~ The *harmonizer*
~ The person who is detail-oriented
~ The task master, or the person who can get the tasks done

You consciously think proactively in these terms. If you do, when a crisis arises, you will have all the pieces in place so the situation is handled with as little disruption as possible. Otherwise, you are working reactively and will feel and appear to be out of control. To be blunt, you will most likely not be an effective leader. Again, the cooperative learning research has been very helpful in both my own learning as a teacher, my practice as a teacher, and then as a principal and superintendent. Now that I am working in teacher education, I have found that the processes are the same.

***

To provide even more details regarding the theoretical context of my practices I draw from some of the key theorists in the field. For example, these and other scholars have influenced my work:

~ Dewey
~ Vygotsky
~ Sergiovanni and his sense of community because it is communities that we are talking about in terms of schools with their unique cultures

As a principal and superintendent I would always share ideas with colleagues. I would give a teacher, for example, an article and ask them if there were ideas in there that were worth considering, or should they be parked or abandoned? I would use this kind of language because I was not interested in wasting anyone's time. If they are not interested, then no problem.

· 6 ·

EDUCATIONAL LEADERSHIP AND CRITICAL PEDAGOGY

An Interview with Lauren Hoffman

Can you talk about yourself and how you came to be an educational leader?

I will begin with my educational background just to situate myself and then share my more personal understanding of how I have come to be the leader I am today. I am currently a professor in educational leadership at Lewis University and direct the Educational Leadership Doctoral Program. This program was explicitly designed with a critical theoretical framework. I have a doctoral degree in educational leadership, and bachelor's and masters degrees in speech and language pathology. Prior to my university work, I worked in K-12 as a speech-language pathologist, speech-language coordinator, special education supervisor, and assistant director of a special education regional cooperative. Not terribly exciting, however, my work in K-12 consistently took on a transformative role with a strong critique of the exclusive and oppressive nature of education.

Early in my career as a speech-language pathologist in K-12, I was recognized as quite unusual because I demonstrated a commitment to both scholarship and practice, questioned current practices, and believed in the power and knowledge of families. In my early leadership work with speech-language pathologists, I worked with academics from across the country to redefine and expand the work of speech-language pathologists to more deeply connect to students' educational, social, and cultural backgrounds. I worked with general and special educators and school leaders to question their labeling and segregating practices of students with disabilities, to recognize the need for augmentative communication for those students who did not have verbal communication, to understand the oppressive nature of special education, to transform school structures and processes that marginalized students with disabilities, and to understand how standardized testing marginalized multiple groups of students, including those with disabilities.

Although my early work focused on students with disabilities, I was always open and sensitive to all forms of marginalization and oppression, especially race, class, gender, and sexual orientation. My more current leadership is much broader, although still concerned with oppression in education. I have done significant work in schools that are in disadvantaged communities with a focus on emancipatory curriculum and family leadership. My leadership work in the university has involved the development of educational programs with a critical theoretical foundation.

Given this brief educational and professional background, my personal background clearly set the foundation for my leadership orientation to equity and social justice. As a young white, privileged child, there were significant events that opened my eyes to injustice and privilege. I questioned why Eunice, the woman who cleaned our home, did this type of work. She was Black and I didn't know why she needed to clean and do our laundry. My Grandmother was a politician in Chicago and demonstrated women do all kinds of things with their lives even when it was quite unusual at the time. My Grandmother also demonstrated a very unusual move by taking a woman with a mild cognitive impairment into her home to live to avoid being put into an institution by her family. Known as NuNu to us, she became a part of our family and although I recognized she was a little different than people her age, she was just another person in my life to love. I could not imagine why her own biological family treated her so differently. One of my first close friends was Cindy and she was not able to walk because she had feet that turned in and required multiple surgeries. Once she began to walk, we took ballet classes together and even though she really could not make so many of the moves and steps, we had so much fun engaging in this together. In addition to these early racial, gender, and disability lessons, I also learned a great deal about class. I grew up during the school year in a blue-collar community where my father was an eye doctor, but we also had a summer home where we lived for the summer with affluent families from the Chicago area. I learned about the privilege of my summer friends and recognized how differently we/they lived from my other friends during the year. Although my summers were great fun, I really didn't like their bullshit and saw through their arrogance. I believe this was the foundation for my development into a critical and socially active leader.

What is your philosophy of leadership? That is, what philosophies, theories, ideas, or ways of viewing the world inform your practice as a leader?

I am clearly aligned with critical theory and critical pedagogy in my work as an educational leader. I have come to learn that the field of educational leadership assumes a non-activist stance and has too long accepted the idea that injustice is natural in education. I had the exceptional opportunity to have Dr. William Foster as one of my professors during my doctoral program; he was one of the first leadership scholars in the USA to bring critical theory into the educational leadership literature. His work immediately resonated with my implicit notions about leadership needing to be focused on social justice. I have made this my philosophy of leadership and firmly believe educational leaders need to understand the competing political, economic, and social forces in education, become less apologetic for their views, and become more confident in resisting the dominant discourses in order to advocate for those typically marginalized and powerless in society. There is a sense of urgency to act, because for the past decade in the U.S., educational discourse has been dominated by neoliberalism, neoconservatism, and authoritarian populism, which, to social justice educators and leaders, had devastating effects on education. These dominant discourses in the U.S. have come together to create an educational system that produces inequalities and has delegitimized critical models of teaching and learning. Current educational leadership theories have failed to discuss the challenges these political coalitions have had on public schooling.[1] With some exceptions, "leadership theories are limited to viewing leadership as 'reengineering' or 'reculturing' schools to build capacity to make them more productive, not expand democratic participation."[2] There is now a sense of urgency to expand views of leadership in the U.S. whereby educational leaders redefine their roles, challenge the inequities in the system, understand and promote more democratic alternatives, and become committed socially and politically active leaders in the process.

Although educational leadership has been typically defined as a non-activist role, in 1992 Henry Giroux emphasized the social responsibility educational leaders have in terms of the wider political and social function.[3] He was concerned that educational leadership historically ignored the language of community, solidarity, and the public good and drew on neoliberal theory; thus promoting a lack of ethical responsibility from understanding the importance of creating systems that help those unemployed, poor, experiencing discrimination, and suffering from institutional abuse. He called for educational leadership to broaden the parameters of concerns so that we are focused on educating students to live in a "multicultural world, to face the challenge of reconciling difference and community, and to address what it means to have a voice in shaping one's future as part of a broader task of enriching and extending the imperatives of democracy and human rights on both a national and global level."[4] Giroux believed that the crisis in educational leadership includes a lack of critical moral discourse in the attempted educational reform movements. The neoliberal and neoconservative focus on markets and accountability offers limited insight into how schools should prepare students to work against oppression and continues to promote scientific management through the rules of management and efficiency as opposed to a discourse of ethics, values, or culture. Although Giroux spoke to this very specific need in 1992, conditions in the U.S. since then have only deteriorated.

Consistent with Giroux's call for political deliberation and transformative work in educational leadership, are some emerging examples where social activism is considered fundamental to the work of educational leaders.[5] Foster suggested *protest leadership* should be explored in response to the limitations administrators experience regarding accountability, standards, and high stakes testing. [6] He described *protest leadership* as exercised against ideas, practices, institutions, and values that form a system. It is extrasystemic in nature and organized to revolutionize and overthrow. It is anti-cultural in its dynamics, meaning as it does to disrupt extant cultures that may be oppressive in nature. Protest leadership is filled with questions and ambiguities.[7] He differentiates protest leadership from our more standard forms of leadership, *institutional leadership*.[8] *Institutional leadership* is:

> Leadership for some established or perceived institutional objectives, goals, purposes, and mission. It is often seen as the means to achieve greater organizational performance. This is the type of leadership that hopes to achieve a cultural influence on the organization, to have organizational members committed to the same vision and goals, and to inspire and achieve. Drawn from the broader anthropological notion of culture, institutional leadership looks for the culture of organization, asking how leaders can create, change, enhance, or otherwise manipulate in some way the ethos of a particular organization.[9]

Foster suggests that the concept of organizational culture has become a romantic notion, based on the idea that the culture can be shaped and manipulated, with no understanding of the complexity of culture as being dynamic, an inherited system of beliefs that arises from power relations and relationships. Such an understanding leads to his perspective that we need to consider the limits of leadership within this organizational cultural orientation especially in light of regulatory standards and high stakes testing. Neoliberal and neoconservative policies and practices are limiting the possibility of institutional leadership, especially given the question of its viability in the first place.

Anderson calls for *advocacy leadership* that assumes schools are sites of struggle over ideas and resources and focuses on advocating for students, families, and communities.[10] Advocacy leaders believe in public education for all students, understand the political nature of education, are willing to take risks, ask questions to get underneath the issues, work outside their comfort zones, understand social inequities exist beyond the school, and not only resist neoliberal and neoconservative reforms, but also create and enact counter proposals.[11] He suggests advocacy leaders engage in new ways of thinking about the relationship between policy and practice, accountability, leadership, and pedagogy.

Smith, Angus, Down, and McInerney encourage educators and leaders to enact social activism by going beyond the classroom and school building and engaging in *relational politics of school and community activism* that values trust, respect, high regard for the knowledge and wisdom of educators and community members.[12] They believe this type of social activist work includes the following beliefs and practices: (1) schools alone cannot solve the complex issues of disadvantage, social inequality and student performance, (2) community organizing and school and community members work together to determine what is needed for the betterment of the community and school, (3) outside experts work with the community rather than for the community (4) strengths and capacities of communities are used as opposed to problems and deficits, (5) community members are regarded as change agents rather than clients, and (6) a democratic participative culture is used in the collaborative work.[13] They have seen schools in a community transform and affirm the power of human agency and activism in the process.

A social activist orientation is also evident in the work of several African American educational leadership scholars who use their cultural backgrounds and experiences to inform their perspectives on educational leadership. For example, Murtadha and Watts wrote about the history of African American leadership and the need to recognize its contributions in educational leadership work today.[14] "In the past, educational leadership for African Americans meant fighting a larger, more complex battle with a moral imperative to overcome the social barriers of poverty and institutionalized racism's inequities within a democratic society."[15] Black educational leaders used strategies of leverage and coalition in the absence of power, organized church groups to support collective interests, and recognized that community strengths were needed to bring about change.[16] The knowledge gained from historical biographies of these African American educational leaders will be useful for educational leaders today to become more socially and politically responsive.[17]

Dantley suggests that the language of social justice has become so common in the literature that it actually might be losing some of the power it was intended to have.[18] He is concerned that the revolutionary attitude and actions that were noticeable at the beginning of the work on social justice seem to be fading and discusses how we might deal with these dominant forces. To recapture the incisive edge of social justice and education it once held, Dantley uses the term *radical* in his writing and argues for critical spirituality in educational leadership in order to inspire school leaders to become grassroots activists for the progressive reconstruction of schools. He believes the intellectual work of an educational leader should not be separated from political work and the work of the leader should become a community endeavor.[19] Dantley refers to the need for race-identifying protest leaders and race-transcending prophetic leaders as described by West.[20] [21] Race-identifying leaders see themselves as contemporary Black activists who focus on Black issues to keep the social justice agenda explicitly in the center of the discourse.[22] Race-transcending leaders not only recognize the issues of African Americans but also turn the questions and problems into political action.[23] He believes leaders must adopt a more radical practice and see schools in a broader social and political context.[24]

Dillard also views educational leadership as transformative political work where advocacy for the individual needs of students is critical.[25] She believes educational leaders need to embrace a critical ideology to offer possibilities of hope and enact a "conscious transformative pedagogy and leadership toward oppressive structures."[26] She recognizes the difficulty of this type of work by discussing how advocacy work for students can create tension and problems with the teachers.

These examples of social activism in educational leadership reflect the political and social nature of leadership as well as the need to learn from African American leaders who historically enacted political forms of leadership within a context of struggle. Given the educational inequalities in the U.S., the need for educators and educational leaders to embrace more politically and socially active leadership practice has not been greater.

What is the purpose of leadership?

I argue for a social activist stance in educational leadership that fundamentally addresses social change and human emancipation. I embrace Foster's four demands for leadership that include the following: (1) being critical to reconceputalize life practices with the common ideals of freedom and democracy, (2) being transformative to promote social change, (3) being educative to discern current circumstances while also envisioning a new future, and (4) being ethical to promote democratic values within a community.

I believe educational leaders need to work for social justice and equity. Educational leaders need to recognize how they are promoting the status quo and find the agency to resist the dominant discourses and marginalizing policies and practices.

Can you talk about your own approach in the context of competing ideas or purposes of leadership?

Because I have developed a decent amount of political clarity during my leadership experiences, I stay the course with a critical orientation in the face of competing ideas about leadership. As Gary Anderson stated, most leadership theories promote ideas related to reculturing, restructuring, or being more productive in teaching and learning. Although this is not necessarily bad, it does not address issues of democracy, neoliberalism, or systems of oppression. Since I have a clear focus on the purpose of leadership being oriented to social change and human emancipation, I am not distracted by these other technical ideas about leadership. I have seen too much energy wasted on ill informed technical procedures to promote certain pedagogical ideas that are sustaining the status quo.

How does educational research regarding teaching and learning inform your own personal approach to policy as an educational leader?

Educational research does inform me as a leader; however, it depends on the type of research. If the research is oriented to positivistic, "evidence-based" technical notions of teaching and learning, the impact for me is to know about it in order to resist and challenge it. I use that type of research to uncover neoliberal and market-driven ideology and how it perpetuates oppression and certain privileged perspectives. I do believe the work of a critical educational leader involves helping people understand this ideology promoted by the dominant discourses and engage them in resisting the perspectives and practices.

If the research is broader, complex, engages multiple methodologies and realities, engages subjugated and indigenous knowledge from diverse social and geographical locations, and produces knowledge that speaks to cultural, political, and social forces, the research will definitely impact my work as an educational leader. I use the knowledge to interrogate current policies and practices, dialogue with others to examine the meaning for our context and determine what we need to follow up regarding the new content. I believe leaders to be highly informed and highly critical of the research that is being generated.

How does educational research regarding teaching and learning inform larger society-wide or statewide approaches to educational leadership?

Unfortunately, too much policy is informed by positivistic, narrow, and "evidence-based" research as I described above. This has narrowed the purpose of education, the focus of curriculum, and the nature of assessment. This type of research has supported the notion of teachers as robots and technicians and educational leaders as managers. This is certainly created a system of oppression that is designed for the success of white, middle class students. We need to engage critically informed research and find creative alternatives for policy.

In what ways, if any, do federal, state, district, and/or institutional policies impact your work as a leader?

I believe critical leaders need to see their work as understanding and focusing on the macropolicies that are structured to marginalize. For example, Anyon suggests that an unjust economy and the policies through which it is maintained create barriers to educational success that are almost impossible to surmount without political and social involvement and change.[27] She argues that the macroeconomic policies controlling such things as minimum wage, affordable housing, tax rates, and transportation create such significant conditions for students and families that school reform or educational policy alone cannot transcend. Education did not cause the problems of poverty and unemployment and cannot be expected to solve them.[28] She argues that school reform alone cannot solve the systemic problems in our educational system no matter how well intentioned and committed our teachers and leaders are to their students and families. She strongly believes "macroeconomic mandates continually trump urban educational policy and school reform."[29] I do believe this type of macopolicy work should impact the work of educational leaders. We need to broaden our work from the narrow perspective of the school to an understanding of the social issues in local communities and global societies.

What challenges does ed leadership in urban education face?

No amount of external leverage on its own can change educational disadvantage.[30] We need to recognize the importance of (1) respecting the knowledge, language, class location, culture and experience of communities of disadvantage, (2) learning that self-esteem and capacity for political action are mutually reinforcing, (3) realizing that people from communities of disadvantage have the right and capacity to challenge authoritative solutions.[31] Leaders in urban education contexts must continually recognize the broader economic, social, and political ideologies impacting school life. Urban education leaders need to acknowledge that the problems of schooling in communities that are disadvantaged are the result of unequal power relationships in our society. Urban education leaders must understand how to build relational solidarity and power with a range of groups in communities. Urban ed leaders need to be highly tuned into the preponderance of pathologizing practices, build a counter narrative in the school, and help others resist deficit images of students, families, and communities. Perhaps one of the largest challenges is to create a sense of hope and be able to imagine and envision a new way of thinking about schools and education. As Giroux suggests, this type of work requires an ongoing process of critique along with a vision of possibility.

What do you see as your own challenges in your work as a leader?

My personal challenge is dealing with my anger about injustice and my frustration and impatience when dealing with people and systems that maintain the status quo. I am frequently disappointed by the lack of moral courage and agency displayed by educational leaders. I am also extremely discouraged by the technical and methods oriented preparation provided in higher education. My challenge is to try to engage people and perspectives, increase awareness, encourage self-reflection, and model ways of being that are inclusive and respectful.

Notes

1. Gary Anderson, *Advocacy Leadership: Toward a Post-Reform Agenda in Education* (New York, NY: Routledge, 2009).
2. Ibid, 14.

3. Henry Giroux, 'Educational Leadership and the Crisis of Democratic Culture,' *UCEA Monograph Series* (1992): 4–24.
4. Ibid.
5. William Foster, 'The Limits of Leadership,' *Journal of Thought* (2002):9–21.
6. Ibid.
7. Ibid, 9.
8. Ibid.
9. Ibid.,10.
10. Gary Anderson, *Advocacy Leadership: Toward a Post-Reform Agenda in Education* (New York, NY: Routledge, 2009).
11. Ibid.
12. John Smyth, Lawrence Angus, Barry Down and Peter McInerney, *Activist and Socially Critical School and Community Renewal: Social Justice in Exploitative Times* (Rotterdam, Netherlands: Sense Publishers, 2009).
13. Ibid.
14. Khaula Murtadha and Daud Malik Watts, 'Linking the Struggles for Education and Social Justice: Historical Perspectives of African American Leadership in Schools,' *Educational Administration Quarterly* (2005): 591–608.
15. Ibid, 606.
16. Ibid.
17. Ibid.
18. Michael Dantley, 'The Critically Spiritual Imperative toward Keeping the Promise,' in *Keeping the Promise: Essays on Leadership, Democracy, and Education*, ed. Dennis Carlson and C.P. Gause (New York, NY: Peter Lang, 2008), 159–176.
19. Michael Dantley, 'African American Spirituality and Cornel West's Notions of Prophetic Pragmatism: Restructuring Educational Leadership in American Urban Schools,' *Educational Administration Quarterly* (2005): 651–674.
20. Ibid.
21. Cornel West, *Keeping Faith: Philosophy and Race in America* (New York, NY: Routledge, 1993).
22. Michael Dantley, 'African American Spirituality and Cornel West's Notions of Prophetic Pragmatism: Restructuring Educational Leadership in American Urban Schools,' *Educational Administration Quarterly* (2005): 651–674.
23. Ibid.
24. Ibid.
25. Cynthia Dillard, 'Leading with Her Life: An African American Feminist (Re)Interpretation of Leadership for an Urban High School Principal,' *Educational Administration Quarterly*, (1995), 539–563.
26. Ibid, 548.
27. Jean Anyon, *Radical Possibilities: Public Policy, Urban Education, and a New Social Movement* (New York, NY: Routledge, 2005).
28. Ibid.
29. Ibid.
30. John Smyth, Lawrence Angus, Barry Down and Peter McInerney, *Activist and Socially Critical School and Community Renewal: Social Justice in Exploitative Times* (Rotterdam, Netherlands: Sense Publishers, 2009).
31. Ibid.

IN THEIR WORDS

Educational Leadership in Higher Education

· 7 ·

THE GENEROSITY OF LEADERSHIP

A Cultural Approach with David Whitehorse

Can you talk a little about yourself and how you came to be an educational leader?

I come from a mixed cultural background which includes Native heritage (Lakota) and Irish as the principal ethnicities. As a child from a very large and economically poor family—there were eight of us siblings—we were often split up, and many of us lived with extended family or fictive kin, as economics dictated. My father was killed in action in World War II, and my mother and my "Uncle" John were my role models.

As I was the eldest male, my mother spent considerable time ensuring I knew the breadth of my cultural heritage including the Lakota language, to the extent that she knew it herself. My mother grew up in an adoptive situation and wrestled with cultural discontinuities, throughout most of her childhood. An often retold anecdote was that my mother's adoptive parents told her (when she didn't behave appropriately), "Don't act like a little savage; we took away from that life, but we can send you back if you don't behave."

Being of mixed heritage, I didn't fit fully into Native culture, and when forced into the mainstream American culture, I often felt like an immigrant in my own land. My mother stressed the importance of education as *the way out* of the so-called cultural double-bind, and socialized us to accommodate the mainstream culture. As a result, I learned a great deal of resilience, and by age ten or eleven, I was expected to be the principal male figure for my siblings when we were reunited as an extended family. In retrospect, I think that was the first time I realized I was in a leadership capacity, more so by default than by design.

Education in the 1940s and early,1950s was not exactly what, today, one would consider to be culturally appropriate, especially for Native people on the reservation. The philosophy underlying my education was thoroughly Eurocentric and paternalistic. In the Catholic mission school, the nuns believed they were doing us a favor by virtue of 'giving' us an education. They thought they were giving us a superior culture and worldview, which would, as a result, save us from ourselves. Using Native language or behaving as a cultural person in any way resulted in punishment, often corporal. Having someone consistently tell you that you are wrong for being yourself does not make for a pleasant experience. However, despite this context and the destructive tendencies of Western education, my mother stressed the importance of mastering it. While my siblings and I performed reasonably well in school, even excelling in many situations, we maintained a strong cultural component that centers on the importance of generosity. That is, you cannot be a leader in our Native community unless you are generous—and not just generous with material things, but generous with your time and your attention. It is a *sharing* culture built around the 'tiyoshpaye,' which some define as an extended family, but it is actually a *'tipi group,'* that is, people who live and move together. When we think about leaders as people who persuade groups to work together toward common goals, within the Lakota context it would sometimes be the responsibility of the 'akicita,' the warriors, to persuade the whole community. This was the job of the men, but the Lakota culture is matri-centered. Consequently, even though the men served leadership functions in subsistence and political arenas, principally, it was the women who had the real power and exercised social and cultural control. The women were the stewards of the land.

Situated within this context, since I was a young child my mother always told me that I was a natural teacher, that is by her definition, a leader. From that young age I always knew that I would work in the field of education in some capacity. Thinking specifically about how I came to be an *educational leader*, I have to say that I do not know because I do not define myself as an educational leader. While I do have a degree in educational leadership and many years of study and practice in the field, I do not define myself in that way. I define myself more as a teacher. If others want to place those labels on me, I do not have a problem with that. After all, I do fill the position of Dean of the School of Education.

Thinking more about how I am perceived as an educational leader, my contribution to the field has been developing standards, models for reviving struggling departments and colleges of education, and creating new education programs. I have therefore received some notoriety for being *the start-up guy*. I can go into a program that is either restructuring or just starting out and apply some innovation and contextualization that has proven to be successful. I am able to help people realize what their strengths are and how they might be most effectively used to create a high quality program. Thinking about my own work as an educational leader provides a transition into my own philosophy and your next question.

What is your philosophy of leadership? That is, what philosophies, theories, ideas, or ways of viewing the world inform your practice as a leader?

For me, I define my particular approach to educational leadership as *cultural leadership*. This approach, which I will elaborate on momentarily, is significantly different from the most other models. The traditional framework for Western educational leadership is based on Durkheim's notion of structural functionalism. The idea is that you have a social structure, which requires social actors to abandon illusions of maintaining an independent existence and fulfill institutional functions as dictated by the naturally superior leaders. The ultimate goal is to achieve institutional harmony. You therefore have a structure and designated functions for institutions, such as schools, which influence the culture of those organizations and the performance of its members or employees (i.e., teachers and educational leaders). We might characterize this as *the command and control model*. It is very similar to military leadership and even our political leadership. That is, the notion that the structure and the behavior of the legislature influence everything else in the society and how it operates. Again, this is a more dated view.

The alternative, focusing on organizational culture as the center, changes fundamentally how we lead and how we practice. The structures and the behaviors become foundational building blocks that support this. The culture then determines performance and how we modify performance. Sergiovanni offers one of the most comprehensive challenges to the structural functionalist paradigms, when he argues that the new model, if we are talking about cultural leadership, is contextual and situational.

Operating from this new paradigm that stresses the importance of contextualization, when I go to faculty meetings here, I could say that I have all these wonderful models that I helped to develop in California that we should put in place here in this context. Doing this would be doing to education what has been done to it before. That is, having someone come in approaching change or the notion of restructuring as an imposition on an existing system. Rather than follow this authoritarian model of dictation—irrespective of the content to be dictated—I am attempting to work with the culture that is already here. This is a more contextualized approach, which is based on a critique of the one-size-fits-all formula. Coming from this perspective I would define leadership as *a persuasive way of having people move forward with shared goals*. Based on this definition, leadership must therefore exist and operate within the organizational structure.

As a result, my leadership in my current position might be fundamentally different than it was when I was doing the same job in California, or when I was a leader doing my job in the Marine Corps, because the context and the culture are different. At the same time, our previous experiences always inform our current experiences. For example, when addressing the faculty and expressing my commitment to advocate for them against an often hostile college administration, I jokingly say that *I have spent thirty-eight and a half months in combat and in the process was wounded five times, what the hell can they do to me?* This says something about leadership because in combat it is command and control. In that context workers (i.e., soldiers) are expected to provide instant responses to commands, orders, and so on, but it was toward a common purpose—*the survival of all members of the group*. I can take those lessons and translate them to the School of Education today. The purpose is the same—the survival of all members of the group in terms of the tenure process, publications, and professional growth.

What my experiences have taught me is that effective leaders have vision. My philosophy of leadership is therefore based on vision and not the deficiency model. That is, when I examine a situation, I do not do a *needs assessment*. Rather, I look at what the assets, the values, and interests of a group are. I approach the situation asking how those assets can be used, consensually, to evoke some kind of change. It has nothing to do with power and position. What I stress to people is that I consider myself to be a teacher. I do not believe that there is this disjuncture between faculty and administration. I see the relationship as interactive and interdependent. This is not easy for many people to *get* or understand because they are used to the notion of power and position. This idea of hierarchy can be seen, for example, when a faculty committee awards travel stipends and other support to disciplines that have historically been situated as valuable and important, such as math and science, but then does not support other fields that have been undervalued like education because *"they are just teachers."*

Rather than ranking the value of people and what they do or study, my approach is based on widespread participation and life-long learning because I believe we are all life-long learners. Some of the literature that I have read that seems to be more in line with my philosophy talks a lot about the concept of empowerment. I do not use that term because I believe people have their own inherent power. In other words, you cannot *give* someone power. This idea of *empowering others* is a paternalistic attitude. Rather, as a leader, you can create the conditions where people can realize their own power or empower themselves. In other words, I attempt to provide the structure and opportunity for people to realize their own potential. This is where the social justice component comes in for me, and it relates back to my own Lakota cultural heritage.

I grew up with the notion of the medicine wheel, which embodies the four principal values in Lakota culture (integrity, courage, endurance, and generosity). Within this context we begin with *integrity*. As an individual you must possess this characteristic, and it is the family group that is expected to develop this quality within its members. Integrity involves *courage*, and I do not just mean the courage of a warrior or a hunter, but moral courage. It is the courage to face the world *as it is* and exercise your own strength to help other people get through the challenges of an unjust world. This, of course, is an essential component of leadership in just about any cultural context. As a leader, you have to be able to demonstrate this courage and integrity consistently over time, which therefore requires a certain amount of *endurance*—that is part of what makes a leader a *good* leader, or perhaps a more effective leader. In practice, this means that leaders should consistently operate at their own optimal level, which is never static. Much of this work requires a great deal of *generosity* on the part of the leader, as previously mentioned.

Consequently, if you take those four values (integrity, courage, endurance, and generosity), which were ingrained in me from a very young age, it is easy to see how my cultural, community-oriented approach to leadership runs contrary to the dominant, structural functionalist, perspective, which is essentially a European model. However, there is *some* truth to the notion that form follows function in terms of how we develop ourselves individually and organizationally. But if you examine a school of education you have to look beyond that structure and function of the academy, and rather view it as a larger community of learners. As a leader I therefore treat the department I lead as a family unit writ large, that is, as a culture. Part of the problem at some small colleges is that they are very insular and therefore do not take in a lot of new information and ideas and, consequently, does not *put out* many innovations except in individual ways.

As a leader, when we go into these kinds of insular environments with the intention of modifying the culture, we must think very carefully about the best way to approach the task because the members of those cultures can exhibit a tremendous amount of resistance if they feel threatened. You therefore have to be careful to ensure people do not feel as though they are having something imposed upon them. One way to begin is to ask the faculty if they want to change the culture within their institution. If the faculty does not want to change their environment, then nothing you do will be successful. You might have wonderful ideas, but if you do not draw on the culture that is already there in that particular institution, it simply will not work. Again, the only way to arrive at the actual work of developing change mechanisms, you must start with where the people you are working with are at, culturally, philosophically, and so. Performance expectations are very closely tied to cultural expectations.

What is the purpose of leadership?

To persuade other people to pursue shared goals. Ultimately, it is *to do good*. If you look at the principal rule of physicians, which is *to do no harm*, for educators, this would translate into *do no harm to any child or student*. In order to *do no harm*, at whatever level, one would have to be a very profound leader. The notion of good here is determined by your own cultural model and by the consensus of the group you are leading. Without this grounding, you will not make changes. For example, without consensus from the faculty, I would not be able to come in and engage them in a discussion about how to adapt models I developed in previous leadership positions.

Can you talk about your own approach in the context of competing ideas or purposes of leadership?

I do not tend to look at it as competing ideas or purposes, that is, as a competition. However, if I were going to situate my discussion of the old structural functionalist model and the newer cultural model within this context of a competition, I would say that it is the older model that is more prevalent or dominant, and the newer one is just starting to gain ground organizationally in the last ten to twenty years. Again, I do not see them as competing because I see them doing fundamentally different things in different ways. My response would be that you suit your leadership style to the cultural context in which you are working. It is not just leadership *style* that I am referring to. If we are talking about persuasion toward shared values, I really need to know what exactly it is we are trying to change, inside and out, and *how* to change it. In other words, the leader needs to have the skills to be able to persuade people that whatever it is we are talking about is in the best interest of the whole group.

How does educational research regarding teaching and learning inform your own personal approach to policy as an educational leader?

If we are talking about a knowledge base and how research frames our context for doing things—for our work as educational leaders—then good leaders must demonstrate a number of interconnected characteristics:

- ~ First and foremost, they have to be knowledgeable about just about *everything* affecting their leadership role, which includes recent research in teaching and learning as well as educational leadership.
- ~ They must take the broad view. Many would say that the best leaders are the ones that are global thinkers.
- ~ They must be capable of simultaneous processing. For example, we are sitting in a faculty meeting discussing the possibility of changing the curriculum and changing capstones so we have programs that are based in educational excellence. At the same time we are talking about that, I am thinking about how that might inform how I construct the budget for next year because every change we make alters the mix and distribution of resources. I am also considering how I might get this into some graduate committee for approval, so I can have the new curriculum in place and provide the necessary resources. Thinking broadly then, I am considering how this all affects strategic planning because all of these components operate on different timelines. This is the simultaneous processing that the leader must be engaged in. Every time I hear a faculty member share an idea about what they would like to do, it alters the whole mix, similar to a ripple effect.
- ~ One of the most important characteristics leaders should demonstrate is the skill of listening. That is, leaders have to be *good* listeners, and it's difficult to listen when you are doing the talking.

What all of this means in the context of research having an impact on educational leadership is that I must be familiar with areas such as *brain-based research*. I must know how children process information so I can help professors examine their own pedagogy and the approaches to teaching and learning they are advocating for in their teacher education courses. We must therefore consistently stay current with this and other areas of inquiry. This process has been described as being a *reflective practitioner* and a *life-long learner*. If we are consistently learning new things over time, then we have to be reflective in ways that allow us to draw on that new experience, modify our behaviors, and move forward.

How does educational research regarding teaching and learning inform larger society-wide or state-wide approaches to educational leadership?

My basic response to this question is that it *should*, but it largely does not. For example, if we took all the research about standardized testing and we applied it on a political level, No Child Left Behind (NCLB) would never have passed. As a result, NCLB attempts to solve a problem by adding on more of the things that created the problem. We therefore have to ask, "How are we going to solve the problem when we keep on doing more of the same old thing?" We are adding standardized testing on top of standardized testing while attempting to argue that it is relevant and meaningful in terms of telling us about degrees of improvement in schools and classrooms. There is nothing that has ever proved that more standardized testing improves learning. What is working, however, is the unstated agenda of setting schools up to fail through imposing unrealistic (and meaningless) standardized testing goals so they can be handed over to private for-profit management companies.

As a result, society-wide or statewide approaches to educational leadership that are grounded in the latest research on teaching and learning do not exist. My School of Education, for example, is accredited by RATE (Regents Accreditation of Teacher Education), and the accreditation process is largely driven by state mandate and state policy. Leadership, as directed by state policy, therefore serves a political function rather than an educational function. If we were interested in doing something that was genuinely relevant, we would use a set of standards that were based on academic excellence. Let's apply something like NCATE (National Council for Accreditation of Teacher Education), or something that was built in by the profession like the INTASC (Interstate New Teacher Assessment and Support Consortium) standards, for example.

Taking a step back considering *national* leadership, every president of the United States that I can remember talked about himself as *the education President*. If that is the case, every presidency has been a failure since FDR (Franklin D. Roosevelt), the first president I ever heard of. If education has gotten better, it has gotten better by default and by its own devices, not by some federal or state policy.

As a demonstration, in California we were subject to a lot of the same kinds of testing and external mandates that exist in all of the other states, such as New York, but we could create programs that were not constrained by a particular number of units or credits. As a result, we did many things in innovative ways. At the secondary level, for example, rather than having individual courses for language and literacy, math and science and social studies, we developed themes that ran through all our offerings. Multiculturalism was the theme that ran through all of our courses.

If we were talking about language and literacy, for example, we might have asked, *what does cultural difference have to do with language acquisition?* A short answer would be *a lot*. We might also ask *what does cultural perception have to do with science?* If you are studying ecology and you believe that you are related to all other living things and the Earth itself is a living thing, such as people with an indigenous ontology then your notion of ecology is going to be vastly different from someone with a Western, dominant-society perspective. This Western philosophy views the world not as an interconnected living entity, but as a vast source of *potential profit,* reducing the world to *regions* and *areas* and resources to be managed and exploited.

Such Western thinking tends to conceptualize environmental degradation as either an inevitable consequence of the *forward march of industrial progress* or as *a problem* because it threatens the perpetuation of wealth extraction. In other words, if there is no forest, there can be no logging; and without logging, there is no industry; and with no industry, there is no profit; and with no concentration of wealth, there is no concentration of power; and with no concentration of power, there is no basis for the few dominating the many; and with no basis for elite social control, there *is* the possibility of genuine democracy *by* the people *for* the Earth. The mainstream, Western environmentalist therefore says *I am green and I can solve these problems by recycling* not by rethinking one's relationship to the Earth, each other, and all living beings—that is, by altering the *style* of leadership, not the *purpose*. Again, this multicultural approach to curriculum design, and these innovations more generally, emerged *despite* state and federal policy.

Does this mean that I reject the notion of state and federal control? *No.* In terms of education and civil rights, I think the government has a large and important role to play in ensuring communities and individuals are not violated or abused by private interests and entities. Mandates that legislate opportunity and equality, for example, have been, and continue to be, very important for people and cultures traditionally oppressed by Euro-centric policies and practices from Western Expansion, on to slavery, and into the capitalist present. However, state and federal policy makers have never really examined the notion of educational equity, which is more than just giving everyone *the same thing*, it is giving people what they *need*, as cultural beings with the inalienable right to exist as distinct human groups. This point of view is sharply distinct from the Euro-centric, paternalistic framework that has been designed to give people what the leaders *think* they need, such as the English language, a bible, and the self-image of a devalued, dehumanized, obedient, hard-working subservient being.

Conscious of this larger context and the underlying values informing it, we—as educational leaders and educators united around common goals and a vision of purpose—can go far beyond what any state board of education requires or mandates for teacher certification. That is, we can transgress these limitations only if we can find a higher set of standards that allows us to put higher quality teachers into schools. For example, the State of New York does not require people who work as teacher educators to have first hand experience in classrooms. As a result, teachers going through teacher education programs might not be prepared for what they will experience in the classroom because their professors have never been in the classroom outside of being a student, which does not provide the same kind of experiential knowledge as being a teacher, administrator, or researcher. In other words, if I do not have experience teaching at the pre-K though grade twelve level, how can I teach someone to work in this context? The State of California, on the other hand, annually, requires all teacher educators to put in forty-five hours of working directly with students in pre-K through grade twelve schools. To me this does not seem to be a lot of time. It is the equivalent of teaching a one-semester course. It is invaluable though because it keeps you connected to what is going on in schools.

The notions of public policy and the notions of command and control are things that the state and the certifying board or body of the State of New York lays on and keeps us from achieving excellence. Our School of Education, for example, because of state policy and legal/legislative factors, and market forces, technically, provides students with a Master's degree and Teacher Certification in a specialty area in as little as eight months. If the New York State Department of Education was composed more of professional educators rather than bureaucrats and political appointees, I think we would have a lot greater opportunities for more effective teacher preparation.

In what ways, if any, do federal, state, district, and/or institutional policies impact your work as a leader?

While this question, to a large degree, has already been answered, I will repeat that one must be the global thinker, the simultaneous processor, and one has to know where those things either become opportunities or constraints. Someone who is doing curricular leadership might be focused more on what happens with the children in the classroom, and are they getting the right information, and can they pass the standardized tests? In this context, the leader examines every course change, analyzing what these other impacts are. That is, the curricular leader is interested in student achievement and what impacts it.

What challenges does educational leadership face?

Thinking about what challenges are faced by educational leaders and leadership I would have to say, time, resources, political will, the will of the faculty, etc. For me, the biggest challenge I face as an educational leader is answering and addressing the question of "whom do we lose in the interim until we get to that state that we talk about in our vision or our mission?" That is, between now and achieving a greater level of academic excellence, are we preparing teachers who are only moderately prepared to go out into that public school world? Are we setting some of our future teachers up for failure because our program is marginal? For example, we have students who meet the minimum grade point average, but because our program is so short, they do not have time to be reflective practitioners. Their student teaching experience is jammed into fourteen weeks or less, so how do we know that they will be good novice teachers? Again, the question is, who are we going to lose until we begin doing things in a better way?

The focus of many teacher education programs is collecting student tuition. In other words, they have been cash cows, but that is changing in some areas because the *market* is shifting. As the market shifts and the pool of potential students decreases, new strategies and visions must be employed. For example, I am convinced, based on decades of experience, that if you build a culture of excellence, students will come—build it and they will come. The reality is that the programs in teacher preparation and doctoral programs that provide the highest standard are the ones that draw the greatest number of applicants. I am not talking about being like Harvard, which does many things that I would not want to see repeated in other teacher education programs.

But I look at the innovatiove, professional, reflective and effective education programs because they focus on academic excellence, and, as a result, they draw many, many people. Consequently, when I was on the NCATE team, visiting a western university, I found out that in their teacher preparation program, they turn away two students for every one they accept. Why were they turning so many people away? Were they being gatekeepers? Were they being selective? *Yes*, they were being selective because they have very high standards for admittance, which accounts for why they have so many people trying to get it. In other words, because of their reputation for academic excellence, people interested in becoming teachers in the region look to that school as offering a degree that will guarantee them future employment.

Based on this knowledge and perspective, I can say that if programs like the one at my current institution, that follows a market, factory model, adapt our leadership style, our planning, and our school culture to be one of academic excellence, we will get more and more people and develop our own cash cow rather than depending on the Canadian market. Of course the college administration has anxiety about surviving through this transition period, but I have a response to them. I ask how long did teacher education serve as the cash cow supporting the development of nursing, the allied health programs, the undergraduate programs, and so on. Now the *cash cow* is nursing and it is *pay back time*, as it were.

Another internal challenge for the institution I am currently at is the governance structure of the college. I think faculty need to look at how we find that complementary critical mass. Why don't we restructure our operations around a faculty senate with elected representatives? They might consider changing the disproportionate representation of their bodies like the Graduate Council. I am really surprised that on things like Strategic Planning, and other key committees, there are people from Budget and Finance, Human Resources, Enrolment Management, Undergraduate and Graduate Admissions, the President's Office, and only one representative from Academic Affairs. If Academic Affairs is central to all of this, then it should have the greater representation and the other areas should be there for support. That is, the structure seems backwards. Internally, therefore, these are really big challenges. If I wanted to distill this down for what it means for my challenges, it becomes philosophical. That is, how do I keep the *will* and keep the *spirit* to do these things in the face of what are some very significant odds?

This brings me to the last challenge or concern that I wish to address, and that is, to what degree can consensus rise in the academy? Colleges and universities are built around an eleventh-century monastic model. Within this structure you have the clerics in their robes who sit in their little disciplinary fields and do all of their work in isolation from the rest of the community. It is only the very successful universities that have broken that model, opening spaces for more consensual practices and cultures. For example, a number of years ago we developed an organization, the Network of Innovative Colleges of Education (NICE), the *nice* group. Working with five or six different colleges and universities we were able to develop more consensual models and flatter, less hierarchical structures. Some of those programs have continued to move forward, and some have collapsed back into their previous steady, *monastic* state.

· 8 ·

THE EDUCATIONAL LEADER AS CRITICAL MENTOR

Mapping the Minefield with Sandy Grande

Can you talk a little about yourself and how you came to be an educational leader?

Until we sat down to do this interview, I had forgotten that I was the chair of the Department of Education at Connecticut College, and therefore, an educational leader. I came to be an *educational leader* because the person who was the department chair before me had held the position for fifteen or twenty years and he did not want to do it anymore. Being a very small department—there are just four of us—I was the only other tenured faculty member eligible to take the position. Consequently, I have to be the chair for the foreseeable future. In some ways it is the least interesting and most unimportant work that I do. But now that I have two new women of color that are going to try to go through the tenure process at Connecticut College, I recognize that there are now serious responsibilities for me that are attached to this position. That is, I do have to take it seriously even though I do not really enjoy it.

This is how I see my role. If they choose to leave, that is one thing, but since we hired them, we have a mutual responsibility to make sure they make it through the process and get tenure. If they do not get tenure, I would feel that I failed as department chair and their mentor, unless, of course, they did not fulfill their commitments. For me, this means many things. It includes mundane activities such as working with them to create teaching schedules. I always put myself last on the teaching schedule. They have to be able to create a teaching schedule that works for them. One of our colleagues, for example, is a single mother, so she needs to be able to create a schedule that works for her situation. She therefore does not teach every day, but puts all of her courses on two days each week. I also do not want to teach during the same time the two untenured faculty members are teaching as in case I need to go into their classrooms for whatever reason, I can. One of the reasons why so many people often do not get tenured is because of the hierarchy and seniority-approach to scheduling that exists in the vast majority of colleges and universities.

Another way I attempt to support our untenured faculty members is through not only allowing them decide *when* they will teach, but also deciding *what* they will teach. That is, probably the two most politicized courses in our program are the first course students take, and then the last class they take as student teachers. The first course is designed to challenge students, the vast majority of whom are white and highly privileged, to self reflect on their conceptions of what it means to be a teacher from a critical pedagogy perspective. Out of all the classes they take, if they are going to get any resistance from students, this is one. After taking this first introductory course, they decide whether to apply to the program or not. We still get resistance throughout, but not as much or as heated as in this first critical pedagogical introduction to education. Then when they are student teaching, they are so steeped in the day to day of teaching, they tend to not want to hear about teaching as an intellectual project anymore. They just want to know *what to do* in terms of classroom management practices. In this context, we always push them to backup and reflect on what they are saying and the assumptions within the point of view they are adopting. Consequently, this is another time they get frustrated with the coursework.

Based on this situation we just had a departmental conversation around what classes what faculty should teach. On one hand I do not want to be patronizing and say that untenured faculty should not teach these courses because they are going to get hurt on student evaluations. On the other hand, however, they are two women of color, so the students are already going to contest them in a way that they would not contest even me, and definitely not my other senior colleague who is a white male. This was a very interesting and worthwhile conversation to have because if they are teaching the first course, which is the most politicized and the biggest class with the most students, it could potentially have the greatest negative impact on their tenure file. As of now, they have chosen not to teach these classes. However, I tell them that after tenure, it is a different story; we are all in the mix, as it were.

Because I am tenured, teaching those classes has no impact on my life and my future. It therefore makes no difference to me if I have to teach them. Again, for them, it matters a great deal because it is not in their interest to get poor student evaluations. It is not that poor student evaluations would not impact my future promotions, but the students do not contest tenured faculty the same way they contest untenured professors. Students are aware of the tenure process and therefore view untenured professors as in a sort of probationary period where they can have a direct influence. As an untenured professor, if you challenge these privileged students, who tend to possess a deeply ingrained sense of entitlement, to consider ideas and perspectives that make them uneasy or uncomfortable, they will vote on your future through their evaluations. Again, for those of us who are tenured, we do not face this aspect of the university and white student culture.

An area that is perhaps even more serious is supporting the scholarly activities of our two untenured professors. They both do work in areas that I am not familiar with. Despite this fact, I can encourage them to be making connections with people who work in their fields. An aspect of this mentoring process is strategizing on who might be potential future leaders and *grooming* them as such. This includes mapping out what they are doing, how they should be doing it, and how much time they should be dedicating to specific tasks. From the beginning they get pulled into doing a lot of service, and so I often advise them to say no to a lot of service-oriented requests. Because time is so scarce, we have to be careful where we place our energy. For example, a lot of the committees (i.e., service) that we are asked to serve on are not endowed with the institutional power required to make a difference and effect change.

One of the primary reasons that I do not like being an educational leader is because so much of my life, my work, and everything I do is relationship based. The way the institutional structure is constructed inhibits me, at least in my mind, in the kinds of relationships I can have with my colleagues. As a teacher and a student I do not like the liberal democratic discourse of *we're all the same, let's have this liberal, democratic classroom* because at the end of the day, the teacher is going to give the student a grade. At the same time, as an educational leader, at the end of the day, I am going to have to write the tenure letter of our untenured professors. My preference would be to have someone else play that role. In this way, I would be able to build relationships with them that did not have this other *boss/worker*-like component. Rather than their super-visor, I would be able to hang out with them as a colleague.

What is your philosophy of leadership? That is, what philosophies, theories, ideas, or ways of viewing the world inform your practice as a leader?

What I *can* say is that I know my philosophy of leadership does *not* include a liberal, democratic view of the world, as previously mentioned, which I had coming up for tenure in both of my different institutions. Both of the chairs I had came from this white, liberal perspective and it was a *disaster*. Their atti-tude was literally expressed to me as, *do whatever you want, Sandy, we are behind you*. I had to tell this woman who was the chair of my department that I did not need anybody *behind* me, especially being a woman of color and get-ting into conflicts on campus, which tends to be inevitable if you are a person of color. What I needed was the chair of my department to be in *front* of me telling people to *back off* or whatever, not standing *behind* me. I did not need anybody supporting me because I had plenty of that from other colleagues.

In the end I feel that the progressive model is a total failure when it comes to teaching and leadership. Sometimes people who are in leadership positions do not want to confront their position and power and therefore attempt to pre-tend that they are just friends and colleagues with those who are, institution-ally and structurally, below them. In my experience, ignoring these structures does nobody any favors, and, again, can be damaging to those who do not have the power. It is true that we genuinely liked and like each other, but I do not like the way a liberal discourse attempts to blur the boundaries, which I do not think you can do.

Going back to my current situation, the two untenured women in my department know these boundaries exist and they cannot be willed out of existence. We do not attempt to blur the boundaries at all. We are always try-ing to recognize the boundaries and map out where they are. In so doing, we also map out the strategies of how to navigate the institution and successfully navigate the tenure process. For example, I will tell the untenured faculty that the tenure committee will always question what you are doing, and I would not have supported them for hire if I did not believe in their work and the way they do things.

I see my job as making it apparent to everyone else that our faculty is com-petent and that they are serious scholar educators. With this larger goal or objec-tive in mind I therefore do not want to come into their classrooms and do observations that generate anxiety by employing methods based on objectivity because I do not believe objectivity is possible. Your teaching can never be accurately represented in one class period anyway. What we do, therefore, is we map out strategies of how to conduct a peer review, and they choose a strategy they are comfortable with, which always includes multiple observations.

What this work leads to is the co-construction of an observation letter that goes in their file even though they are probably not supposed to see it. Again, however, I do not believe in the notion of objectivity, which the traditional framework is based upon, so why would I practice it? I do not believe that it is any more rigorous if I take secret notes on their teaching practices, construct a secret letter, and discretely place it in their tenure file. It is arguably more rigorous to do it the way we do it because it not only takes more thought, but it tends to improve their teaching practices, which is a good thing and what the tenure committee looks for.

After my observations, after each observation, we will have a discussion and I will share with them what I observed, and what I think they need to work on. The letter I write therefore becomes a narrative of their growth over time concerning their classroom teaching. This seems to be a much more honest evaluation of their pedagogy. I never submit the letter until they understand and acknowledge the content. What I tell them is that the tenure committee will be looking for growth over time. The last thing you want is a glowing letter your first year about your teaching. There should be something in there about areas you need to work on. This is another reason why the liberal model is a failure because it is always so positive and flowery, talking about how great everyone is, which, in the long run, is not helpful.

Summarizing my approach I would say it includes the following repeating and overlapping steps:

~ Being aware of existing power dynamics
~ Working to make these power dynamics transparent
~ An honest attempt to negotiate these dynamics and structures of power

What is the purpose of leadership?

I think leadership functions the same way in higher education as it functions in public schools, K through grade twelve, which is a form of social control and gate keeping. For me, however, as an educational leader, I am constantly attempting to level the playing field, which means creating access and opportunity for people who get shut out by traditional forms of leadership. I therefore see my role *not* as a gatekeeper, but as a *gate opener*. However, the notion of being a *gate opener* here is not conceived in the liberal sense where the view is *we are all the same and everything you do is great*, but to guide professors in and through ensuring they understand what they have to do to survive and get tenure. This does not mean assimilation, but negotiation and survival within the system, which is strategically required to transgress the system.

How does educational research regarding teaching and learning inform your own personal approach to policy as an educational leader?

Ideas from critical pedagogy about teaching and learning inform my practice. To illustrate this I can share a recent story about an awful chairs meeting we had. Supposedly the meeting was going to be about this horrible article on minority faculty, and it was one of the worst discussions I have ever had to sit through. One of the topics of the discussion was about how minority faculty members have to be socialized into institutions of higher education as the only way they will survive. I was so infuriated by the discussion that it only reaffirmed my commitment to ensure that the women in my department do not have to assimilate into the department or the institution. What I *can* let the new faculty know is what is *out there*, that is, what the internal culture of the academy is like.

This act of *naming the world* is a central aspect of mapping the minefield of the institution. There are certain mines that I may feel as though they should step on them and *blow them up*, but this is my opinion and they must be aware of what the consequences are going to be one way or another. My job is therefore not always to avoid the mines, although there are some that should definitely be avoided. However, sometimes there are mines that are worth blowing up and dealing with.

For example, they might be in a meeting or on a committee, and, as usual, they are the only faculty of color in the group. In such a context it is not uncommon for a topic to emerge with Euro-centric or racist undertones. When this occurs critical faculty have to decide if they should keep their mouths closed or if they should say something and blow it up. Sometimes the situation demands a *blow up*. Other times, however, I will just tell the committee chair that *such and such professor* cannot be on the committee anymore for some reason like a scheduling conflict. The decision, whichever way it goes, is always strategic and weighed according to relevancy, personal costs, and potential for change.

Hypothetically, for example, let's say one of our untenured faculty members was on a committee, and they were talking about restructuring the whole curriculum, my advice would be that they should definitely speak up. At the same time she would speak up, I would feel obligated to have a meeting with the Dean of the Faculty and explain to him what it means for an untenured faculty member in my department to sit through these meetings. For something this significant, myself and the other tenured faculty member would probably choose to become active and be a part of it because she should not be out there by herself. However, the point here is that there are always choices to be made and sometimes they are worth it, and sometimes they are not. Of course they would have to make the decision for themselves whether they wanted to speak out or not, but if they asked my advice, I would give them my opinion and try to map out the consequences for them.

Again, my practice and philosophy of practice or praxis here are informed by critical pedagogy, which subscribes to a theory of learning that always acknowledges the larger political context in which knowledge is constructed. My work as an educational leader draws inspiration from the ways Freire engaged with the people he was organizing to carve out spaces for political engagement. This is what I have been describing, that is, the ways I work with faculty to carve out spaces for political engagement as an active co-construction while navigating the minefield and the power dynamics of the academy. This is how I have constructed the *purpose* of educational leadership according to my own critical pedagogical approach to teaching and learning.

In what ways, if any, do federal, state, district, and/or institutional policies impact your work as a leader?

The roles and responsibilities of deans and chairs and the whole structure, for example, are definitely dictated by large organizations like the National Council for Accreditation of Teacher Education (NCATE) as well as federal legislation like the Higher Education Opportunity Act having an even bigger impact on the institutional roles of leaders in particular. This has been especially apparent since the conservative swing, or recovery movement, and the emergence of the No Child Left Behind Act (NCLB). While it was directed at pre-K through grade twelve, it has infiltrated higher education to a considerable degree.

For example, beginning in the fall of 2010 every faculty member will be mandated to send to every Dean of every college of education the list of books they are using in their courses so they can be posted on the college's web page. Supposedly, this is intended to allow students to have access to that information so they can buy books at a more reasonable rate. However, I do not get the sense that people *really* believe that this is the real reason. At my institution, for example, a large majority of the students are very privileged and will therefore continue to just go to the bookstore and buy their books, unconcerned with how much they cost. At a federal level, it seems as though they want to be able to keep track of what faculty are teaching.

As chair I therefore had to let my faculty know that they would have to provide me with a list of what books they are using so I can report back to the dean as well as post them on our web site. To know exactly what was required I went and looked at the federal legislation and discovered that only the ISBN number had to be published. I was therefore able to direct my faculty as such. As a strategic decision I decided that if someone was interested enough to know what books we were using they could go look up the ISBN numbers. This is an example of one of those issues that I would not choose to resist and deal with the consequences of resisting because I do not think it is that big of a deal to post our ISBN numbers on the internet.

What this *does* suggest, however, is that one of the responsibilities of a critical pedagogical leader is that you have to be well informed regarding the policies you are charged with enforcing. That is, you cannot assume that policies are always going to be interpreted accurately by whatever agency or administrator that hands them *down* to you. As suggested throughout this chapter, this perspective challenges the educational leader to *sometimes* take on the role of an activist by resisting, but to *always* assume the *mindset* or *consciousness* of an activist—an activist-leader—by investigating, analyzing, discussing, coalition building, and supporting less powerful colleagues.

While there is a lot of good research on higher education and teaching and learning, I do not think it is driving educational practices at any level. Federal policy and corporate interests, which overwhelmingly tend to be political not educational, are driving higher education, as well as primary and secondary education through NCLB (discussed more fully in previous chapters). Even though the creators of NCLB, the Bush administration, are no longer in office, it remains unclear *how* and *if* this might change under the new presidency, the Obama Cabinet, with its Secretary of Education, Arne Duncan. Again, it remains to be seen if the NCLB policies, which have proven useful for corporations on many different levels, will continue to dictate what goes on in schools *and* in colleges and universities although to a lesser, although notice-able, extent.

What challenges does educational leadership face?

What goes on in most educational leadership doctoral programs is very tradi-tional and not informed at all by the work done by critical theorists and criti-cal pedagogy, which I think would make a huge difference. The goal of an educational leadership program informed by critical pedagogy would not just be about figuring out how to be in compliance or even creating access. It would ask, access *to* what and *for* what? Asking and answering these larger ques-tions are what critical theory really has to contribute.

Even the people in higher education working to generate more access for African Americans and other traditionally oppressed peoples into institutions, which is important work, often do it without considering these larger questions. This is dangerous because the hegemony, or the perspective assumed to be nor-mal and natural, is Euro-centric and pro-capitalist. Consequently, the presup-position behind the notion of *access* therefore means assimilation and accommodation of that which exists—white supremacy, patriarchy, and capi-talism, for example. The language that is usually employed to justify efforts to increase institutional *access* for oppressed people is usually around notions of creating *productive citizens*. In a consumer-corporate driven society, such as what exists in the United States and elsewhere, the definition of a *productive citizen* is far too obvious and devoid of any social justice-oriented content. The goal is to therefore create the *opportunity* for more people to enter that world. Critical pedagogy, on the other hand, challenges us to critique the destructiveness and dehumanization of that world.

Again, because of the way educational leadership programs are currently structured, they are not producing leaders with the fund of knowledge or the skills to critique the system. On the contrary, they are being schooled to repro-duce the hegemonic system. It is very similar to teacher education, which also tends to produce teachers who will serve as social reproducers, not social reconstructionists or critical conscious navigators of the minefields of capital-ist society. From my point of view, this is a big problem.

Another example is Harvard who recently created a new doctoral-like program and a new degree in educational leadership, which they call a doctor-ate in Educational Leadership (EDLD) that appears to be a very corporate model. It is not a Ph.D. or an ED.D., but something entirely new and different. It is designed to *integrate the fields of education, business, and public policy in inno-*

vative ways. To enter the program, you do not need a background in education, but they are going to produce educational leaders for placement in charter schools and other schools taken over by private, for-profit management companies. What is impressive about this new degree and program is the audacity with which they are flaunting the fact that education and business are in bed together. There is *no* shame here in disregarding the notion that education should serve humanistic interests uncorrupted or influenced by private interests.

CONCLUSION

· 9 ·

POLICY AND THE SOCIAL CONSTRUCTION OF EDUCATIONAL REALITY

The *preconstructed*…is everywhere. This means that we see not so much what there is to see but more what we have come to see in the course of our past experiences… Engaging in research without knowing how our common ways of seeing the world mediate what we are perceiving and doing means that we no longer *know* in explicit ways what we are perceiving and doing—some learning scientists talk about the *tacit nature of knowing*. That is, our ways of knowing normally are hidden from view and therefore invisible. If we do not question ourselves and our ways of seeing, we merely record during our research what we already know implicitly rather than opening up ourselves to new learning. (Roth, 2007, pp. 56–66)

Throughout *Doing Teacher-Research: A Handbook for Perplexed Practitioners* Roth (2007) continues to stress the importance of being aware of the socially constructed schemas that mediate the knowledge production process of individuals rendering the notion of *objective science* absurd. Making this point Roth (2007) reminds his audience, "the most dangerous enemy to a researcher are his or her own presuppositions (ideologies)" (p. 88). Because we are all exposed to roughly the same dominant cultural texts and messages through the mainstream media, as researchers and educators or teachers/researchers, we find consistent and predictable similarities of the schema of most people within a given society. Reflecting back on Chapter Two the notion of "news framing" identified by Rhoades (2008) as "the promotion or adoption of an intention-

al and cohesive narrative structure in news reports" and "presenting a particular perspective on an issue, replete with a set of identified problems, solutions,
and guilty parties" (p. 180), is particularly useful for understanding how our
beliefs and ideas about education, that is, our schema, are socially constructed
by the news media. That is, education tends to be framed in a way that supports
the policies and leadership practices of corporate power wielders.

For policy makers to get away with forcing a domesticating education on
the majority of students, the public has to be convinced that such treatment
is warranted. Working classes, immigrants, and students from other historically oppressed, colonized, and enslaved cultural or ethnic backgrounds and communities are therefore portrayed, in various context-specific ways, as *criminal*,
or *potentially criminal* and *depraved*, *out of control* and in need of external conditioning for *their own good* so they can *pass the standardized tests* and *compete
on the global market for a livable wage*. This conditioning contributes to the formation of a working class identity based on consenting to the labor-capital relationship as inevitable and good. In this context education is framed, or socially
constructed by the media, as a *paternalistic gesture* made by the *benevolent leader*
who *makes the hard decisions for the ignorant masses*, who, because of their *ignorance*, are *unable* to comprehend the rationalization behind the policies they are
subjected to, so are angry at the bosses for *oppressing* them. *The boss, because he
is wise and kind, continues his policies even though it renders him unfavorable among
the ignorant masses for which he has so much love, so much* tough *love*. This is the
social construction or framing of educational reality, which is informed by an
implicit, built-in hierarchy. It becomes a presupposition. The hierarchy is not
even mentioned. It is taken for granted, just a normal and natural aspect of
objective reality no more significant than the fact that the Earth is seasonal and
therefore has a perpetually shifting environment. What amounts to *a biased* perspective therefore becomes a socially constructed reality and therefore invisible to the uncritical observer.

For example, in a recent essay by Oxford economist Paul Collier, "The
Politics of Hunger," which appeared in the November/December 2008 edition
of *Foreign Affairs*, available in bookstores and airports throughout the United
States. Collier's (2008) article represents the standard argument that poor
people, indigenous communities in the *third world* in particular, are too stupid
and lazy to manage their own affairs, freely consenting to the corporatization
of their traditional agricultural-based economies. He goes on to argue that only
romantic liberals support "peasant agriculture" because of their fetish for the
organic as a "luxury brand." Making his case Collier (2008) argues that because

of sustained hunger third world peasants' "mental potential is impaired," which, he argues, "can be handed down through the generations" (p. 70). In the end, Collier makes the case that romantic elites are hurting the third world's ability to feed themselves by preventing more commercial farming, which is assumed to be a benevolent gift from the intellectually superior class who have a natural inclination for entrepreneurship. Because this use of media is part of the way the world is socially constructed, it demonstrates the need for critical media literacy because we are in an age of neoliberal hierarchy that cloaks itself in paternalistic favors.

The task is therefore to uncover the hegemonic veil that renders one unable to comprehend the philosophy behind the practice of modern, capitalist, Euro-centric practices and perspectives. The process of de-hegemonizing our minds, our schemas, which serve as a lens through which we construct and interpret knowledge and experiences, requires many interrelated conceptual tools and insights to reflect upon. This engagement with life-long critical learning and practicing might include discussion of the following analyses and observations:

~ Challenging the assumption of an external objective reality that can neutrally be comprehended refocuses the debate from issues of *accuracy* to questioning *certainty*. While this shift may seem qualitatively insignificant, its ontological implications have immense pedagogical and curricular consequences. If knowledge exists outside the realm of human intervention, then *truth* can be absolutely known and externally imposed. However, critical constructivism argues that knowledge is socially constructed by historically contextualized knowers with particular relationships to dominant modes of power and authority.

~ Invalid research conclusions and cultural biases built into reform language. For example forty percent of students in Boston public schools are classified as "limited English proficiency," which, it has been argued, is based on a racist, paternalistic, savior pedagogy situated in the context where bilingual education has been all but banned. Seventy-five percent of linguistic-minority students reside in low-income urban areas. What impact has the changing demographics of the U.S. had on educational policy development? Many students whose first language is not English have developmentally critical language needs that are being unmet. In Boston, for example, forty percent of students have a first language other than English. Most of these students are placed in

Sheltered English Immersion, a national trend due to NCLB setting annual test score goals that do not exclude learners who have Limited English Proficiency. Because bilingual education has been banned, students and parents interested in such programs need special waviers to be placed in bilingual programs, even though research suggests bilingual approaches are far more effective than immersion models.

~   The political design that predetermines failure with 4 to 1 funding inequalities, for example, is ignored. "This is where urban school reform rhetoric has missed the mark. It has presumed that urban schools are broken. Urban schools are not broken; they are doing exactly what they are designed to do" (Duncan-Andrade & Morrell, 2008, p. 1).

~   If knowledge is objective, then "under-performing" urban students and school districts—and *urban* here implies an association between criminality and blackness and brownness—are assumed to be objectively inferior (hierarchy of intelligence).

~   Policy tends to reflect the imposition of external interests not validated within affected communities. For example, English only laws in the U.S. are designed to phase out other languages and cultures, especially Spanish in the twenty-first century, which hegemony is designed to manufacture consent for. The results have been an increase in student resistance, social movements but also passivity and a fear of freedom.

What Have Been the Implications of This Context?

~   As mentioned in Chapter Two the No Child Left Behind Act (NCLB) has not served the interests of school leaders, such as principals and superintendents who maintain an interest in working as professionals, and less so the more critical they are.

~   Transfers power over goals and outcomes of school from teachers and administrators to federal government. Thus unconstitutional: Congress is not intended to legislate education, that responsibility was left to individual states

~   Sanctions for missing AYP (Adequate Yearly Progress) target, measured through standardized, high stakes testing

~ The loss of funds and control to private management corporations (i.e., Edison) as a result of NCLB sanctions has had a negative impact on curriculum and multicultural education.

~ However, not even research supports testing and sanctions as adequate school improvement strategies.

~ Critics have charged NCLB as being nothing more than a "backdoor maneuver" (Kohn, 2004, p. 84), allowing private for-profits to take over public education—paving the way for *market reform*. Profit in testing market: 50 million tests: Billion dollar industry

Thinking about the most current political context in the United States, let us turn our attention to U.S. President Barack Obama and the approach to education his Secretary of Education, Arne Duncan, is offering.

~ Obama on education, conflicting messages? He has taken the position that too much time is devoted to testing. However, he has also said that "the goal of the law (NCLB) was the right one."

~ Arne Duncan, unfortunately, suggests an unfavorable answer concerning Obama and the corporate takeover of public education. In Chicago, when Duncan ran the city's public school system, teachers protested: "he spent a lot of time using NCLB and test scores to close down quite a few public schools and turn them over to charters" (Malone & Sadovi, Dec. 17, 2008).

~ "How can policy makers deal effectively with educational problems without a decent understanding of what school is like for those who teach there?" (Eisner, 1998, p. 118)

Despite Obama's obvious continuation of the policies and practices that support dominant forms of wealth and power, many white teacher education students continue to ask questions such as; "Historically whiteness has been a hegemonic construction of the ruling capitalist class, but with a newly elected Black president, will this be true in four years, in ten years, or in twenty years?" What these kinds of questions suggest is that the social construction of educational reality is so mis-informative that many people do not understand where power lies and how it is exercised. That is, while Obama, as the president, can propose legislation, his ideas are meaningless without the approval of Congress, a predominantly white male body long since bought out by corporate lobbyists.

What we are beginning to uncover here are the ways teacher education students have been conditioned to understand the world. That is, it provides a window into how future teachers tend to socially construct the world, which speaks to their media, schooling, and family experiences. What follows is therefore a discussion on student ideas, which is indispensable for the critical leader interested in engaging students from where they are coming from, as a place of critical departure.

Teacher Candidates and Their Social Construction of Educational Reality

The social construction of educational reality unavoidably includes ideas about the larger society and its historical development. After reading and discussing critical texts, and reflecting on the dominant Euro-centric view of the world held by members of her family, one white female student from Ontario comments:

> Even some of my family members believe that since the British were more powerful and defeated the local Huron and Ojibwa and Iroquoian bands, they deserve to live on reserves, because they lost the war. They believe that since so many non-whites in our area at least are poor, they must all be drug dealers or gang members or something.

What this suggests is that the old rigid dichotomy crudely portraying wealthy whites as pure and poor people of color, Native Americans in particular, as depraved, is, unfortunately, still very much alive. Another student reflects on the Euro-centric portrayal of Columbus she observed at the elementary level:

> I recently observed a first grade class. The students were told that it was the month to recognize the Native American heritage. The teacher handed out that class an article about the Native Americans and settlers during the time of Christopher Columbus. The majority of the lesson was about how the settlers came to America to find religious freedom and pointed out how the Indigenous people dressed different from the settlers. The remainder of the lesson went over what the ships were called that Columbus traveled on and where they first made land. To say the least, I was disturbed; not only by the content of the lesson (which had very little information about Native Americans) but that the teacher had nothing to add. She literally read the lesson right out of the teacher guide attached to the meaningless article. I know a good way to start changing the curriculum so that is more inclusive, throw away material that is incorrect and clearly repressive. Instead, give your student something worthwhile to learn.

This means that teachers need to be creative with making up their own ways to present material that is appropriate, accurate, and truly multicultural.

As a response to this racism, many white students will adopt a "we are all the same" stance, which, from a biological point of view is correct, but from a cultural point of view, which includes schemas and worldviews, and therefore is at the center of knowledge production, is incorrect and the cause for a lot of misunderstandings. Adopting this paradigm, one recent, white Canadian student noted, "Mr. Obama is just as human as the rest of us, so why shouldn't he be president?"

Do we believe that there is a necessity to congregate different ideas when teaching empirical subjects such as math and science? These subjects require one correct answer without explanation.

While this perspective represents the dominant paradigm of objectivity and is therefore widespread, other students were able to engage with critical texts and challenge it. The following exchange between two students is indicative:

> *Question*: To me, Critical pedagogy is the spark of open-mindedness that allows progress, growth, and creativity to flourish. Is there any place within education that critical pedagogy would not be a valid approach?

> *Response*: As has been illustrated in previous readings, as well as in this particular assignment, critical analysis can be accomplished in any type of subject matter, even those areas thought to be purely objective. Understanding the idea that our perceptions create certain realities is crucial to engaging in critical thought. Teaching this broader understanding is important for our students, our nation and our world. In every instance critical analysis is employed, we can find progressive answers, thoughtful, positive change, and social justice as a result.

Sometimes, however, students reject critical approaches outright. The following passage demonstrates how critical pedagogy has made one student feel threatened:

> People tell white teachers that they should incorporate more multiculturalism in the classroom, and then when they do they are accused of trying to come across as superior when that is not their intention at all. I have heard others from minority groups trying to explain that they know the "white" culture just because they watch television but shows like *Friends, Roseanne,* and *The Simpsons* do not reflect my culture or me. Also in my undergraduate years there were professors who taught Christianity who were not Christians and they made ignorant sweeping assumptions and of course no one bats an eye to this offensive behavior.

This *pick yourself up by the bootstraps and quit complaining about the system* discourse does represent the most advanced stage of human civilization, even if it does have a few minor flaws like a propensity for genocide and perpetual war, economic exploitation, environmental degradation, white supremacy, a bitter hatred for all that is not Western European, heterosexual, male, and wealthy, etc.

Behaviorism and Learning

Question: Considering the tenets of behaviorism, how do you see its application in the classroom, what are the pros and cons to such a theory?

Response: Behaviorism is the conditioning of a desired behavior by using extrinsic rewards to reinforce the likelihood that that behavior will occur again. Classroom management is important for learning to occur. If the students are behaving inappropriately then they will not have the proper concentration/ focus needed to learn.

Appropriate classroom management involves techniques of Behaviorism. Some teachers that I have observed use behavioral conditioning methods accurately. For example, when students sit quietly and listen to the teacher while she is giving instruction, the students are immediately rewarded by being given a point that is put towards a prize. I was working with a first grade student who was having trouble following along with the math class worksheet. It was the end of the day and he was either not motivated to do his work or he was too tired. I told him if he could follow along with me as I showed him how to do the problem, then he would be able to play for a little while with his cars. I addressed my expectations and the desired behavior and it also gave him motivation to concentrate on the math. The student was attentive long enough for learning to occur, I rewarded the behavior even though he needed my assistance. Behaviorism does not guarantee that learning will occur. It should only be used to control behavior. The cons of this theory are a result of the misuse of the techniques, such as using external conditioning to improve the cognitive learning process. Students' personalities and unique learning potential should be kept in mind when choosing methods of teaching and when to use behavioral conditioning.

This behaviorist construction of educational reality is one of the most indoctrinated ideas regarding education permeating the entire dominant society. Another student in the following short quote reproduces this idea:

I think the greatest enemy of mankind is ignorance, and ignorance can be simply defined as a lack of knowledge or education. People can only progress as quickly as they can acquire knowledge. Most people have attained a certain level of progression because of teachers who have instructed, educated, and mentored them. Pedagogy, then, is one of the most important professions because teachers are charged with the responsibility of educating and instructing our children.

Again, what we find here is another techno-mechanical conception of learning. That is, in this behaviorist paradigm learning occurs as a result of transmission. Consequently, the quantity of raw knowledge one has acquired is what determines a person's worth, whether they are ignorant or enlightened. This point of view ignores the relational knowledge one cannot simply be told, but must be constructed through the practice of critical pedagogy. Learning is not just memorizing but requires actively engaging with ideas and other people. Not being racist, according to a mechanical conception of learning, is therefore understood as the result of memorizing the right ideas. Studying, however, is only part of the process and sometimes not even a required part. What *is* always required is interaction and practice living against racism in every domain of one's life. Sometimes students state this transmission conception of cognition even more plainly:

> The school is a unique environment because it is the most important way of transferring information to young minds.

Again, challenging the assumption that learning is a mechanical exercise of memorization is not easy. Especially when the epistemological foundation of your education schema rests on the psychological banking concept. It is much easier for a future teacher to visualize how she or he will fit into the system as a teacher of teaching is viewed as a technical act of depositing rather than a complex challenge of guiding students on an active process of construction, deconstruction, and reconstruction for liberation against the ongoing process of capitalism as colonialist plunder. For many people, this is scary, and it challenges everything they have learned about the world. If this were not enough, getting a new job and taking on new responsibilities, like the learning and growth of young minds, is also a very scary prospect.

We might therefore speculate that for some prospective teachers the rejection of critical pedagogy and MCE has a lot to do with coping and the attempt to get relaxed and not stressed out or overly anxious. These are real psychological processes and responses that critical pedagogy must be sensitive to. Also at play, and widely reported in the literature, is students' fear of being alienated from their families as a result of adopting the values of critical pedagogy, such as community and sharing. For example, I am raising my daughter with values that are antithetical to the values of capitalist society.

My mother, who I love and respect, has not rejected the values of the dominant capitalist society. As a result, when my mom is at our house, and my daughter, Jayne, is getting into things that she is too young for, my mom tells her "that is not yours," or "no Jayne, that is grandma's." I feel compelled to tell my mom that we are not raising our daughter with those individualistic values of ownership. I tell my daughter she is too young for whatever it is she should not be destroying, and that when she is old enough, I will teach her how to use whatever it is. It might seem minor, but it is fundamental to her ontological development, that is, how she understands the relationship between people and the material world. However, this decision to raise my family with the values of what we hope will be a post-capitalist, more democratic and loving world, creates real tension and animosity between me and my immediate family. Again, for many this price is simply too high, which, from a psychological perspective, is understandable.

In the following excerpt a white student expresses a common rejection of critical pedagogy for a more familiar behaviorism due to a sense of feeling threatened.

> A student-centered classroom is one where students are actively involved in their learning. Instead of having teacher directed lessons students are encouraged to participate in group dialogue and learning centers designed to have students probe further. A teacher of this type of classroom acts as a guide rather than an instructor. Critical Pedagogy encourages this type of learning environment because it empowers the student. It allows students to come to their own conclusions about a concept rather than having them recite facts that the "oppressive, evil" white teacher is giving them. These two concepts are not interchangeable. It is possible to have a student-centered classroom without supporting the critical pedagogy theory.

This student could just not get past an individualistic understanding of the world. She was stuck in the *bad apple* paradigm, and was therefore upset because she interpreted challenges to white supremacy as *all white people are bad apples*, that is, "oppressive and evil," to use her words. But I guess that is part of whiteness; we think everyone is talking about us. She had difficulty understanding how whiteness is problematic because it is embedded within institutions and social structures, which, as a result, privilege whites and inform the identity of everyone in those white-dominated Western societies. Consequently, whites grow up with an unjustified sense of entitlement and a host of other psychological maladies. In other words, while whiteness privileges white people, it is not good for *anyone*, not even whites—from a psychological health point of view. Just because white people benefit materially and socially from it does not mean it is the best system for those who fit within conceptions of whiteness. This is important because a lot of the literature on whiteness assumes that the system that exists, capitalism, is good for whites. Change is therefore stuck within the hegemony of capital. Real change must transgress the process of value production as part of anti-whiteness pedagogy. The response of whites to the call to transgress whiteness and capital (and patriarchy) should therefore not be one of fear and anxiety, but one of joy and happiness.

The Question of Student Growth

My initial approach to learning was based on the Westernized methods that were typically used in the schools that I attended throughout my life....As a future Special Education teacher, I find that critical pedagogy will awaken my sense of creativity to hone in on practicing epistemologies that will offer choice, cultural relevance, individual meaning, and social justice. (student 1)

After completing this philosophy course, I have discovered the many social injustices that our world faces today....Before taking this course I severely underestimated the importance of our profession. I have now come to realize that teachers have a professional and social responsibility to help young people learn and promote social justice. Today, capitalism has become a crippling evil. Oppression, ignorance and racism are just a few examples of what this type of system has done to our societies. It is important for educators to educate our young about these real life issues and advocate changing to a socialist economy. (student 2)

My perception of the characteristics that embody a great teacher has incredibly changed this semester....The Euro-centric way of teaching that our North American schools are very fond of might be a great barrier to how we teach our students. (student 3)

At the beginning of the semester I argued that a realist philosophy was valid in math and the pure sciences where ideas and hypotheses can be empirically tested and thus considered "right" or "wrong." Whereas the social studies were not so "cut and dry," a constructivist approach would prove beneficial as there were virtually no "absolute" truths. However, at the end of the semester, I argued that math and the pure sciences were in fact subjective studies, where "knowledge" has been defined according to the dominant paradigm. A comprehensive study of critical pedagogy effectively paved the way for constructivism to emerge from the confines of the social studies classroom. (student 4)

These *testimonials*, if you will, are representative of the comments I, and countless other critical pedagogues throughout much of the world, receive every semester. That is, the vast majority of students in our classes, after reviewing and discussing multiple perspectives and evidence, consistently acknowledge that there are many critical approaches to education that do far better jobs of staying true to our most cherished democratic values than does the decontextualized banking model that continues to dominate public education. Not only do many future teachers develop sophisticated and complex knowledge systems to better understand and make sense of the world, they also frequently display great humility, courage, and dignity as they commit to developing critical pedagogies because they believe that students have a right to the best possible education, even though such an education happens to be counter-hegemonic.

While it is true that any *student* who can decode a critical text can regurgitate ideas and make radical statements and declarations of allegiance and commitment, it is, nevertheless, for many, *a first step*. Even if students do not fully understand, or *believe*, what they are saying, and even if they are just trying to tell the teacher or professor what they think she or he wants to hear to get a good grade, they have at least engaged with critical perspectives, and therefore are more inclined to continue reflecting on the merits of the critical tradition than if they had never constructed such declarations.

As critical pedagogues I therefore do not believe it is our task to police the *authenticity* of student comments, but rather, to create spaces for such statements to be made and reflected upon. If we spend our energy attempting to control student behavior and punishing them for not being *as authentic as we think we are*, then we will have failed to act democratically, and we will continue to blame students for their resistance and stubborn grip on their antiquated beliefs. When we *do* fall victim of *critical banking*, as I have referred to it elsewhere, we teach students that critical pedagogy is just another dogma externally imposed upon them from another set of behaviorists-in-denial. Unfortunately, this contradiction is often enough to turn students off the critical tradition entirely. Our task, as critical pedagogical leaders, is therefore to demonstrate our own excitement and conviction for our democratic values, and the evidence that supports our conclusions, and to treat student comments as if they were genuine even if we know they are not. In so doing we are providing yet another opportunity for students to reflect on the validity and usefulness of the critical tradition, rather than locking them into their conditioning, which, given the necessary amount of time and guidance, they will become conscious of. This awareness is central to seeing the world through non-biased eyes. Obtaining this skill is central to understanding Eisner's (1998) observation that larger "since the early 1980s (and earlier), there has been widespread concern about the quality of public schools" (p. 118). The following two excerpts speak to this analysis:

> Urban schools are producing academic failure at alarming rates…inside a systematic structural design that essentially predetermines their failure. This is where urban school reform rhetoric has missed the mark. It has presumed that urban schools are broken. Urban schools are not broken; they are doing exactly what they are designed to

do. A social justice approach shifts the blame from the victims of an unjust system onto the fiscal, political, and ideological policies that deliberately undercut and demean urban schools. (Duncan-Andrade & Morrell, 2008, p. 1)

The wealthiest U.S. public schools spend at least 10 times more than the poorest schools—ranging from over $30,000 per pupil at the wealthy schools to only $3000 at the poorest. (Darling-Hammond, 2004, p. 6)

The Mind and Critical Pedagogy: Looking at Kincheloe

One of the most powerful bodies of work making significant contributions to exposing the social construction of educational reality are the sixty books and hundreds of chapters and journal articles written by Joe Kincheloe. Not only is Kincheloe's pedagogy contextualized within the larger structures of power that teaching and learning are always situated in, but it is also contextualized within the individual spirit of each individual learner/teacher. In other words, Kincheloe understood that education is not merely a technical or mechanical act between *depositors* and *depositees*. But rather, in its most sophisticated manifestations, education is a full body libidinal experience filled with emotion as the *spirit-ness* of the *free will* dances and experiments with the body's senses, and biological endowments dialectically engage with the larger social context and its own social conditioning. Summarizing this point in their text outlining the *postformal basics*, P.L. Thomas and Joe Kincheloe (2006) note that their postformalism is intended to foster "an intoxicating cognition that repositions our relationship to the world and other people" (p. 14). The authors go on to argue that through the practice of education and the critical engagement with texts that "we can use the magic of words to move human beings to a new cognitive frontier" (p. 14).

It is this focus on contextualization that runs throughout Kincheloe's philosophy of education. It is the hyper-*de*contualization of schools and curricula that the need for a contextualized approach becomes evident. It is the attempt to argue that knowledge is neutral and objective that prevents policy makers from stating (or being aware of) the real goal of this kind of education, that is, "to perpetuate the dominance of 'mainstream' culture—white supremacy, Christian ascendancy, patriarchal hegemony, class elitism, heteronormativity, and so on" (Kincheloe, hayes, Rose, & Anderson, 2006, p. xxx). When schools are organized in ways that reduce teaching and learning to technical and mechanical acts, as noted above, but validate knowledge produced from the perspective of the dominant culture as objective truth and therefore treated as a non-perspective, the vast array of religious, ethnic/cultural, linguistic, immigrant, social class epistemologies are belittled as wrong or inferior. Lost is the contextualized understanding that "learning cannot be separated from an individual's identity" and the social, historical, political context in which it exists (Kincheloe, hayes, Rose, & Anderson, 2006, p. xxix). Kincheloe's critical pedagogy/constructivism is therefore based on challenging the false hierarchy of intelligence dominant within mainstream schooling in favor of a contextualized approach to learning that celebrates epistemological diversity as counter-hegemonic and transformative.

***

Because Kincheloe's critical approach to education is complex enough to untangle/teach against the vast contradictions and *dark/curious hegemonic alliances* between the oppressed and the oppressors that are part and parcel of the colonization/hegemonization process (see Kincheloe, 2005, 2008; Malott 2008), it deserves much celebration and reflection. Our first clue is that it embraces diverse ways of knowing, allowing educators and students to "hang out in the epistemological bazaar listening to and picking up on articulations of subjugated knowledges" (Kincheloe, 2005, p. 127) excluded by Western reductionism (Kincheloe, 2001, 2005, 2008). That is, if knowledge production is going to serve the interests of democracy, then the experiences and insights from those most oppressed become invaluable for understanding and transforming unjust social structures and institutions.

    This insight is particularly important from a critical constructivist (Kincheloe, 2005) perspective because the act of learning or acquiring knowledge here is understood *not* to be the passive and objective transmission of predetermined *facts* that occurs when we "detach" the "mind from the senses," as Descartes (1637/1994) argued was possible, which led him to believe that he was able to "abstract my mind from the contemplation of [sensible or] imaginable objects, and apply it to those which, as disengaged from all matter, are purely intelligible" (p. 103). Challenging this Cartesian idea that the mind and the production of knowledge can be disconnected from the social context of "corporeal objects," Kincheloe (2005) has observed that because humans are inherently social beings, everything we do, including learning, occurs in the highly political terrain of society—*the mind and society* can no more be disconnected from one another than can *the mind and the body*. Learning is therefore never objective or vacuous and can thus be described as an active process of creation that is unavoidably and always situated in a social-political context.

Because the mind is designed to socially develop *schema* for the production of thought—schema that are not predetermined, and therefore always subject to change—the process of becoming conscious of the content of our schema is of extreme importance. That is, for critical constructivism and critical pedagogy (Kincheloe, 2004; 2005) self-awareness is indispensable. For example, if we are not aware that we have been indoctrinated with self-destructive schema and thus are not aware that we are acting self-destructively, we cannot be expected to independently alter our behavior. The normalized and naturalized, that is, hegemonized, belief that everything assumed to be non-white, Western, and European is inferior or savage, has a direct consequence of producing self-destructive knowledge and perpetuating the practice of oppression.

That is, when we de-hegemonize our schema through the never-ending process of critical self-reflection and action (Freire, 2005; Kincheloe, 2005), we pave the way for dehegemonizing the knowledge we produce. For example, when the Euro-centric history curriculum is reformed and the central roots of Western science are accurately understood as essentially African, the production of anti-Black knowledge and practices face severe challenges. We can describe this as social justice scholarship, which is the choice of critical pedagogy because it serves the best interests of humanity—and we conclude that it is in the best interest of humanity to be united around democratic principles, such as an appreciation of diverse epistemologies, paving the way for universal self-actualization.

This conclusion stems from our rejection of the myth of natural hierarchy, which is based on the assumption that the establishment of social equality can only ever be an attack on freedom because it prevents the naturally superior individuals or groups, however conceived, to rise to their predetermined state of domination. Consequently, teachers' loyalties, critically conceived, should be to the communities they serve, based not on one of Descartes' (1637/1994) hierarchies or paternalism, but on one of his positive contributions, that is, that "good sense is, of all things among men, the most equally distributed" (p. 3). Kincheloe's (2004) postformal cognitive theory, mentioned above, is based on a similar conclusion, that "most students who don't suffer from brain disorders or severe emotional problems can (and do) engage in higher-order thinking" (p. 19) in their daily lives, not necessarily at school.

Again, the danger of Cartesian reductionism in education is the tendency to disconnect the production of knowledge from the social political context in which it is situated. Conceiving the world as chopped up into areas of study or disciplines is another fundamental feature of Western reductionistic and thus decontextualized education. Ignoring the political implications of the scientific method of knowledge production informing industrialism, for example, has been catastrophic. Reducing humans, geography, and all forms of life to their wealth generating potential through the disinterested science of capital is the result of the mechanistic and thus utilitarian view of the body after it has been disconnected from the soul or the mind. Summarizing this "machine cosmology" (Kincheloe, 2005), Descartes (1637/1994) theorizes:

> If the body of man be considered as a kind of machine, so made up and composed of bones, nerves, muscles, veins, blood, and skin, that although there were in it no mind, it would still exhibit the same motions which it at present manifests involuntarily, and therefore without the aid of the mind [and simply by the dispositions of its organs] (p. 126).

Rejecting this dichotomy, Kincheloe's vast body of work provides a unified, interdisciplinary approach to the production of knowledge and conceptualization of the world and all that it encompasses. Transgressing the narrow epistemological borders of the dominant, Euro-centric paradigm Kincheloe's critical pedagogy/constructivism rejects the notion that knowledge is objective existing independently of the mind. This is where most self-proclaimed revolutionaries miss the mark. That is, in an act of critical banking, many fail to transgress dominant assumptions of learning, only replacing the content or substance to be transmitted or indoctrinated. Kincheloe's consistent emphasis on identity and self-reflection can therefore not be overstated.

Critical constructivist educators are consequently "concerned with the processes through which certain information becomes validated knowledge" as well as "the processes through which certain information was not deemed to be worthy or validated knowledge" (Kincheloe, 2005, p. 3). Again, from this critical pedagogical perspective, the goal "is not to transmit a body of validated truths to students for memorization," but rather, "engaging students in the knowledge production process" (Kinchelo,e 2005, p. 3). Teachers who are successful at this show a great capacity to create the conditions where students can spark their own epistemological curiosities (Freire, 2005) which tends to be marked by the creation of a classroom "where students' personal experience intersects with academic knowledges" (Kincheloe, 2005, p. 4). Kincheloe (2005) offers some insight into what this might look like in practice, noting that "in their search for ways to produce democratic and evocative knowledges, critical constructivists become detectives of new ways of seeing and constructing the world" (p. 4). Put another way, critical scholars, dedicated to not only understanding the world, but contributing to uplifting its democratic imperatives, tend to be perpetually searching for new interpretative frameworks (philosophies) or "ways of seeing" that can better serve these ends—hence, the *epistemological bazaar* (Kincheloe, 2005).

Rather than viewing content as an entity that can be objectively known, the critical constructivism of Joe Kincheloe (2001, 2004, 2005) points to the ways in which power works to shape our understanding of *the facts*, that is, knowledge about ourselves in relationship with others and the rest of the material world. Language or discourse, from this paradigm, does not merely reflect *material reality* or *the truth* but informs our actions *in* and *on* the world. For example, the knowledge constructed about the world, and the subsequent practice in that world, from the perspective of the oppressed, is going to be antagonistically related to the ideologies constructed by the oppressors. From here we can begin to understand why a ruling class would seek to restrict the meaning of language through propaganda. The complexity of the contemporary era can therefore be understood as the product of the experience and practice of subjugation and oppression and the attempts to foster false consciousness within the oppressed populations through media outlets and schooling institutions, and the many ways in which people assert their own humanity despite tremendous odds.

Kincheloe (2005) argues that Western bias is representative of a larger tendency within modern science, noting that, "with the birth of modernism and the scientific revolution, many premodern, indigenous epistemologies, cosmologies, and ontologies were lost, ridiculed by European modernists as primitive" (p. 84) because dominance, the hallmark of modern European civilization, was equated with superiority. In other words, because indigeneity tends not to view nature and the world reductionistically and mechanistically, but as interconnected living systems, during the period of American and African colonization, for example, they were discursively reduced to an inferior status by the colonizing European forces.

Ironically, contemporary Western scientists are beginning to look at the wisdom of Indigenous peoples and therefore attempting to finally catch up to their advanced level of scientific/philosophical sophistication. These subjugated knowledges are the substance of Kincheloe's epistemological bazaar. They are the gifts that dominant society schools are designed to hide. Through his vast body of work, Kincheloe ceremoniously offers his audience many windows of perception to view the paradigm shifting nature of this *bazaar*. Elaborating on this point of view Kincheloe (2005) makes the following observation:

> The advantage of subjugated perspectives, the view from below, has been termed the *double consciousness* of the oppressed. If they are to survive, subjugated groups develop an understanding of those who control them; at the same time they are cognizant of the everyday mechanisms of oppression and how they shape their consciousness. (p. 144)

Conclusion: A Place of Departure

Focusing on the connection between education and research positions us to better understand and intervene in the validation process.

~ If you are studying to be an educational leader, how might this volume inform how you see your future practice?

~ If you are studying to be a professor or a public school teacher, how has this volume informed how you see your future practice?

~ How are students, teachers, and other educational workers subjected to the policies and management styles of educational leadership?

~ What do these examinations reveal to us about the relationship between citizenship and education within the current global capitalist system?

~ What is the connection between educational leadership and philosophy? In other words, how is educational leadership, first and foremost, a philosophically informed intervention in the world of education?

~ Why might critical pedagogues argue that the very notion of educational leadership presupposes an ontology of hierarchy?

REFERENCES

Abu-Jamal, M. (2000). *All Things Censored*. New York: Seven Stories.

Abu-Jamal, M. (2003). *Faith of Our fathers: An Examination of the Spiritual Life of African and African American People*. Trenton, NJ: Africa World Press.

Adams, D. (1995). *Education for Extinction: American Indians and the Boarding School Experience 1875-1928*. Lawrence, Kansas: University Press of Kansas.

Ajogún. www.myspace.com/ajogun

Banks, C.M. (2007). Gender and Race as Factors in Educational Leadership and Administration. In *The Jossey-Bass Reader on Educational Leadership*. 2nd ed. San Francisco: Jossey-Bass.

Banks, J. (2003). *Teaching Strategies for Ethnic Studies*. New York: Allyn and Bacon.

Bergstrom, A., Cleary, L., & Peacock, T. (2003). *The Seventh Generation: Native Students Speak About Finding the Good Path*. Charleston, West Virginia: Clearinghouse on Rural Education and Small Schools.

Bernal, M. (1987). *Black Athena: The Afroasiatic Roots of Classical Civilization*. New Brunswick, NJ: Rutgers University Press.

Bigelow, B., Harvey, B., Karp, S. & Miller, L. (2001). "Introduction." In Bill Bigelow, Brenda Harvey, Stan Karp, and Larry Miller (Eds.). *Rethinking Our Classrooms: Teaching for Equity and Justice: Volume 2*. Williston, VT: Rethinking Schools.

Bigelow, B. (1998a). "Discovering Columbus: Re-reading the Past." In Bill Bigelow and Bob Peterson (Eds.), *Rethinking Columbus: The Next 500 Years*. Milwaukee, WI: Rethinking Schools.

Bogdan, R. & Biklen, S. (1998). *Qualitative Research for Education: An Introduction to Theory and Methods*. New York: Allyn and Bacon.

Butler, S. (1935/2003). *War Is a Racket*. LA: Feral House.

Chance, P. (2009). *Introduction to Educational Leadership & Organizational Behavior: Theory into Practice*. Second edition. Larchmont, NY: Eye on Education.

Chandler, W. (1992/2002). Trait-Influences in Meso-America: The Africa-Asian Connection. In Ivan Van Sertima (Ed.). *African Presence in Early America*. London: Transaction Publishers.

Childs, S. (2003). "Summer Camp" for Teachers: Alternative Staff Development. In Linda Christensen and Stan Karp (Eds). *Rethinking Schools Reform: Views from the Classroom*. Milwaukee, WI: Rethinking Schools.

Chomsky, N. (1987). *The Chomsky Reader*. James Peck (Ed). New York: Pantheon.

Chomsky, N. (1999). *Profit over People: neoliberalism and global order*. New York: Seven Stories.

Chomsky, N. (2002). *On Nature and Language*. Cambridge: Cambridge University Press.

Chomsky, N. (2005). *Imperial Ambitions: Conversations on the Post-9/11 World*. Interviews with David Barsamian. New York: Metropolitan Books.

Chomsky, N. (2007). *What We Say Goes: Conversations on U.S. Power in a Changing World*. Interviews with David Barsamian. New York: Metropolitan Books.

Christensen, L. & Karp, S. (Eds). (2003). *Rethinking School Reform: Views from the Classroom*. Milwaukee, WI: Rethinking Schools.

Churchill, W. (2004). *Kill the Indian, Save the Man: The Genocidal Impact of American Indian Residential Schools*. San Francisco, California: City Lights.

Cleary, L. & Peacock, T. (1998). *Collected Wisdom: American Indian Education*. London: Allyn and Bacon.

Clegg, L. (1992/2002). The First Americans. In Ivan Van Sertima (Ed.). *African Presence in Early America*. London: Transaction Publishers.

Coles, G. (2003). Learning to Read "Scientifically." In Linda Christiansen and Stan Karp (Ed.). *Rethinking School Reform: Views from the classroom*. Milwaukee: Rethinking Schools.

Collier, P. (2008). The Politics of Hunger: How Illusion and Greed Fan the Food Crisis. *Foreign Affairs*, November/December, pp. 67–79.

Collins, J. (2007). Level 5 Leadership. In *The Jossey-Bass Reader on Educational Leadership*. 2nd ed. San Francisco: Jossey-Bass.

Cone, J. (2003). Preface. In Mumia Abu-Jamal. *Faith of Our Fathers: An Examination of the Spiritual Life of African and African American People*. Trenton, NJ: Africa World Press.

Daily, D. (2004). *Battle for the BIA: G.E.E. Lindquist and the Missionary Crusade against John Collier*. Tucson: The University of Arizona Press.

Darling-Hammond, L. (2004). From "Separate but Equal" to "No Child Left Behind":

The Collision of New Standards and Old Inequalities. In Deborah Meier and George Wood (Eds.). *Many Children Left Behind: How the No Child Left Behind Act Is Damaging Our Children and Our Schools*. New York: Beacon.

Darwin, C. (2007). *The Descent of Man, and Selection in Relation to Sex: The Concise Edition*; selections and commentary by Carl Zimmer. New York: Plume.

Descartes, R. (1637/1994). *A Discourse on Method: Meditations and Principles*. London: Everyman.

Diop, C. A. (1955/1974). *The African Origin of Civilization: Myth or Reality*. Chicago: Lawrence Hill Books.

Du Bois, W.E.B. (1989). *The Souls of Black Folk*. New York: Penguin.

Duncan-Andrade, J. & Morrell, E. (2008). *The Art of Critical Pedagogy: Possibilities for Moving from Theory to Practice in Urban Schools*. New York: Peter Lang.

Durkheim, E. (1893/2000). *The Division of Labor in Society*. In Timmons, Robert and Amy Hite (Eds.). *From Modernization to Globalization: Perspectives on Development and Social Change*. New York: Blackwell Publishers.

Eisner, E. (1998). *The Enlightened Eye: Qualitative Inquiry and the Enhancement of Educational Practice*. New York: Prentice Hall.

Flynn, J. (2007). *What is Intelligence?* London: Cambridge University Press.

Foster, W. (1989) The Administrator as a Transformative Intellectual. *Peabody Journal of Edcation*, v66n3, pp. 5–18.

Freire, P. (1998). *Pedagogy of the Oppressed*. New York: Continuum.

———(1999). *Pedagogy of Hope: Reliving Pedagogy of the Oppressed*. New York: Continuum.

———(2005). *Teachers As Cultural Workers: Letters to those who dare teach*. Boulder: Westview.

Friedman, M. (1955). "The Role of Government in Education." [Online] Available at: http://www.schoolchoices.org/roo/fried1.htm.

Friedman, M. (1962/2002). *Capitalism and Freedom*. London: University of Chicago Press.

Gresson, A. (2004). *America's Atonement: Racial Pain, Recovery Rhetoric, and the Pedagogy of Healing*. New York: Peter Lang.

Hess, F. & Petrilli, M. (2008). *No Child Left Behind Primer*. New York: Peter Lang.

Hill, D. & Kumar, R. (2009). Neoliberalism and Its Impacts. In Dave Hill and Ravi Kumar (Eds). *Global Neoliberalism and Education and its Consequences*. New York: Routledge.

Holder, W. (2007). *Classroom Calypso: Giving Voice to the Voiceless*. New York: Peter Lang.

hooks, b. (1994). *Teaching to Transgress: Education as the Practice of Freedom*. New York: Routledge.

Hursh, D. (2008). Neoliberalism. In David Gabbard (Ed). *Knowledge & Power in the Global Economy: The Effects of School Reform in a Neoliberal/Neoconservative Age*.

Second Edition. New York: Lawrence Erlbaum Associates.

Jean-Marie, G., James, C., & Bynum, S. (2006). Black Women Activists, Leaders, and Educators: Transforming Urban Educational Practice. In Joe L. Kincheloe, kecia hayes, Karel Rose, and Philip M. Anderson (Eds.). *The Praeger Handbook of Urban Education: Volume 1.* London: Greenwood Press.

Johnston, H., Laraña, E. & Gusfield, J. (1994). Identities, Grievances, and New Social Movements. In Enrique Laraña, Hank Johnston, and Joseph R. Gusfield (Eds). *New Social Movements: From Ideology to Identity.* Philadelphia: Temple University Press.

Jossey-Bass reader on Educational Leadership, The. 2nd ed. (2007). San Francisco: Jossey-Bass.

Karp, S. (2004). NCLB's Selective Vision of Equality: Some Gaps Count More than Others. In Deborah Meier and George Wood (Eds.). *Many Children Left Behind: How the No Child Left Behind Act Is Damaging Our Children and Our Schools.* Boston: Beacon.

Keynes, J.M. (1936/1997). *The General Theory of Employment, Interest, and Money.* Amherst, NY: Prometheus.

Kincheloe, J. (1991). *Teachers as Researchers: Qualitative Inquiry as a Path to Empowerment.* New York: Falmer.

Kincheloe, J. (2001). *Getting Beyond the Facts: Teaching Social Studies/Social Sciences in the Twenty-first Century: Second Edition.* New York: Peter Lang.

Kincheloe, J. (2004). Why a Book on Urban Education? In Shirley Steinberg and Joe L. Kincheloe (Eds.). *19 Urban Questions: Teaching in the city.* New York: Peter Lang.

Kincheloe, J. (2005). *Critical Constructivism Primer.* New York: Peter Lang.

Kincheloe, J. (2008). *Critical Pedagogy Primer: Second Edition.* New York: Peter Lang.

Kincheloe, J. hayes, k., Rose, K. & Anderson, P. (2006). Introduction: The Power of Hope in the Trenches. In Joe L. Kincheloe, kecia hayes, Karel Rose, and Philip M. Anderson (Eds.). *The Praeger Handbook of Urban Education: Volume 1.* London: Greenwood Press.

Kincheloe, J., Slattery, P. & Steinberg, S. (2000). *Contextualizing Teaching: Introduction to Education and Educational Foundations.* New York: Longman.

Kohn, A. (2004). NCLB and the Effort to Privatize Public Education. In Deborah Meier and George Wood (Eds.). *Many Children Left Behind: How the No Child Left Behind Act is damaging our children and our schools.* Boston: Beacon.

Kozol, J. (2005). *Shame of a Nation: The Restoration of Apartheid Schooling in America.* New York: Random House.

LaDuke, W. (2005). *Recovering the Sacred: The Power of Naming and Claiming.* Cambridge, MA: South End Press.

Leistyna, P. (2002). *Defining and Designing Multiculturalism: One School System's Efforts.* Albany, NY: SUNY.

Leistyna, P. (2007). Neoliberal Non-sense. In Peter McLaren and Joe L. Kincheloe (Eds.). *Critical Pedagogy: Where Are We Now?* New York: Peter Lang.

Lincoln, E.C. (1984). *Race, Religion, and the Continuing American Dilemma*. New York: Hill and Wang.

Lippmann, W. (1920/2008). *Liberty and the News*. Oxford: Princeton University Press.

Lippmann, W. (1922). *Public Opinion*. Boston: Little, Brown and Company.

Lippmann, W. (1927). *The Phantom Public: A Sequel to "Public Opinion."* New York: Macmillan Company.

Lippmann, W. (1937/2005). *The Good Society*. London: Transaction.

Lippmann, W. (1943). *U.S. Foreign Policy: Shield of the Republic*. Boston: Little, Brown and Company.

Loder, T. L. (2006). Dilemmas Confronting Urban Principals in the Post-Civil Rights Era. In Joe L. Kincheloe, kecia hayes, Karel Rose, and Philip M. Anderson (Eds.). *The Praeger Handbook of Urban Education: Volume 1*. London: Greenwood Press.

Lynd, S. & Grubacic, A. (2008). *Wobblies & Zapatistas: Conversations on Anarchism, Marxism, and radical history*. Oakland, CA: PM Press.

Macedo, D., Dendrinos, B. & Gounari, P. (2003). *The Hegemony of English*. Boulder: Paradigm.

Malone, T. & Sadovi, C. (2008). Head of the class: city school reform goes national. In Dec, 17th Chicago Tribune.

Malott, C. (2007). "Cuban Education in Neo-Liberal Times: Socialist Revolutionaries and State Capitalism." *Journal for Critical Education Policy Studies*. 5(1). [Online] Available at: http://www.jceps.com/?pageID=article&articleID=90.

Malott, C. (2008). *A Call to Action: An Introduction to Education, Philosophy, and Native North America*. New York: Peter Lang.

Malott, C. (2009). Education in Cuba: Socialism and the Encroachment of Capitalism. In Dave Hill and Ravi Kumar (Eds.). *Global Neoliberalism and Education and Its Consequences*. New York: Routledge.

Malott, C., Waukau, L. & Waukau-Villagomez, L. (2009). *Teaching Native America Across the Curriculum: A Critical Inquiry*. New York: Peter Lang.

Malott, D.M.C. & Malott, C. (2008). Culture, Capitalism and Social Democracy in Jamaica. In Brad Porfilio and Curry Malott (Eds.). *The Destructive Path of Neoliberalism: An International Examination of Education*. Rotterdam, The Netherlands: Sense.

Marable, M. (1996). *Speaking Truth to Power: Essays on Race, Resistance, and Radicalism*. Boulder, CO: Westview.

Marshall III, J. (2004). *The Journey of Crazy Horse: A Lakota History*. New York: Penguin Books.

Maslow, A. (1968). *Toward a Psychology of Being*. New York: Van Nostrand Reinhold.

McLaren, P. & Farahmandpur, R. (2005). *Teaching Against Global Capitalism and the New Imperialism*. New York: Rowman & Littlefield.

McNeil, L. (2003). The Educational Costs of Standardization. In Linda Christensen and Stan Karp (Eds.). *Rethinking School Reform: Views from the Classroom*.

Milwaukee, WI: Rethinking Schools.

Meier, D. & Wood, G. (2004). *Many Children Left Behind: How the No Child Left Behind Act Is Damaging Our Children and Our Schools.* Boston: Beacon.

Menchaca, M. (1997). Early Racist Discourses: The Roots of Deficit Thinking. In Richard Valencia (Ed). *The Evolution of Deficit Thinking: Educational Thought and Practice.* New York: Routledge.

Miner, D. (2003). For Profits Target Education. In Linda Christensen and Stan Karp (Eds.). *Rethinking School Reform: Views from the Classroom.* Milwaukee, WI: Rethinking Schools.

Mohawk, J. (2000). *Utopian Legacies: A History of Conquest and Oppression in the Western World.* Santa Fe, New Mexico: Clear Light.

Murphy, J. (2007). The Unheroic Side of Leadership: Notes from the Swamp. In *The Jossey-Bass reader on Educational Leadership.* 2nd ed. San Francisco: Jossey-Bass.

Neihardt, J. (1932/2004). *Black Elk Speaks: Being the Life Story of a Holy Man of the Oglala Sioux.* London: University of Nebraska Press.

Neuman, L. (1994). *Social Research Methods: Qualitative and Quantitative Approaches.* New York: Allyn and Bacon.

Nisbett, R. (2009). *Intelligence and How to Get It: Why Schools and Cultures Count.* New York: Norton.

Obama and Biden. (accessed 10–04–08). "Education." http://www.barackobama.com /issues/education.

O'Reilly, K. (1994). *Black Americans: The FBI Files.* New York: Carroll & Graf.

Orfield, G. (2003). Schools More Separate: A Decade of Resegregation. In Linda Christiansen and Stan Karp (Eds.). *Rethinking School Reform: Views from the Classroom.* Milwaukee, WI: Rethinking Schools.

Peterson, B. (2003a). Teacher Councils: Tools for Change. In Linda Christensen and Stan Karp (Eds). *Rethinking School Reform: Views from the Classroom.* Milwaukee, WI: Rethinking Schools.

Peterson, B. (2003b). Survival and Justice: Twin Goals for Teacher Unions. In Linda Christensen and Stan Karp (Eds.). *Rethinking School Reform: Views from the Classroom.* Milwaukee, WI: Rethinking Schools.

Pinar, W., Reynolds, W., Slattery, P. and Taubman, P. (2000). *Understanding Curriculum: An Introduction to the Study of Historical and Contemporary Curriculum Discourses.* New York: Peter Lang.

Porfilio, B. & Malott, C. (2008). Introduction: The Neoliberal Social Order. In Bradley Porfilio and Curry Malott (Eds.). *The Destructive Path of Neoliberalism: An International Examination of Urban Education.* Rotterdam, The Netherlands: Sense.

Pratt, R. (1892). "The Advantages of Mingling Indians with Whites" http://historymatters.gmu.edu/d/4929/ accessed November third, 2009.

Rhoades, K. (2008). Educational Research. In David Gabbard (Ed.). *Knowledge & Power in the Global Economy: The Effects of School Reform in a Neoliberal/Neoconservative*

Age. Second Edition. New York: Lawrence Erlbaum Associates.

Rist, R. (1998). Influencing the Policy Process with Qualitative Research. In Norman Denzin and Yvonna Lincoln (Eds.). *Collecting and Interpreting Qualitative Materials*. New York: Sage.

Robertson, L. (2005). *Conquest by Law: How the Discovery of America Dispossessed Indigenous Peoples of Their Lands*. New York: Oxford University Press.

Roth, W.-M. (2007). *Doing Teacher-Research: A Handbook for Perplexed Practitioners*. Rotterdam: Sense.

Sergiovanni, T. (1979). Rational, Bureaucratic, Collegial, and Political Views of the Principal's Role, *Theory into Practice*, 18(1), 12–20.

Sergiovanni, T. (2007). Leadership as Stewardship: "Who's Serving Who?" In *The Jossey-Bass Reader on Educational Leadership*. 2nd ed. San Francisco: Jossey-Bass.

Shawki, A. (2006). *Black Liberation and Socialism*. Chicago: Haymarket.

Sizer, T. (2004). Preamble: A Reminder for Americans. In Deborah Meier and George Wood (Eds.). *Many Children Left Behind: How the No Child Left Behind Act Is Damaging Our Children and Our Schools*. Boston: Beacon.

Skinner, B.F. (1971/2002). *Beyond Freedom & Dignity*. Indianapolis, IN: Hackett.

Smith, A. (2005). *Conquest: Sexual Violence and American Indian Genocide*. Cambridge, MA: South End Press.

Spillane, J. (2003). *Educational Leadership, Educational Evaluation and Policy Analysis*, (254), 343–346.

Steel, R. (2008). Foreword. In Walter Lippmann. *Liberty and the News*. Oxford: Princeton University Press.

Taylor, F. (1911). *The Principles of Scientific Management*. New York: Harper & Brothers.

Thomas P.L. & Kincheloe, J. (2006) *Reading, Writing, and Reading: The Postformal Basics*. Rotterdam: Sense.

Thorndike, E. (1910). *Educational Psychology*. Albany, NY: Teachers College, Columbia University.

Tierney, W. and Foster, W. (1989). Introduction: Educational Leadership and the Struggle for the Mind, *Peabody Journal of Education*, 66(3), 1–4.

Tippeconnic III, J. (1999). Tribal Control of American Indian Education: Observations Since the 1960s with Implications for the Future. In Karen Gayton Swisher and John W. Tippeconnic III (Eds.). *Next Steps: Research and Practice to Advance Indian Education*. Charleston, West Virginia: Clearinghouse on Rural Education and Small Schools.

Tyler, D.A. (2006). African-American Teachers: The Dying Group. In Joe L. Kincheloe, kecia hayes, Karel Rose, and Philip M. Anderson (Eds.). *The Praeger Handbook of Urban Education: Volume 1*. London: Greenwood Press.

Vizenor, G. (1990). *Crossbloods: Bone Courts, Bingo, and Other Reports*. Minneapolis: University of Minnesota Press.

von Wuthenau, A. (1992/2002). Unexpected African Faces in Pre-Columbian

America. In Ivan Van Sertima (Ed.). *African Presence in Early America*. London: Transaction Publishers.

Watkins, W.H. (2001). *The White Architects of Black Education: Ideology and Power in America, 1865–1954*. New York: Teachers College.

Wildcat, D. (2001). Indigenizing Education: Playing to Our Strengths. In Vine Deloria, Jr. and Daniel R. Wildcat (Authors), *Power and Place: Indian Education in America*. Golden, Colorado: Fulcrum Resources.

Wilentz, S. (2008). General Editor's Introduction. In Walter Lippmann. *Liberty and the News* (1920/2008). Princeton: Princeton University Press.

Yazzie, T. (1999). Culturally Appropriate Curriculum: A Research-Based Rationale. In Karen Gayton Swisher and John W. Tippeconnic III (Eds.). *Next Steps: Research and Practice to Advance Indian Education*. Charleston, West Virginia: Clearinghouse on Rural Education and Small Schools.

Zimmer, C. (2007). Selections and Commentary. In Charles Darwin. *The Descent of Man, and Selection in Relation to Sex: The Concise Edition*. New York: Plume.

INDEX

Plessy v. Ferguson 82
Pratt, Captain Richard Henry 12, 95–100

R

Rist, Ray 66
Robertson, L 49
Roth, Wolf-Michael 73, 175

S

Sergiovanni, Thomas 19, 20, 126, 136, 151
Skinner, Burrhus Frederic 12, 30–33, 54
Systems theory 12, 17, 35, 36, 40

T

Taylor, Frederick 12, 19–25, 30, 33, 54

Taylorism 35
Thorndike, Edward 27–30

V

Vygotsky, Lev 26, 136

W

Washington, Booker T. 86

Z

Zapatistas, the 5, 6, 51, 52, 55, 116

M. Christopher Brown II. *General Editor*

The *Education Management: Contexts, Constituents, and Communities* (EM:c³) series includes the best scholarship on the varied dynamics of educational leadership, management, and administration across the educational continuum. In order to disseminate ideas and strategies useful for schools, colleges, and the education community, each book investigates critical topics missing from the extant literature and engages one or more theoretical perspectives. This series bridges the gaps between the traditional management research, practical approaches to academic administration, and the fluid nature of organizational realities.

Additionally, the EM:c³ series endeavors to provide meaningful guidance on continuing challenges to the effective and efficient management of educational contexts. Volumes in the series foreground important policy/praxis issues, developing professional trends, and the concerns of educational constituencies. The aim is to generate a corpus of scholarship that discusses the unique nature of education in the academic and social spaces of all school types (e.g., public, private, charter, parochial) and university types (e.g., public, private, historically black, tribal institutions, community colleges).

The EM:c³ series offers thoughtful research presentations from leading experts in the fields of educational administration, higher education, organizational behavior, public administration, and related academic concentrations. Contributions represent research on the United States as well as other countries by comparison, address issues related to leadership at all levels of the educational system, and are written in a style accessible to scholars, educational practitioners and policymakers throughout the world.

For further information about the series and submitting manuscripts, please contact:

Dr. M. Christopher Brown II | *em_bookseries@yahoo.com*

To order other books in this series, please contact our Customer Service Department at:

(800) 770-LANG (within the U.S.)
(212) 647-7706 (outside the U.S.)
(212) 647-7707 FAX

Or browse online by series at www.peterlang.com